JAPAN
53 Kasumigaseki
54 Fujioka

INDIA
55 Royal Calcutta

HONG KONG
56 Royal Hong Kong

SINGAPORE
57 Singapore Island

MALAYSIA
58 Royal Selangor

INDONESIA
59 Bali Handara

AUSTRALIA
60 Royal Melbourne
61 Royal Adelaide
62 Royal Sydney

NEW ZEALAND
63 Paraparaumu

SOUTH AFRICA
64 Durban Country Club
65 Royal Johannesburg

MOROCCO
66 Royal Rabat

THE
WORLD ATLAS OF
GOLF COURSES

THE
WORLD ATLAS OF
GOLF COURSES

BOB FERRIER

**MALLARD
PRESS**

Half title page: *The beautiful 5th hole at Muirfield Village, Jack Nicklaus' creation in his home state of Ohio.*

Title page: *The difficult 16th hole at Augusta, one of the most famous golf courses in the world and the permanent home of the U.S. Masters tournament.*

Above: *Cypress Point, and two of its famous holes – the 16th and 17th – showing to good effect the dramatic Monterey scenery.*

MALLARD PRESS
An Imprint of BDD Promotional Book Company, Inc.
666 Fifth Avenue
New York, N.Y. 10103

"Mallard Press and its accompanying design and logo are trademarks of BDD Promotional Book Company, Inc."

Copyright © 1990 The Hamlyn Publishing Group Limited

First published in the United States of America
in 1990 by The Mallard Press
by arrangement with The Hamlyn Publishing Group Limited,
a division of The Octopus Publishing Group,
Michelin House, 81 Fulham Road, London SW3 6RB, England

ISBN 0–792–45284–4

Produced by Mandarin Offset
Printed in Hong Kong

CONTENTS

INTRODUCTION

Golf is a solitary, subjective game, a fact enhanced by the truths that every golf course is different from the other, no golf hole ever plays twice in quite the same way, and no single golf shot can be repeated exactly. The weather, if nothing else, will see to all of that. True, golf courses have a few basic elements in common – trees, greens, hazards and, throughout most of the world, grass on the fairways. But they inhabit a wide variety of landscape – moorland, heathland, linksland, meadowland, parkland. They have prospered in humdrum suburbs and along magnificent cliff tops. Some of the greatest are public courses – Pebble Beach, Carnoustie, St Andrews. Some of the greatest are entirely and severely private – Augusta, Muirfield.

In establishing 'greatness', a treacherous quality, among the world's golf courses, we have tried to use certain basic criteria. Perhaps the most important is balance, and that is perhaps best expressed in the philosophy of Donald Ross, the Dornoch man who emigrated to the United States and over a span of some 40 years proved himself an outstanding designer involved in hundreds of golf courses. He believed that 'The championship course should call for long and accurate tee shots, accurate iron play, precise handling of the short game, and finally, consistent putting. These abilities should be called for in a proportion that will not permit excellence in one department of the game to affect too large deficiencies in another'. The championship course should ask the player from time to time to take risks, rewarding him if he is successful and punishing him if he is not; the reward should be in proportion to the size of the risk, and the punishment should reflect the extent of a failure to overcome it. The holes should have variety of length and direction, straight holes, dog-legs either way, uphill, downhill and so on, with varied green sizes and shapes, and hazards. The scenic quality of the course and its surroundings should add to the pleasure of the player, and the course should have history to sustain it.

In designing golf courses, the architect must work to the same norm as does the handicap committee of the club – that of the scratch golfer. All our references to the playing of these great golf courses have been based on the abilities of the scratch golfer – indeed, the championship golfer. If this is necessarily unfair to the average golfer, who is more likely to have a handicap of 18, nevertheless the average player can get immense pleasure from these courses even if he does not play them from the championship tees.

Our selection has been based on the observations, experiences, convictions of the most respected players, architects and observers of the great game, and from our own persuasions, prejudices and total golf experience. We trust that among them will be your favourites.

Bob Ferrier

Michael Allen on the 16th tee during the Scottish Open, held on the King's course at Gleneagles, the premier Scottish golf 'resort'. Allen, an American, went on to win the tournament.

THE AMERICAS

Golf imitates life in North America, where the vast mass of the United States, the energy and vision of its people, the sheer affluence of its society, have made it golf's world leader.

There was 18th century golf, in colonial America, at Savannah and Charleston, but the game was formalised in the 1880s; half a dozen select clubs formed the U.S. Golf Association. Canada was slightly ahead. Royal Montreal, 1873, is the oldest extant American club.

The game then expanded hugely in the 1920s, and again in the 1950s and subsequently, with the televising of great championships and champions such as Ben Hogan, Arnold Palmer, Jack Nicklaus, Lee Trevino and Tom Watson. The result is that there are several million golfers in the U.S., playing at clubs which range from the highly exclusive and fearsomely expensive, to the hundreds of public courses. In North America, golf is everyman's game.

The variety of terrain – desert, mountain, prairie, forest, beach – has enabled American golf architects to produce imaginative and often beautiful courses, the financing of which has often been sustained by sophisticated hotel and resort development, and property sales.

By contrast, the game in South America has remained aristocratic and expensive and is perhaps most advanced in the countries which consider themselves to be most 'European' – Argentina and Chile.

View from the tee of the short but treacherous 16th hole at Augusta where many a contender's challenge has come to nothing.

SHINNECOCK HILLS

Of all the great championship courses in America, Shinnecock Hills is the least known and the least played. Yet, it has a most distinctive place in the history of American golf. It was one of the five founding clubs which in December 1894 formed the Amateur Golf Association of America, which quickly became the American Golf Association, and then the United States Golf Association.

The other founding clubs were the St Andrews Club of New York, The Country Club, at Brookline, near Boston, the Newport Golf Club of Rhode Island and the Chicago Golf Club at Wheaton. Samuel Parrish from the Shinnecock club became the first treasurer of the USGA. The following year, they were able to stage the first Open and Amateur championships, at the Newport Club, and in 1896 it was Shinnecock's turn.

The club had its origins in a visit made to Biarritz by three Long Island gentlemen of means, wintering in France in 1890–91. They were William K. Vanderbilt, Edward S. Mead and Duncan Cryder. They came across young Willie Dunn, a Scottish professional who had

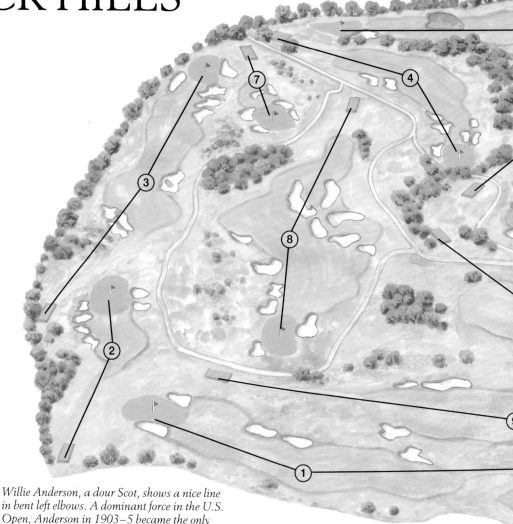

Willie Anderson, a dour Scot, shows a nice line in bent left elbows. A dominant force in the U.S. Open, Anderson in 1903–5 became the only man to take the title three years in a row.

ambitions as an architect and who was designing 18 holes at Biarritz. It was arranged that Dunn should cross to Southampton – a fashionable summer resort at the eastern end of Long Island – when he had finished at Biarritz, and find a piece of land suitable for a course he would then design.

Dunn arrived in March 1891 and was taken on a tour of the Southampton area, eventually settling on a treeless area of scrubland among low-lying sandhills by the south shore of Great Peconic Bay, and only a couple of miles from the ocean. The site was to provide a course unique in American golf. It was within a few minutes of the Southampton resort, and hard by the railroad which had brought the area within 2½ hours of Manhattan, a good 100 miles away.

SHINNECOCK HILLS			
Card of the course			
1	399 yards par 4	10	412 yards par 4
2	221 yards par 3	11	159 yards par 3
3	454 yards par 4	12	470 yards par 4
4	379 yards par 4	13	367 yards par 4
5	498 yards par 5	14	445 yards par 4
6	450 yards par 4	15	399 yards par 4
7	185 yards par 3	16	513 yards par 5
8	336 yards par 4	17	167 yards par 3
9	418 yards par 4	18	425 yards par 4
3,340 yards par 35		3,357 yards par 35	
Total 6,697 yards par 70			

Indian Reservation

Dunn recruited a crew of 150 Indians from the nearby Shinnecock reservation, from which the club took its name, and

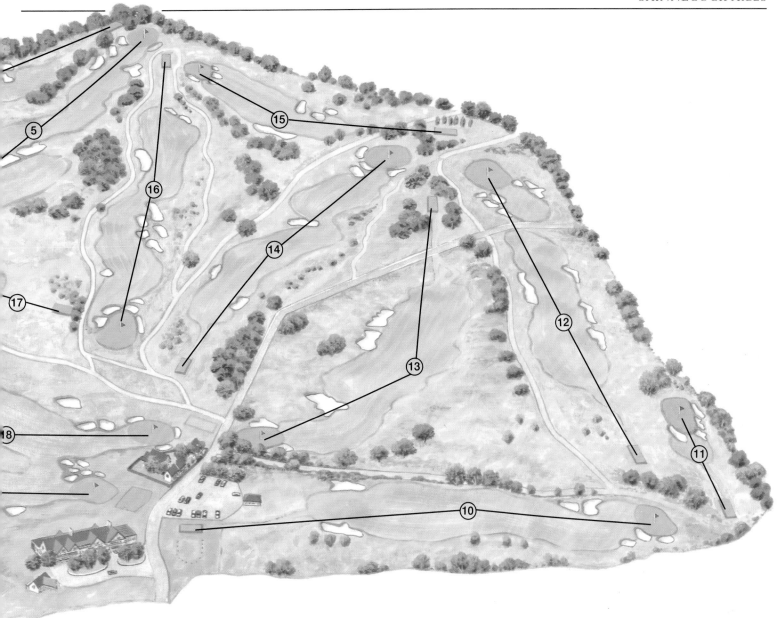

with their sweat and a few horse-drawn drags, by mid-summer he had cleared out a 12-hole course. Fairways and greens were certainly much less cosmetic than their modern counterparts, but Vanderbilt and his friends were delighted. His faith in the venture was justified. By September, 44 members had bought all the available debentures and the club was incorporated. Southampton took to the game avidly, so much so that within a year, they were extending their course to 18 holes and had opened their grandiose clubhouse, the work of one Stanford

Stanford White's clubhouse overlooks the 9th and 18th greens, and is fronted by a natural grandstand for the final green.

White, an eminent architect of the day. White produced a great white rambling palace, which still stands on its rise dominating the Southampton area. It had grill rooms, showers, comfortable locker rooms and was the very last word in luxury. It was the first true American golf clubhouse.

'Newport Swells'

In general, the first American golfers were drawn from the upper reaches of society the '400', men who might winter in Europe and spend their summers or summer weekends away from the heat of the city. Southampton and the 'Hamptons' out on Long Island, and Newport were the most swank of these summer

resorts, providing cottages and villas for the privileged. When the five clubs which formed the USGA took to meeting for play, the St Andrews boys – the famous Apple Tree Gang – were more than abashed when they saw the Shinnecock

fellows and the 'Newport swells' decked out in uniforms of red coats, white knickers and gaiters.

A New Course

Dunn's original course was less than 5,000 yards long. It was lengthened over the years. But by 1931, when part of the club's land had been lost to a new highway, and with the coming of the steel shaft era, it was time for change. Dick Wilson, a highly capable architect with an impressive body of work to his credit, was invited to modernise the course. This he did brilliantly by, in the first place, sitting down and considering what he had – a course no more that two miles from an Atlantic Ocean which produced a regular supply of salty south-west winds; an open, sandy terrain with a good deal of rolling movement in it; virtually no trees, certainly no trees 'in play' as they are in almost all American courses; severe rough; and crisp light turf, reminiscent of Scottish links turf.

Wilson designed a course that demands solid, accurate driving, as all great courses must. His fairways are undulating, often with ridges that have to be carried or passed for the player to reach the optimum position for the second shot. The second shots demand a variety of clubs, and to greens often protected by swales and dips at the fronts or sides, as the old links courses were; and the greens are defended by strong bunker positionings. The rough is of long, clinging grass.

The four short holes, so often an indication of a course's quality, are very fine, and closely trapped. All of them lie across the prevailing wind to varying degrees. Wilson artfully arranged that all the shorter par-4 holes play into the prevailing wind, while the longer par-4 holes play down the wind. The 15th hole, at 399 yards, is a good example. It plays more or less east to west, a dog-leg to the right with a rash of bunkers in the angle. If the drive carries a rise in the fairway by the angle, it will find a valley from which the shot to the green is fairly straightforward. But to get there, the drive must be long and true.

With no more than occasional primping and polishing since, Wilson's design remains thoroughly modern. The late

Above: *Raymond Floyd, the oldest champion (43 years, 9 months, 11 days), plays an old-fashioned running chip on his way to victory at Shinnecock Hills in the U.S. Open of 1986.*

Left: *Shinnecock Hills hosted the U.S. Open in 1896 and 1986. This hole, the 1st, could be at Sunningdale or at any first-rate sand-based inland course in England.*

Thirties and World War II saw Shinnecock suffer a decline; but the club and the course were saved by re-financing in 1948; and Ben Hogan, having visited it in the early 1960s, declared it 'one of the finest courses I have played'. Pulled out to 6,900 yards – not overlong for a modern championship course – it proved itself in the U.S. Open of 1986. The course shrugged off the onslaught of the world's finest players.

On the first day, when the wind blew, not one player could better the par of 70, and only one player was under par at the end of 72 holes. That player was one of the most talented, most mature of American professionals, a previous winner of the U.S. Masters and the U.S. PGA and a future American Ryder Cup captain – Raymond Floyd, aged 43, who scored 279. Shinnecock Hills was alive and well, unscarred and at peace with the world.

THE NATIONAL

The National Golf Links of America vies with its near neighbour at Shinnecock Hills as the least-known, least-played great golf course in America. Yet the National is nothing less than a monument and at the same time a milestone. It is a monument to a remarkable man, Charles Blair Macdonald, and it represents a milestone in American golf architecture, having set a style for American courses that still holds good, at least in the golfing public's mind, today. So critical was Macdonald to so many aspects of the early game in America, and in particular its courses, that he demands some consideration.

Charles Blair Macdonald, from Chicago, was sent by a wealthy father to the University of St Andrews in 1872. Still in his teens, he became enchanted by the game of golf, sitting at the feet of, and occasionally playing with, Old Tom Morris and other leading players. As the years passed, he became a very good player. In his prime Macdonald was a big man – powerful, intelligent, intolerant, aggressive, a man to have his own way. Back home in the Middle West he hustled his friends and extracted cash from them in order to start the Chicago Golf Club – building a course at Wheaton, to the west of the city. He went on to represent the club at the foundation of the U.S. Golf Association in 1894 and became the first official amateur champion.

When designing the Chicago club, one of the first in the country with 18 holes, Mcdonald had the course measure 6,200 yards, the same length at that time as the Old Course at St Andrews, which he worshipped. Golf course design in the U.S. at the end of the last century was fairly basic, often carried out by anyone who could spin a tale of his talents to the committee of one of the dozens of clubs which were springing up all over the place. Often it meant the 'architect' spending a day on the site, putting down markers for tees and greens, with straight fairways, bunkers thrown across them some 150 yards out, and flat greens with bunkers on either side, the whole thing

Charles Blair Macdonald, who studied at St Andrews, helped form the U.S. Golf Association, became the first U.S. Amateur Champion and built the classic National golf links on Long Island.

laid out on a piece of open farmland, or parkland. Macdonald was less than satisfied with this.

He had been greatly impressed by the subtle features of St Andrews and other great links courses in Scotland and by the way the more famous holes offered the golfer options in the playing of them. He came to believe that he could design holes that would equal or even improve on these features, and that indeed he should design and build the first great American golf course. It would be definitive, a classic. Thus in the early years of the 20th century Macdonald made several trips to Britain, making notes and collecting drawings of the outstanding holes on the major links courses of Scotland and England. At the same time, he searched along the eastern seaboard states for a suitable site. He found it some three miles from Shinnecock and Southampton, at the end of Long Island – more than 200 acres of rolling duneland, on a point between Sebonac and Petonic Bays.

A Taste of Scotland

On this ground, he built his masterpiece. Several of its holes are closely reminiscent, if not quite copies, of British holes. The National's 3rd might well be Prestwick's 17th (Macdonald gave his the same fanciful name, 'The Alps'), with a blind second shot over high dunes to a sharply contoured green, with a bunker guarding its front. The 4th, named after North Berwick's 'Redan', is also a par-3 with its green angled across the line of shot, and screened by a bunker. And the National's 7th, named 'St Andrews', is a lookalike of the famous 17th on the Old Course. A large area of scrubby bunkers and wasteland takes the place of the old railway sheds on the drive, while the infamous Road Hole bunker, centre-left of the front of the green, is repeated. The 13th, a fine par-3 over water, has copies of the Hill and Strath bunkers fronting St Andrews' 11th – Macdonald naming his hole the 'Eden'.

The outstanding feature of the National, apart from the positive movement which Macdonald put into the ground, is the strategic quality of the design. On every tee shot, including those of the short holes, the golfer has an alternative line and an alternative target area. There is, however, one notable exception, the 14th, a hole that has been copied all over the world. Macdonald used it on other courses which he designed. It is a drive and pitch hole of 359 yards, but the drive, over water, must be precisely placed into one small area to clear bunkering on the right, stay short of rough and bunkering on the left, and open the dog-leg approach to the right to a circular green surrounded by sand. It is the perfect illustration of penal golf – the drive must be hit in one direction and to one length. There is no alternative. It is a lovely but demanding golf hole.

A Powerful Test in the Wind

Construction of the National started in 1907, the course was in play in 1909, but thereafter Macdonald made constant revisions, fine-tuning many of the holes. It

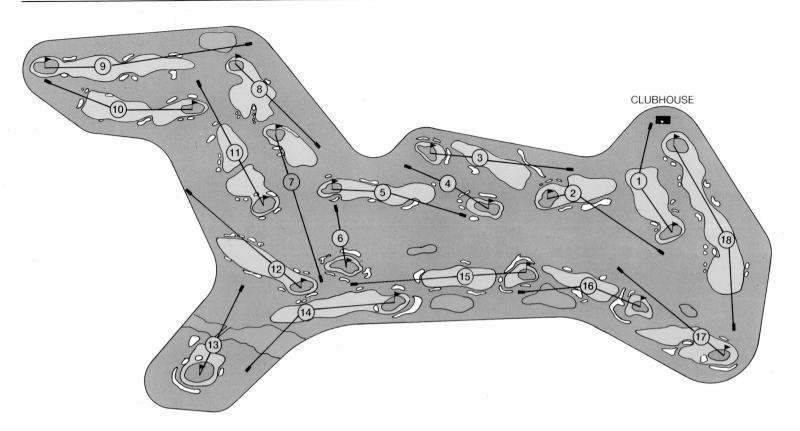

CLUBHOUSE

Right: *View of the tee of the formidable 3rd hole, which requires a long, accurate tee shot and a blind approach over high dunes.*

THE NATIONAL				
Card of the course				
1	320 yards	par 4	10	457 yards	par 4
2	271 yards	par 4	11	431 yards	par 4
3	426 yards	par 4	12	437 yards	par 4
4	196 yards	par 3	13	170 yards	par 3
5	476 yards	par 5	14	359 yards	par 4
6	130 yards	par 3	15	392 yards	par 4
7	478 yards	par 5	16	401 yards	par 4
8	390 yards	par 4	17	368 yards	par 4
9	540 yards	par 5	18	503 yards	par 5
3,227 yards	par 37		3,518 yards	par 36	
Total 6,745 yards par 73					

can now play at 6,700 yards and with the wind blowing, as it almost always is from Long Island Sound to the north, or the Atlantic Ocean to the south, the National is a powerful test of golf.

From the moment of its birth, dozens of golf architects have made the pilgrimage out to Long Island. Perhaps its remoteness has been responsible for the fact that the first Walker Cup match, in 1922, between the amateurs of the United States and of Great Britain and Ireland has been the only major event staged at the National. However, its design and construction, a product of the keen observations and vivid imagination of Charles Blair Macdonald, brought a new dimension to golf architecture in the United States, demonstrated how the natural movement of land can be used to great effect, and showed the way to a succession of other great U.S. courses.

OAK HILL

The East course of the Oak Hill Country Club at Rochester, New York State, may just be as close to perfection as any course in America. Perfection in this sense means that the course is beautifully balanced as to the shot values inherent in every hole, that its layout is varied and attractive and that the course is without any weakness, yet is never either overpowering or pretentious. Oak Hill is simply excellent.

The club dates from 1901, but the course on its present site dates from 1926, and was designed by Donald Ross, the architect of Pinehurst. It retains many of his signatures – the slightly raised greens with honest gradients, the little swales and valleys around the greens, inviting a variety of chip shots, the bunker set short of the green to make judgement of distance that much more difficult, yet fairways bunkers contoured so that ambitious recovery shots are possible. One club member at the time of its construction was Dr John R. Williams, a local physician with a compelling interest in botany. He raised hundreds of seedlings, developed 28 different varieties of oak tree and was responsible for planting the

Above: *In the 1989 U.S. Open Curtis Strange (seen here on the 72nd green) retained the trophy, but a drenched Oak Hill restricted him to a two-under-par 278.*

new course, and consequently giving it its name. Now the property is said to carry more than 30,000 trees: presumably someone has counted them.

A Tough Challenge

Oak Hill is an honest golf course, but it demands that the golfer get down to work at once. The 1st hole is a tight par-4 of 445 yards with a creek, which wanders through the entire property, crossing the fairway in front of the green. The green is small and closely trapped. The 2nd hole is a medium-length par-4 of around 400 yards, but with a desperately narrow landing zone for the tee shot and bunkered on either side. The 3rd is a par-3 of more than 200 yards. It is an opening sequence which offers few favours.

The climax to the course is even more severe. The three closing holes are par-4s of 441, 463 and 449 yards, and the 18th is particularly indicative of the problems they pose. At around 260–270 yards, the fairway turns to the right. In the angle of the turn is a huge bunker of florid outline. From there the hole runs uphill to a slightly raised green – three huge bunkers on the right and another on the left front

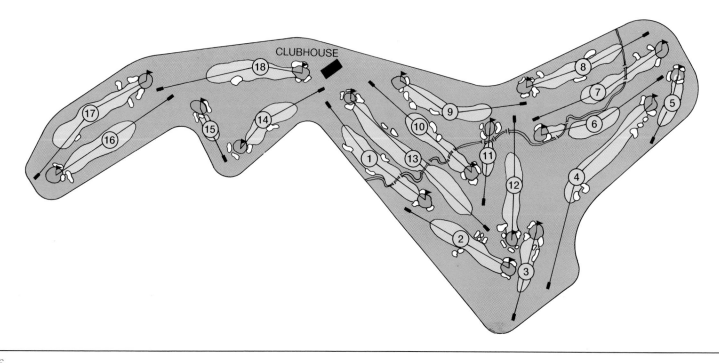

creating a less than generous entrance to the putting surface.

In 1956 Cary Middlecoff won Oak Hill's first (and his second) U.S. Open championship with a score of 281. In 1968, Lee Trevino won the Open with 69, 68, 69, 69 for a 275, equalling the Open's record low aggregate at five under par and becoming the first man to play every round under par in the U.S. Open. Rain had softened the Oak Hill course, making its 6,962 yards controllable. Trevino was playing in only his second Open, but it was clear to the keener observers of the game that here was a very special talent, perfectly illustrated by his manful play on the 72nd hole. He drove into the left rough, advanced the ball but still in the rough, then hit a defiant wedge shot a few feet from the flag, and holed out.

Oak Hill and the USGA seemed embarrassed. The course needed to be

OAK HILL					
Card of the East course					
1	445 yards	par 4	10	420 yards	par 4
2	390 yards	par 4	11	192 yards	par 3
3	206 yards	par 3	12	380 yards	par 4
4	571 yards	par 5	13	602 yards	par 5
5	180 yards	par 3	14	327 yards	par 4
6	440 yards	par 4	15	163 yards	par 3
7	443 yards	par 4	16	441 yards	par 4
8	432 yards	par 4	17	463 yards	par 4
9	416 yards	par 4	18	449 yards	par 4
3,525 yards par 35			3,437 yards par 35		
Total 6,962 yards par 70					

less benevolent. Architects George and Tom Fazio were retained to tighten things up and they changed some holes in the middle of the course, notably the 5th, 6th, 15th and 18th, in time for the PGA Championship of 1980. However, change

Above: *The testing 449-yard 18th viewed from the green, the bunker on the inside angle of the elbow in the background. Ian Woosnam (joint second) birdie putts the 72nd hole in the 1989 U.S. Open.*

does not always mean improvement. Traditionalists like Trevino and Tom Watson were critical of them. The course was only a couple of yards longer, and in the 1980 event, in good conditions, Jack Nicklaus scored 70, 69, 66, and 69 for a 274, giving him victory by seven (!) strokes from Andy Bean, and setting yet another Oak Hill record score.

When conditions are right, Oak Hill, as any other course in the world, cannot resist the talents of the world's finest players; but for all that it remains a beautiful, stylish golf course on a lovely, gently rolling property, and is well worthy of the greatest champions.

BALTUSROL

The fairways of Baltusrol march along in stately fashion, more than half of the holes running straight while the doglegs are always less than severe. Its noble woodland never crowds the player. Its greens are neither ancient dwarf nor contemporary giant, and all are reasonably contoured. The use of water as a hazard is restrained – a small lake fronting the 4th green, and a narrow stream coming into play on another five holes. Yet, despite a pervasive and pleasing sense of grand understatement, Baltusrol's chief attribute is variety – not only in the demands the course makes in its range of shots into the greens, but also in the fact that while half a dozen of its holes require no more than a drive and a pitch, the 17th, at a hulking 623 yards, is the longest hole in U.S. championship golf. Altogether, every aspect at Baltusrol is grand, and every prospect pleases.

The club, at Springfield, New Jersey, and no more than a one hour drive from Manhattan, takes its name from a wealthy farmer of Dutch extraction, a Mr Baltus Roll, who owned the land more than 150 years ago. In 1831, he was dragged out of his house on a nearby hillside by two thieves, who murdered him in the presence of his wife in the belief that there was money hidden in the house. Towards the end of the century, the Baltusrol lands, still being farmed, were owned by one Louis Keller, a gentleman who founded and published the *New York Social Register*. He had been smitten by the game, playing with his smart society friends at Newport and Southampton, and resolved to have his own golf course.

U.S. Open 1980: winner Jack Nicklaus plays out of the back bunker on the 4th, where Robert Trent Jones scored an ace after remodelling the hole.

In 1885 he extracted an initiation fee of $10 from several of his cronies (Baltusrol charges have increased somewhat) and in no time had nine holes in play. By 1921, the club had enough extra land to invite A.W. Tillinghast to design 36 holes.

Baltustol had already become prominent in the affairs of American golf, and was sufficiently well thought of to have staged two U.S. Opens, in 1903 and 1915. The first of these was won by Willie Anderson, the club's first professional, who won four Opens in the space of five years. Only Bobby Jones, Ben Hogan and Jack Nicklaus were to equal his record of four Championships. The second was won by Jerome Travers, the wealthy Long Islander who won two Opens and four U.S. Amateur championships. The time had come for Baltusrol to advance, and in Tillinghast they selected one of the two outstanding golf course designers of the first quarter of the 20th century. The

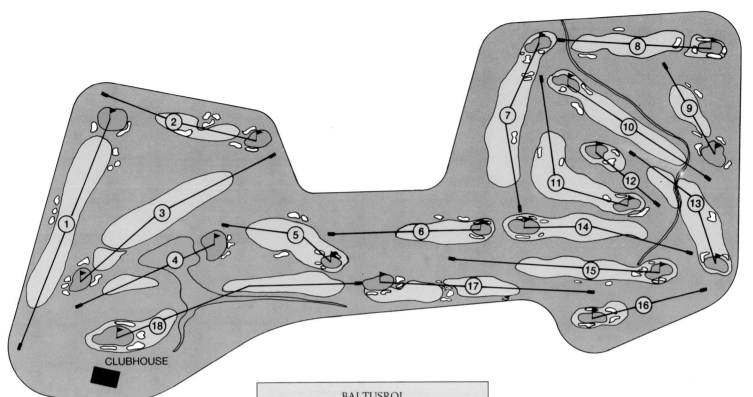

BALTUSROL					
Card of the Lower course					
1	469 yards	par 4	10	449 yards	par 4
2	390 yards	par 4	11	410 yards	par 4
3	438 yards	par 4	12	193 yards	par 3
4	194 yards	par 3	13	383 yards	par 4
5	388 yards	par 4	14	399 yards	par 4
6	470 yards	par 4	15	419 yards	par 4
7	470 yards	par 4	16	214 yards	par 3
8	365 yards	par 4	17	623 yards	par 5
9	206 yards	par 3	18	524 yards	par 5
3,390 yards		par 34	3,632 yards		par 36
Total 7,022 yards par 70					

CLUBHOUSE

other was Donald Ross, and the two men could hardly have been less alike; Ross, the quiet Scot of Presbyterian inclination who designed courses almost until the day he died, and Tillinghast, the *bon viveur* who ended his days as an antique dealer in Hollywood and had amongst other things been a magazine editor and a dabbler in photography and, whatever he was doing, had always enjoyed a dram or two.

Tillinghast built powerful but fair golf courses, among them Winged Foot in New York and Five Farms at Baltimore. His driving lines might be tight, but they were never penal. He believed that a 'controlled shot to a closely guarded green is the surest test of any man's golf'. His greens might be closely guarded but they never had ridiculous slopes, and he would quite often place fairway bunkers centrally, some 20 or 30 yards short of the green, demanding that the player make a positive carry over. Moreover, he used water for hazards only when it was already there – naturally.

Tillinghast's Baltusrol shares with Merion and Oakmont the distinction of having staged six U.S. Open Cham-

pionships. However, it has been revised over the years, and for the 1954 event Robert Trent Jones was called in to strengthen the course. The story of Jones at Baltusrol is almost too good to be true, but not too good not to be re-told. He re-worked Tillinghast's short 4th – paradoxically a water hole. It became a shot over water to a green narrow from front to back, wide from left to right. The water came right up to the putting surface, which was edged by a stone wall. The green sloped from left to right, from front to back, and was screened by tall, mature trees – all oddly reminiscent of the 12th at Augusta. The carry could be as much as

200 yards from the back tee. The club officials and the USGA people thought that Jones had made it much too difficult. He disagreed and offered to pay for any subsequent changes that might be necessary. He led the club president, the chairman of the USGA championship committee, and Johnny Farrell, Baltusrol's famous professional, to the tee and they all hit shots. When it came to Jones' turn he hit a shot that rolled straight into the hole, and said: 'As you see gentlemen, this hole is not too tough'!

Ed Furgol won the '54 Championship with 284. In 1967, Jack Nicklaus won with a record 275 and a last round of 65. In 1980, Jack Nicklaus won again with yet another record 274, which included a round of 63. No man ever enjoyed a victory more than this one. Jack sat in the Press Centre for hours afterwards, saying: 'I don't want this day to end'.

If the conditions are right, the modern champions can overwhelm any course, even one longer than 7,000 yards, like the modern Baltusrol. But for all that Baltusrol undoubtably remains as one of America's finest parkland courses.

THE COUNTRY CLUB

The Country Club at Brookline, now a suburb of Boston, Massachussetts, is by way of being an American institution. It was established in 1860, and was the first of its kind. It saw no need, therefore, to qualify its title – it was and is simply 'The' Country Club. In the early days, horses were the thing – exercising them, racing them, a bit of polo from time to time. ... It was 30 years before the club laid out six holes of golf, but that was enough in the 1890s to permit it to become a founder member, as one of the five original clubs, of the United States Golf Association. The club's match with Royal Montreal, first played in 1898, was the world's first golf match between teams of different countries. But above all else, The Country Club became a shrine of American golf because of the U.S. Open Championship of 1913. It was then that the local boy, Francis Ouimet, aged 20, the Massachussetts Amateur Champion, defeated the Englishmen Harry Vardon and Ted Ray, who were beyond any reasonable doubt the two finest players in the world.

Earlier American Opens had been dominated by British-born, if American-resident, professionals who, it must be said, were scarcely outstanding players. True, a couple of years earlier, young Johnny McDermott had become the first U.S.-born champion; but Ouimet, on that cold, wet September Saturday in 1913 began an American domination of world golf that lasted for more than half a century. The Country Club produced other champions but Ouimet's victory is an almost unique instance of one single event having an immense and permanent effect on an entire sport. The nearest parallel in golf might be the victory of the Japanese team in the Canada Cup (now World Cup) of 1957, and the effect it had on the game over there.

Ouimet went on to have a remarkably fulfilled life. He was twice Amateur Champion of the U.S., a Walker Cup player and American Walker Cup captain. He became President of the USGA and the first non-British captain of the

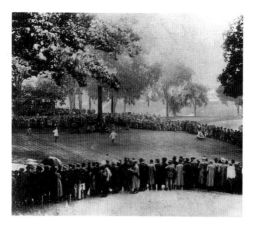

Francis Ouimet, crouching on the left, lines up the winning putt of the fateful U.S. Open of 1913, when he beat the British favourites, Harry Vardon (nearest Ouimet) and Ted Ray, in a play-off.

Royal and Ancient club. He had a prosperous business career as a stockbroker in Boston and throughout his life maintained a simple country boy image. Few in golf have ever been more highly regarded.

The Country Club is not an imperious, breath-taking course. Rather, it is old-fashioned to the point of being almost homely. But when the USGA, with a keen sense of history, took their championship back to Brookline, 50 years on from Ouimet, the course was far more sophisticated than the open spread the young Francis knew. The horses had gone. Trees and heavily-wooded areas on the property were now very much in play and time had put the stamp of maturity on one of the world's great courses. However, in 1963 history repeated itself. Again there was a three-way tie, and a play-off, this time involving Julius Boros, Jackie Cupit and Arnold Palmer. Palmer, at the height of his powers, was expected to make a breakfast of the others. But during the night before the play-off, he was stricken with some kind of food poisoning, and next day came to the tee weak as a kitten. The outcome was Boros 70, Cupit 73 and Palmer 76. And when the USGA went back to Brookline yet again, in 1988, there was yet another tie.

This time, Curtis Strange beat Nick Faldo in the play-off.

In all of these great events, the 17th hole has played an extraordinary and eventful role. Ouimet made a birdie there on his final round, helping to set up the tie with the Englishmen. The hole is 365 yards, slightly dog-legged to the left, with a bunker in the angle. From there it is uphill to the green. In the play-off round, with Ray out of it, Ouimet played nicely

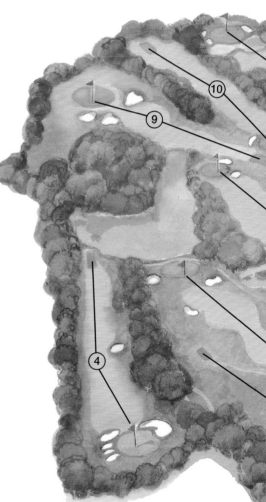

down the fairway, pitched on the green and made his birdie. Harry Vardon, on the other hand, pressing for the birdie he needed – he was a stroke down to Francis – caught the bunker with his drive, scored five, and lost the Open. In 1963 at the 71st hole – Palmer bogeyed, Cupit double-bogeyed, while Boros birdied to set up the play-off. And in 1988, Strange three-putted the 71st, to allow the tie, while Faldo, in the play-off round, overshot the green with his second – a fateful hole indeed.

For the '88 Open, the USGA had invited Rees Jones, younger son of Robert Trent Jones, the most famous of modern golf architects, to revise the course. The original design dates back to 1909, and Jones quickly saw that the course would have to be strengthened for modern championship players. Searching through the club's archives, he found some of the early work plans and talked to the oldest

members and staff as to what they could remember of the original layout. Taking all of this into account, Jones came to the conclusion that he should virtually restore the old course, but in a modern context. He thus created a course that was some 700 yards longer than the Ouimet course.

Jones also discovered that the 17th green of 1913 was long gone. Because of road widening, a new green had been built in 1958, so he set about building a new green, closely guarded by front bunkers and rather flat at the back. His work certainly sustained the critical quality of the hole.

Curtis Strange plays a bunker shot at the 17th in his playoff with Nick Faldo in the 1988 U.S. Open at The Country Club. His greenside play and holing-out work were important factors in his victory.

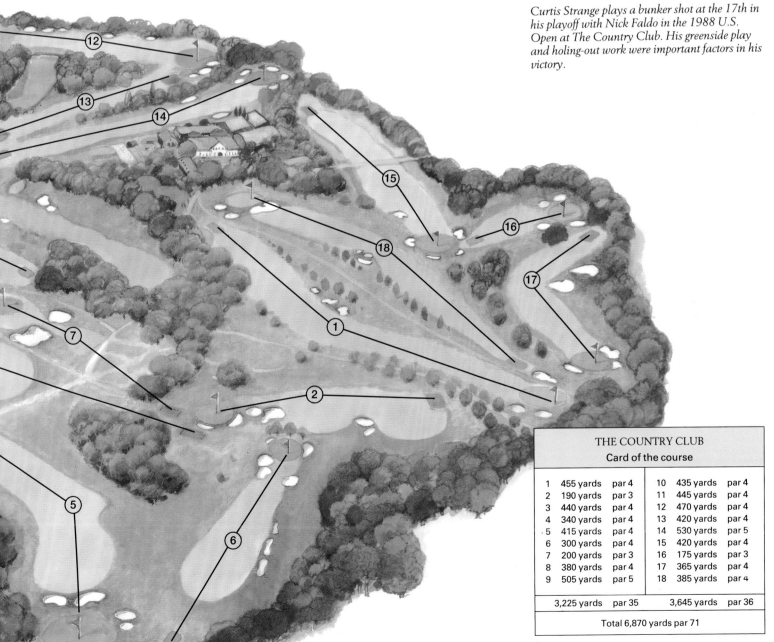

THE COUNTRY CLUB					
Card of the course					
1	455 yards	par 4	10	435 yards	par 4
2	190 yards	par 3	11	445 yards	par 4
3	440 yards	par 4	12	470 yards	par 4
4	340 yards	par 4	13	420 yards	par 4
5	415 yards	par 4	14	530 yards	par 5
6	300 yards	par 4	15	420 yards	par 4
7	200 yards	par 3	16	175 yards	par 3
8	380 yards	par 4	17	365 yards	par 4
9	505 yards	par 5	18	385 yards	par 4
3,225 yards	par 35		3,645 yards	par 36	
Total 6,870 yards par 71					

OAKMONT

Behind every great venture is a singular man. So it was with the creation of the course at Oakmont, a village some dozen miles north of Pittsburgh, and one Henry Clay Fownes (pronounced 'phones'), its architect, creator and the first president of the Oakmont Country Club. Perhaps in this case two men should get the credit – the second being Henry's son, William. Henry, a successful Pittsburgh industrialist and near-contemporary of Andrew Carnegie, took up golf in 1899 when he was already in his forties. Playing on the short, modest courses of the Pittsburgh Field Club and the Highland Country Club, he became adept enough to qualify for the U.S. Amateur Championship of 1901.

His son, William C. Fownes Jr, was introduced to the game with his father and surpassed him. He won the U.S. Amateur Championship of 1910, played at The Country Club, Brookline, beating Chick Evans in the semi-final after being two down with three to play. He qualified for the championship 25 times in 27 years, served for many years on U.S. Golf Association committees, and was USGA president in 1926 and 1927.

Father Henry soon came to see that Pittsburgh needed a 'proper' golf course, and by 1903 he had put together a syndicate to finance such a venture. The word was out that he was seeking a suitable piece of land, within reach of the city. Eventually a friend, George S. Macram, who lived in Oakmont village, reported that a 225 acre plot nearby was available. Fownes bought it. A railroad cut through the property, but the Fowneses simply ignored that – they threw a bridge over the tracks, and laid out holes on either side. And much later, when the Pennsylvania Turnpike, one of America's earliest super-highways, threatened the course, it was routed alongside the railroad track, so that the Oakmont course was left virtually untouched.

An 18-Hole Purgatory
On the morning of 15 September 1903 the first sod was broken by the Fownes workforce of 150 men and 25 mule teams, and six weeks later, before the hard northern winter had set in, 12 holes had been cleared, tees and greens had been built, greens and fairways seeded and a drainage system put in place. The

following spring a further six holes were prepared, and by the autumn of 1904 Oakmont was in play.

It was immediately clear that the Fowneses, father and son alike, took a puritanical, hair-shirted attitude to the game of golf. Their creed was that any shot less than perfect must be punished.

Father Fownes had most of the existing trees ripped out to give the landscape that 'empty', British-links appearance. (Since those early years there has been some planting, but Oakmont retains an open look.) Within a year or so of its opening, Oakmont boasted some 350 bunkers. Since the course was 6,600 yards in length, at a time when the world of golf was only just becoming accustomed to the Haskell wound ball, which was replacing the gutty, and 25 years before the steel shaft, it must have been purgatory. It

Larry Nelson lets it go on the first tee of the last round of the 1983 U.S. Open. Although it was interrupted by a storm, it was one of the great finishing rounds, a 67.

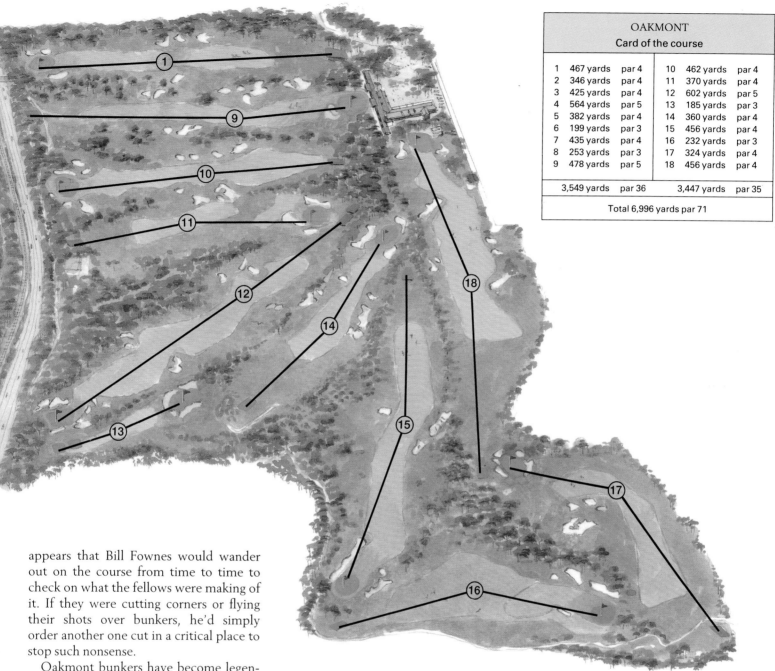

OAKMONT					
Card of the course					
1	467 yards	par 4	10	462 yards	par 4
2	346 yards	par 4	11	370 yards	par 4
3	425 yards	par 4	12	602 yards	par 5
4	564 yards	par 5	13	185 yards	par 3
5	382 yards	par 4	14	360 yards	par 4
6	199 yards	par 3	15	456 yards	par 4
7	435 yards	par 4	16	232 yards	par 3
8	253 yards	par 3	17	324 yards	par 4
9	478 yards	par 5	18	456 yards	par 4
3,549 yards		par 36	3,447 yards		par 35
Total 6,996 yards par 71					

appears that Bill Fownes would wander out on the course from time to time to check on what the fellows were making of it. If they were cutting corners or flying their shots over bunkers, he'd simply order another one cut in a critical place to stop such nonsense.

Oakmont bunkers have become legendary in American golf, and not just for their numbers. The 8th hole boasts 'the Sahara' bunker which is 75 yards long and 35 yards wide and needed eleven truck loads of sand to fill. It guards the left fairway of this par-3 of 253 yards and then runs up to and along the left side of the green. But most famous of all are the 'Church Pews', a block of eight lateral bunkers like lines of infantry, separating the 3rd and 4th fairways, in each case neatly nailing pulled drives.

Even more memorable in terms of the Fownes's penal design philosophy was the

'Oakmont Rake'. The course had been built on heavy clay soil. From a drainage point of view it was not feasible to build deep bunkers after the fashion of British links. The Oakmont bunkers, shallow as they were, were loaded with heavy river sand. Starting in 1920, the Fowneses had the bunkers furrowed by special rakes that had teeth 2 in long and 2 in apart. As a result the heavy sand stood up neatly in ridges, like a ploughed field, and left the

golfer no option but to splash the ball a few yards out with a routine shot.

The Fastest Greens in America

But more lethal than anything in thwarting the great champions have been the Oakmont greens. They have been described as the fastest, the truest, the most difficult in America. To make them fast in the early days the Fownes had them rolled with a 1500-pound roller, which required eight men to pull. The grass was cut to 3/32 in (about 2.5 mm). The wonder was that they were able to retain grass on such greens, especially in high summer.

Bill Fownes became president in 1935, when his father died, and served until 1949, a year before his own death. Before that, although a committee had taken over the running of the club, Bill remained chairman of the greens committee. Over the years, 'his' greens have taken a fearful toll. In the U.S. Open of 1927, against a par of 72/288, Tommy Armour's winning score was 301. In the 1935 Open, Sam Parks, a Pittsburgh man who knew Oakmont intimately, won with 299, the only man under 300. In the previous decade, U.S. Open-winning scores at other venues had often been well under these totals. In the 1929 U.S. Amateur, on the 14th green, Chick Evans three-putted without even lipping the cup – then holed out with the handle of his umbrella!

Postwar Softening

By 1953, when Oakmont held its first postwar U.S. Open, things were different. The club committee and the USGA agreed to make Oakmont slightly less malevolent: some fairways in the driving area were widened; the number of bunkers was reduced to less than 200, and now they had fine white silicone sand.

Above: The first age of Nicklaus. Jack, crewcut, hefty and immensely powerful, lets fly in the U.S. Open of 1962, when he beat Arnold Palmer in a play-off, 71 to 74.

Right: The well-guarded 18th green makes a fitting climax to this hugely difficult course. Even in his annus mirabilis, the great Hogan was only one under par when winning the 1953 U.S. Open.

Below: Arnold Palmer, caught in the 'Church Pews' bunkers at Oakmont in the 1983 U.S. Open, goes for a typically aggressive, swashbuckling recovery.

Perhaps most important of all was that 1953 was the enchanted year of Ben Hogan. He came to Oakmont as the Masters Champion, and promptly played a first round of 67 which broke the back of the competition. He won the championship by six strokes from Sam Snead, with 283 – five under par and at no time in the entire year (he went on to win the British Open) was the marvelously ruth-

less precision of his shotmaking better illustrated than in the last three holes of his final round. At the 16th, a par-3 of 232 yards, he hit a four-wood into the heart of the green – two putts for a 3. At the 17th, a par-4 of some 300 yards, he drove the green – again, two putts for 3. At the 18th, a very powerful finishing par-4 of 456 yards, the second half of the hole uphill to the green, he hit an immense drive, a mid-iron a few feet to the right of the flagstick, and holed the putt – for a 3.

In the 1973 Championship, Johnny Miller, with a scarcely credible 63, played the lowest last round the Open had known, and some said the finest round of golf ever played. In the 1983 championship, Larry Nelson played the final 36 holes in 65, 67 for a record 132. It took such feats of derring-do to win the championships for these men. But in each case, at each championship, torrential rain had taken all the fire out of the Oakmont greens over the two closing rounds. Oakmont is a fearsome course. It has been described as 'the toughest golf course in the world'. It may well be overwhelming, but is it fair? 'Fairness', in the philosophy of the Fownes, 'has nothing to do with it'.

MERION

Merion is a classic, a treasury of design, imagination, craftsmanship and style. The demands it makes of the golfer are all there for him to see, with nothing hidden. But they are rigorous indeed. It is an exacting test for any class of player, and in that respect recalls the great Scottish links course at Muirfield.

The Merion Golf Club and its championship East course at Ardmore, a fashionable suburb of Philadelphia, emerged from the Merion Cricket Club, which was founded during the Civil War. As golf became popular in America, club members first used the estate of one Clement A. Griscomb for this new game; but in 1896 the club purchased 100 acres three quarters of a mile from the cricket ground and laid out nine holes. Four years later another nine were added, and on this course the U.S. Women's Amateur Championships of 1904 and 1909 were played. However, with the advent and spread of the Haskell ball from the turn of the century, it was clear that the course would quickly become obsolete. Consequently, the Merion members bought an abandoned farm at the town of Ardmore for a new course, though the property was less than stunning and included an old stone quarry long out of use, dense with trees and shrubbery.

Contrary to the fashion of the day, the design of the course was vested in a committee of five members, which included Hugh Irvine Wilson, an immigrant Scot, graduate of Princeton, local insurance broker and adequate golfer. The committee made several visits to The National, at Southampton on Long Island, where it became clear that Wilson had a special feeling for design. They sent him over to Scotland and, as Charles Blair Macdonald had done, he spent several months making drawings and maps, talking to people and looking around. When he went to work on Merion East, he copied not specific golf holes that he had seen, but concepts. For example in front

The tell-tale board hails David Graham's near-immaculate 67 – this birdie putt on the last hole grazed the cup – on the final round of his 1981 U.S. Open Championship at Merion.

Above: *View to the par-4 16th green across the overgrown quarry, whose size enforces a long-iron or fairway wood approach shot.*

of his 17th green a – ferocious par-3 – he left a big depression like the Valley of Sin in front of the 18th at St Andrews. And he used the quarry to create the climax of his round – holes 16, 17 and 18 playing over it.

The White Faces of Merion
When Wilson's work was completed in 1912, Merion East was seen to be a course of high distinction and beauty. It was built on open parkland with just enough trees to soften and enhance the landscape. There were 128 bunkers, beautifully shaped – the famous 'white faces of Merion' – some of them graced with islands of tall, spiky grass. Wilson used baskets rather than flags atop the flag-sticks, an idea he was supposed to have found at Sunningdale (qv), but which actually originated in a Scottish custom of using lobster pots!

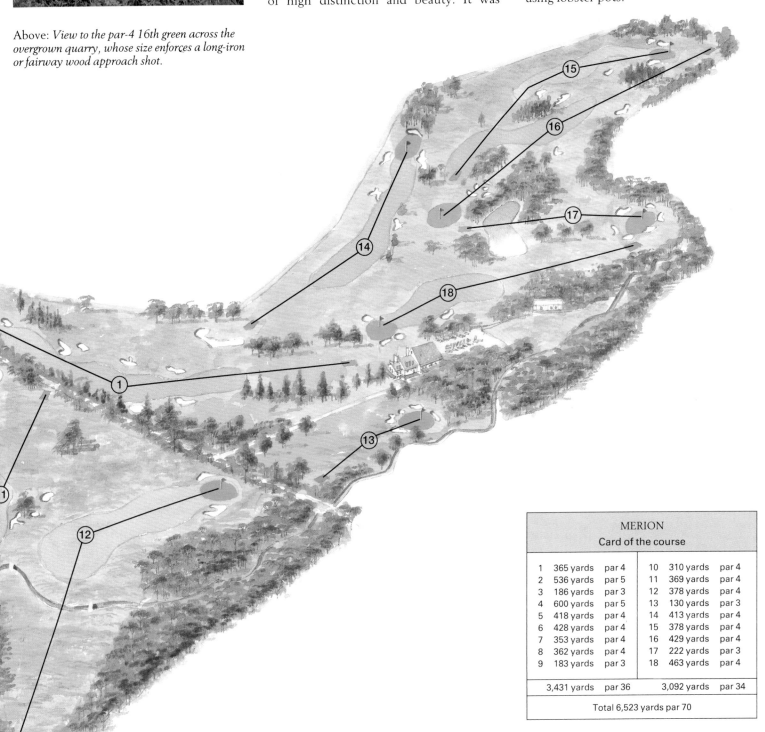

MERION					
Card of the course					
1	365 yards	par 4	10	310 yards	par 4
2	536 yards	par 5	11	369 yards	par 4
3	186 yards	par 3	12	378 yards	par 4
4	600 yards	par 5	13	130 yards	par 3
5	418 yards	par 4	14	413 yards	par 4
6	428 yards	par 4	15	378 yards	par 4
7	353 yards	par 4	16	429 yards	par 4
8	362 yards	par 4	17	222 yards	par 3
9	183 yards	par 3	18	463 yards	par 4
	3,431 yards	par 36		3,092 yards	par 34
	Total 6,523 yards par 70				

Merion has persisted in holding its place in the forefront of championship golf in America – it has staged more national championships than any other course – even though its off-course facilities leave a lot to be desired.

The course has always defied the greatest players of the day. At the first Open played there in 1934, Olin Dutra won with 293, 13 over par. In 1950, Ben Hogan, Lloyd Mangrum and George Fazio tied on 287, 7 over par. In fact, it was not until the Championship of 1981 that par was broken – by five players. Overnight rain had made the greens receptive, and the championship was distinguished by the final round of David Graham of Australia – a 67.

Make or Break on the Greens

Wilson's greens at Merion hold the key. Ample when receiving a long shot, small when receiving a pitch, beautifully shaped, artfully contoured, sometimes on two levels, sloping with the shot or against it, at their optimum speed they are as fast as the greens at Oakmont.

The first hole runs from the clubhouse towards Ardmore Avenue. The entire hole, which turns to the right, can be seen from the tee and it is no more than a drive and pitch. But the drive must be exactly right, placed between flanking bunkers in the driving zone to open up the widest approach to the green. It may look innocuous, but placement of every shot is essential – it is the essence of Merion. Across Ardmore Avenue is something quite different: a hulking 536-yard par-5 along the most slender of fairways. With a drive that must carry a brook, with Wilson's bunkering artfully placed at key points along the left side and with out-of-bounds hard along the right.

The 3rd is a par-3 over a valley to a plateau green; and then we are into a 600 yard par-5. This one has a slightly wider fairway, but presents a comprehensively defended green. A narrow brook crosses in front and the rest of the green is ringed

Tall, spiky grass adds whiskers to many of Merion's 'white faces'. Here Jerry Pate escapes from the left-hand greenside bunker at the par-4 10th.

with five bunkers.

The sequence of holes 10, 11 and 12 is fascinating, proving yet again that sheer length need not be a primary factor in golf-course design, even considering the sophistication of contemporary golfers and their equipment. The 10th is 310 yards downhill. It bears to the left and its major defences are at the turn, on the left. The rectangular green is inclined across the approach shot. An enormous, optimistic drive will probably find trouble of its own making rather than the putting surface, and the trick is to drive far enough and find a place on the right side of the fairway.

The 11th, at 369 yards, is the 10th in reverse. The second shot is critical. The drive is down into a valley, then up to a pear-shaped green and over a stream which also runs along the right side of the green; a very strong bunker covers the left front and centre. The hole is famous above all for being the very last championship hole that Bobby Jones played. He stood on the green eight up with eight to play against Gene Homans in the final of the U.S. Amateur Championship of 1930. He had already won the British Amateur at St Andrews, the British Open at Hoylake and the U.S. Open at Interlachen (Minnesota). Two putts on Merion's 11th green made Jones immortal – the only man to win all four of these championships in one year.

Yet perhaps the most famous holes at Merion are the last three, playing as they do across the quarry and making a frightening finish to the round. The 16th is celebrated Quarry Hole. It is 429 yards and the downhill teeshot must be held short of the quarry. The second shot will require a 4-iron or something stronger to carry the quarry, and reach up the hill to the split-level green. The 17th is a par-3 of 222 yards, requiring a very big shot should it be into the wind. The shot is across the quarry to a green set lower than the tee, but with twin levels neatly framed by five bunkers. Here, Ben Hogan holed a birdie putt of 50 feet in the 1950 Open Championship play-off.

A long and perfect drive on the 18th, 463 yards, will carry the corner of the quarry, than demand a long shot across a dip in the ground to a raised green.

PINE VALLEY

According to Pine Valley records, the club had its origins in the fact that a group of golfers from the Philadelphia Country Club, at Bala, Pennsylvania, occasionally took what was then the Reading Railroad to play nearer the ocean at the Atlantic City Country Club. A Philadelphia hotelier, George A. Crump, was the leader of this happy band. En route one day, Crump noticed a piece of land along the railroad that he thought would be suitable for golf, and he and Howard Perrin, who was to become the first president of the Pine Valley club, investigated. They spent some days tramping over the property. It was virgin forest of pine, swamps and dense undergrowth, but on sandy soil and with a good deal of movement in the land. Crump, by some inexplicable miracle, saw it as the perfect landscape for an 'inland links'!

He formed a syndicate and persuaded 18 of his friends to contribute $1000 each – enough, they felt, to build 18 holes. In 1912 they bought 184 acres of the land from Sumner Ireland, its owner, and by January 1914 the *Philadelphia Inquirer*, a friendly newspaper always ready to publicise the venture, was able to report: 'The land there, comprising 184 rolling acres is, or was, the highest ground in southern New Jersey, 200 feet at points above the sea level, being more than 100 years ago the home to the Delaware Indians. It is the watershed between the Tuckahoe and Delaware rivers. The first blow of the axe was struck there last February; in the ten months since, $40,000 has been spent by the holding company under the direction of George A. Crump, chairman of the greens committee, to whom more than any other man is due the credit for the wonders wrought'.

PINE VALLEY Card of the course					
1	427 yards	par 4	10	146 yards	par 3
2	367 yards	par 4	11	392 yards	par 4
3	181 yards	par 3	12	344 yards	par 4
4	444 yards	par 4	13	448 yards	par 4
5	232 yards	par 3	14	184 yards	par 3
6	388 yards	par 4	15	591 yards	par 5
7	567 yards	par 5	16	433 yards	par 4
8	319 yards	par 4	17	338 yards	par 4
9	427 yards	par 4	18	428 yards	par 4
	3,352 yards	par 35		3,304 yards	par 35
		Total 6,656 yards par 70			

A Labour of Love
Like an Old Testament prophet marching into the wilderness, Crump abandoned the good life, and took to a spartan bungalow he erected on site. There he literally hacked out one of the greatest golf courses in America. He directed the felling of trees, the clearing of stumps, the building of dams to form lakes, the run of the fairways and the positioning of greens; he lived on the site of the course for the best part of six years.

Crump died rather suddenly in January 1918, after a short illness. He had spent some $250,000 of his own money with little thought of repayment. When he died, 14 holes had been finished and his estate left enough to complete the last four. Hugh Wilson, admired for his work particularly at Merion, and his brother Allen directed the work on these final holes, and by the end of 1918 the club had the complete set of 18.

Before then, the world of golf had come

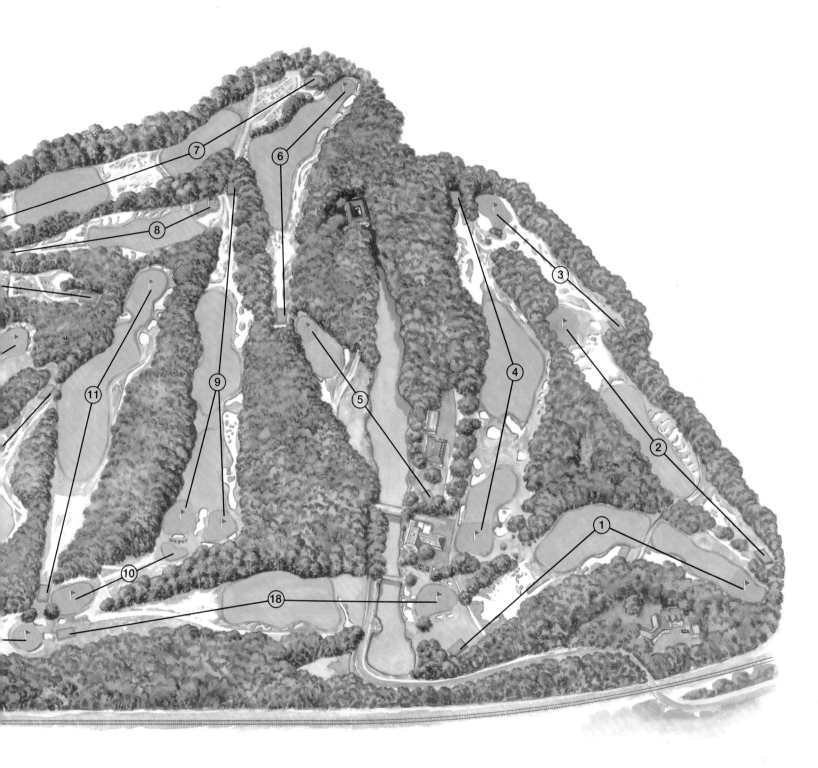

to realise that Pine Valley was an extraordinary golf course. Donald Ross of Dornoch and Pinehurst, one of golf's greatest architects, said plainly: 'This is the finest golf course in America.' Ben Sayers of North Berwick said on first seeing it: 'Why, it is Colt and Sunningdale!,' without knowing that Harry Colt,

the distinguished British architect who was largely responsible for Sunningdale and other fine courses, had been imported by Crump to check on his routing and bunkering. Yet Colt made very few changes to Pine Valley. And Francis Ouimet, Charles Blair Macdonald, Walter Travis, Jerome Travers, Chick Evans, and

Jim Barnes, all outstanding players of the time, sang its praises.

Pine Valley was blessed by another outstanding personality to follow George Crump. John Arthur Brown, a Philadelphia lawyer, joined the club just after the first World War, became president in 1929 and served for more than 30 years,

Left: *Howling wilderness gathers the sliced tee shot on the 367-yard 2nd hole. The sandy escarpments guarding the raised green can be seen at the top left.*

Pine Valley – there are simply large expanses of sand where on other courses fairways would be, and sandy areas surrounding greens. And all this sand is unraked – indeed, unrakeable: there is just too much of it. You simply take your chances with the lie.

Pine Valley is fierce but fair; fierce in the sense that it is absolutely penal ('it's not penal', said one victim, 'it's a penitentiary') in giving the golfer a single option on each shot, one route only, and punishing him severely if he fails; and fair, if any golf course can or should be described as fair, if the shots are played properly and sensibly. Then, its rewards are reasonably forthcoming. Bernard Darwin, the famous golf correspondent of *The Times* and an able (though irascible) player as a young man, was level par after seven holes. After a good drive to the 8th, he found himself 12 over par when he had holed out, and immediately became a spectator. There are even more horrifying stories of high scoring. John Brookes, a member and at one time president of the

guiding the club through some dire financial times during the Depression. Pine Valley has always been a golf club, nothing more. It has never held a major championship. For one thing, the members have not sought such a thing; for another, the layout of the course prohibits the movement of large crowds. At the Walker Cup Match of 1936 a gallery of some 3,000 was more than the club could easily handle.

Islands in a Sea of Sand

The Pine Valley course is set in a forest of pine and larch and oak. There are two good-sized lakes on the property. Each hole exists in isolation from the others – the design philosophy being that the golfer is obliged to play from one island to another; the islands are set in a sea of sand. This is the ultimate manifestation both of golf as a point-to-point game, and

of penal design. The golfer plays from a tee to an area of fairway which has been tailored to receive his drive and hold it there, in the correct place for his next shot. This may well be to a green which is entirely surrounded by sand. On a long par-4 or a par-5 hole, the second shot may be to another island, or peninsula, of sand. Thus there are few bunkers as such at

Right: *The par-3 14th hole is a beautiful one-shotter over water. Here Montogomerie and Sigel (U.S.) shake hands during the 1985 Walker Cup match.*

Left: *The 14th, at 184 yards, is the last of Pine Valley's gorgeous short holes. With 50 feet of water and bunkering fronting the green, and more water at back left, it demands rare confidence and precision from the tee.*

Burning Tree Club in Washington D.C., once played the 14th hole in 44 recorded strokes.

Pine Valley is a beautiful monster. The very essence of this golf course is that both the idea of it and the fact of it can overwhelm the golfer. He will find no solace in trying to persuade himself that it looks tougher than it is. It is not. It is just as tough as it looks. More than anything it is a test of a golfer's courage. If he brings a negative, defensive attitude to the course, the sandy wastes with their little bushes and shrubs and deep footprints will devour him. If he brings an arrogant, aggressive attitude to Pine Valley, the same thing will happen. But if he brings a positive attitude to the course, a sound reliable swing and some decent current form, he may find that the carries are after all not so fearsome and that there is much

pleasure to be found out there.

Most golf courses, on less inspiring land and designed by less inspired people, might have six very good holes, six good holes and six less than good holes. Pine valley has 18 gorgeous holes. The course has a splendid opening of four holes that swing back to the clubhouse. The very first stroke of the very first hole provides a declaration of what the player must digest at Pine Valley – a wasteland of sand spreading out 100 yards or so in front of the tee. The fairway island is ample, and contains the angle of the dog-leg to the right. Most of the rest of the way there is

The 'most awesome challenge' at Pine Valley, the 232-yard par-3 5th where only 'God can make a three'. The drive carrys a wide creek and a belt of scrub to a two-level green.

fairway to a raised green. On the 2nd hole the approach shot is the key. The drive should carry 175 yards onto a long, rectangular fairway island. The hole is 367 yards, not overlong, but the second shot must carry up to a green raised on top of a ridge, so that escarpments of sand beneath it face the player. The 3rd, a par-3 of 181 yards, has an elevated tee, and plays down to a waisted green, which is tilted to the left. Between tee and green lies nothing but an ocean of sand. The 4th is a long par-4 of 444 yards. It turns sharply to the right and there is sand in front of the tee, but Crump left 40 yards or so of fairway short of the green, for the golfer lacking a bit of length.

So the course goes on, one jewel following another. The 5th hole is a marvel, but perhaps no more than a first among equals in the one-shot holes. It is a

hulking 232 yards; when the wind is against him even the highest class of player will need a wood off the tee. The first half of the hole is over a lake, the second half over a modest piece of fairway, then a swatch of sand and then a raised green.

Hell's Half Acre

The par-5s are huge. They must be the only pair of par-5s that do not require bunkering in the ordinary sense. The 7th, at 567 yards and known as the Sahara, for fairly obvious reasons, is of sand, with three islands, one to receive the drive, one to receive the second shot and one containing the green. Between the first and second islands, a stretch of more than 100 yards, lies 'Hell's Half Acre'. The green is completely surrounded by sand and thus, it is said, no

man has ever reached it in two strokes.

The 15th on the other hand, at 591 yards, requires a drive briefly over a lake and onto the only continuous fairway on the course. All the way to the green it goes, up an avenue of pine, but narrowing insidiously as it approaches a small green.

The 13th is an exceptional hole, with less of the rigidity of some on the course. It provides an element of strategic choice – being one of the four final holes completed by Hugh Wilson. The hole is a strong, 448 yards par-4, played out to an island fairway. It turns to the left, and the drive must be to the centre or right to give

The 17th is only 338 yards long but is uphill all the way and the final 70-odd yards to the green are virtually desert scrub. This view from the green was taken during the 1985 Walker Cup.

a sight of the green. The heroic approach, directly on to the putting surface, must carry sand all the way. To the front right-hand side, there is an area of fairway to receive the approach if the drive was short. This route leaves a pitch to the flagstick and the hope of one putt. Most reasonable men would be content to score four on this hole, however they did it, and would not be devastated to score five. The course then has an appealing finish. The 17th is 338 yards, but it is uphill and played across water to a rather small green. The 18th is a fine, attractive final hole of 428 yards, played to an island fairway, then across water and yet more sand to one of Pine Valley's larger greens.

Pine Valley is unique: it is as penal as Oakmont; it is as beautiful as Augusta or Muirfield Village. It is one of the world's greatest courses.

PINEHURST

The resort village of Pinehurst, more or less midway between Charlotte and Raleigh in the sandhills of North Carolina, is a paradise. Surely no community in the world, St Andrews in Scotland included, is more obsessed with the game of golf, and Pinehurst's No 2 course is its masterpiece. The eminence of Pinehurst and its development as a shrine of world golf, with seven courses and a permanent resident population of little more than 3,000, is linked to the lives of famous

men, to the village of Dornoch in Scotland and to fate.

James Tufts of Boston and the American Soda Fountain Company did not enjoy the best of health and at the end of the last century had taken to spending much of the bleak New England winters in the much drier, milder climate of North Carolina. With the idea of developing at Pinehurst a winter resort that other New Englanders might find attractive, he bought, at one dollar an acre,

some 5,000 acres of almost barren timberland, and had an unpretentious course laid out on land that, though little appreciated at the time, was ideal for golf – its sandy subsoil and short crisp fairway grasses being about as close to links conditions as anyone could hope for.

In 1900 came two events of deep and lasting significance for Pinehurst. First, Harry Vardon, the great English champion who later in the year was to win the U.S. Open, came to the village in the

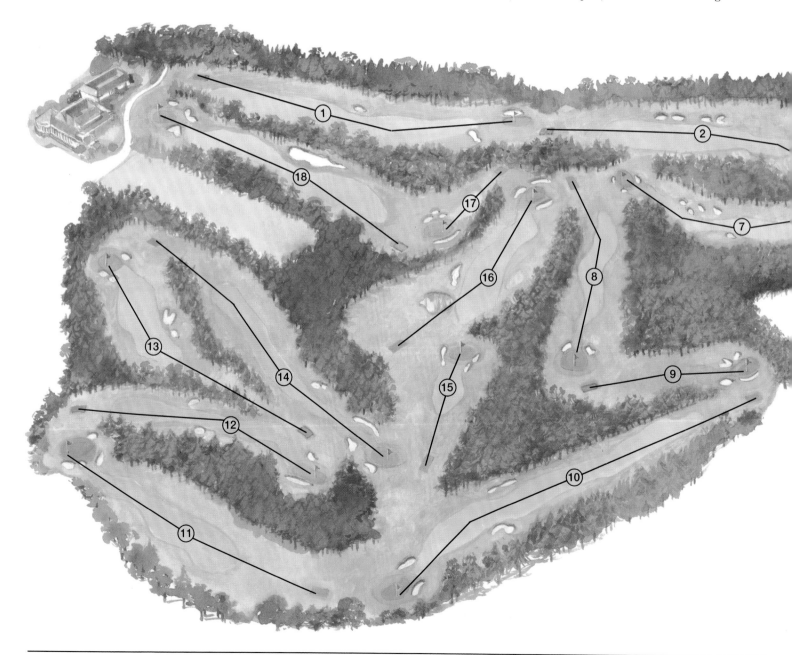

PINEHURST Card of the No. 2 course					
1	396 yards	par 4	10	578 yards	par 5
2	441 yards	par 4	11	433 yards	par 4
3	335 yards	par 4	12	415 yards	par 4
4	547 yards	par 5	13	374 yards	par 4
5	445 yards	par 4	14	436 yards	par 4
6	212 yards	par 3	15	201 yards	par 3
7	401 yards	par 4	16	531 yards	par 5
8	487 yards	par 5	17	190 yards	par 3
9	166 yards	par 3	18	432 yards	par 4
	3,430 yards	par 36		3,590 yards	par 36
	Total 7,020 yards par 72				

spring and played four exhibition rounds. The artistry of the great man, the simplicity with which he swung the club and his unerring control over his shots made a powerful impression on the locals and visitors alike. Second, later that year Donald Ross arrived to become Pinehurst's new professional and greenkeeper.

Links with Royal Dornoch

Donald James Ross was born in 1873 in Dornoch, a lovely Highland village of little more than 1,000 souls, some 50 miles north of Inverness in Scotland. He was apprenticed to a local carpenter and became an enthusiastic and talented golfer. Golf had been played at Dornoch for hundreds of years, but in 1877 the Dornoch Golf Club was formed at the instigation of an exceptional local man, John

The well guarded green on the 5th, a long and difficult par-4. The tee shot should be down the right half of the fairway to allow a clear way into the angled green.

Sutherland, and in 1886, Sutherland invited Old Tom Morris from St Andrews to define 18 holes of 'championship quality' at Dornoch. Sutherland arranged for young Ross to go to St Andrews and learn the clubmaking craft from Old Tom. He spent two years there.

At this point, Robert Wilson, a professor at Harvard University, visited Dornoch and became a pupil of Donald Ross. He told the young Scot of the tremendous interest in golf in America, and encouraged him to emigrate. Thus in 1898, Ross knocked on the Wilson door in Cambridge, Massachussetts and went to work at the Oakley Club, in nearby Waterstown. Here, our Bostonian James Tufts completes the chain. He observed Ross in action, admired his conduct and was impressed by his feelings for the traditions of golf and his attitude to course design. He invited Ross to become the winter professional at Pinehurst, and the young Scot arrived there in December of 1900. Ross got to work on improving the existing course, and in his very first year had started to lay out Pinehurst No 2. At the same time, Tufts had instituted a tree-planting programme.

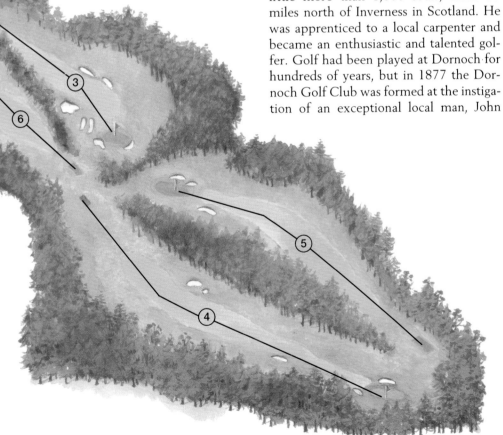

Ross's Triumph

Ross finished Pinehurst No 2 in 1907, in the sense that 18 holes were completed reaching to not quite 6,000 yards; but he continually improved and polished his work over the years as better greenkeeping and maintenance methods and equipment became available. The course as we know it today is a triumph, a links in a forest. It has a par of 72 at around 7,000 yards, and demands of the golfer virtually every shot in this repertoire. It has in abundance what we now think of as Ross characteristics: rather small greens with subtle rather than severe contouring, and with verges and swales around them to demand finesse when chipping the ball or playing a pitch-and-run to the flag.

Ross wanted golf to be a pleasure, not a penance. Unlike Fownes at Oakmont, Charles Blair Macdonald at The National, or – above all – George Crump at Pine Valley, Ross did not feel that a hazard should necessarily be penal. Rather, the player should have the possibility of redeeming his wayward shot with the chance to play an imaginative recovery. Ross's thinking was that a championship course should demand 'long and accurate

Above: *The delightful 17th hole is a medium length one-shotter whose pine-fringed green is bunkered everywhere, except the left front.*

Right: *The par-5 4th curves gently left on its uphill journey to the green, which is normally reachable in two good shots. The World Golf Hall of Fame (opened in 1974) is beyond the green.*

tee shots, accurate iron play, precise handling of the short game, and consistent putting'. He built all of these requirements into Pinehurst and other fine courses with which he was involved, such as Oak Hill, Seminole, Oakland Hills and Scioto, where Nicklaus learned the game.

Donald Ross built two further 18-hole courses at Pinehurst, but Pinehurst No 2 remained his favourite: the 'fairest test I have ever designed'. The 1st hole is a par-4 of 396 yards turning slightly left; a reasonable hole which should give anyone a comfortable start to the round. The 2nd is another par-4, this time of 441 yards turning slightly to the right and slightly less reasonable, and the 3rd, at 335 yards, is a very closely guarded drive and pitch hole. Thus the course leads the golfer into

its treasures with progressively more testing holes. The 4th is 547 yards, a big par-5 uphill to the green at the most distant corner of the course, but it is the par-4s which hold the key to scoring.

The course has an interesting finish, full of birdie opportunities for the accomplished player. The 15th is a short hole of 201 yards, a straight shot to a fairly open green. No 16 is a par-5 of some 531 yards, with a drive over a pond – the only water hazard on the course. On a direct line, the tee shot here calls for a carry of 180 yards over the water, but Ross provides an alternative fairway line to the right. No 17 is another par-3 of 190 yards, and the last hole is 432 yards, back up to the elegant, spacious clubhouse.

Although the sandy ground has given it the flavour of a links, Pinehurst No 2 is in an odd way the summation of the American parkland course. The pine trees, which are never overbearing, nevertheless screen each hole from its neighbour; isolating the player from the world as a links never does. All in all, it is an entirely stimulating experience, particularly when the blossom blooms in the Carolina springtime.

OAKLAND HILLS

'I'm glad I brought this course, this monster, to its knees'. Thus spoke Ben Hogan at the presentation ceremonies of the 1951 U.S. Open Championship at Oakland Hills, which he won with a final round of 67. His remark has passed into the folklore of the game. Whether or not Oakland Hills is a monster is a moot point. Certainly at the time it was a brutal course, and Hogan's win, like Hogan's comment, remains something of a milestone in the game.

Oakland Hills, in Birmingham, Michigan, on the edge of 'greater' Detroit, was built in 1917, the club having been formed by wealthy executives of the Ford Motor Company. The course was designed by Donald Ross of Pinehurst fame. In 1918 Walter Hagen became the head professional on a handsome retainer. But after he won the U.S. Open of 1919 he decided that a club job, however rewarding, was not to be compared with the delights of exhibition matches and public appearances awaiting him all over the world, and he quit.

The course was considered a fine Ross design and a good test, and it staged the Opens of 1924, when Cyril Walker, the little Englishman originally from Hoylake,

beat Bobby Jones into second place; and of 1937, which was won by Ralph Guldahl, for a few short seasons just about the best player in America. By the time of the next Open, scheduled for 1951, the members felt that the course needed 'modernisation' – in those days the host club and not the USGA was responsible for course preparation. The architect, Robert Trent Jones – some of the players thought that he was the monster – was called in, and he made clear that his intention was that the course should 'catch up with the players'. Jones had studied the play and collected data at several earlier Opens. He was convinced that contemporary players, now with steel shafts and much improved golf balls, were simply gobbling up golf courses which dated from the 1920s.

Thus Jones filled in all the fairway bunkers in the 200–220 yards range – the players were simply driving over them. He cut new bunkers 230–260 yards out from the tees, and allowed the rough to grow in on either side of the fairway so that the landing zone for tee shots in some cases was little more than 20 yards across. And the bunkering around the greens was tightened, the result being a course that

OAKLAND HILLS Card of the South course					
1	446 yards	par 4	10	459 yards	par 4
2	521 yards	par 5	11	420 yards	par 4
3	202 yards	par 3	12	567 yards	par 5
4	439 yards	par 4	13	173 yards	par 3
5	442 yards	par 4	14	468 yards	par 4
6	368 yards	par 4	15	388 yards	par 4
7	408 yards	par 4	16	408 yards	par 4
8	458 yards	par 4	17	201 yards	par 3
9	227 yards	par 3	18	459 yards	par 4
3,511 yards	par 35		3,543 yards	par 35	
Total 7,054 yards par 70					

punished the slightest error severely, demanded extreme accuracy, and rewarded rational thinking in the sense that players would prosper if they slavishly followed the only route to each hole that Jones was prepared to allow.

Hogan opened his '51 Open with a 76, a round of some indecision and uncertainty in the face of Jones' changes. But he improved every round and, deciding that attack was the only way to subdue the monster, he tore into the course and produced a brilliant last round of 67. He later called it the finest round of his career. He finished it with an arrogant, defiant flourish. The 18th hole is 459 yards, turning to the right. Hogan hit an immense drive, then a mid-iron that stopped 15 feet from the flagstick, and holed the putt.

After the controversy over the difficulty of the course for that Championship, the USGA increasingly took responsibility for the preparation of all their championship courses. But there is no doubt that Trent Jones produced the makings of a very good course – even a great one, the more so that it has now matured impressively. At 7,054 yards it is a big, open parkland course, not over-wooded, featuring two lakes and a stream and

The 16th hole at Oakland Hills, par 4, 408 yards, demanding a brave and accurate second shot across or around water. Andy North and T. C. Chen on the green during the U.S. Open of 1985, which North won.

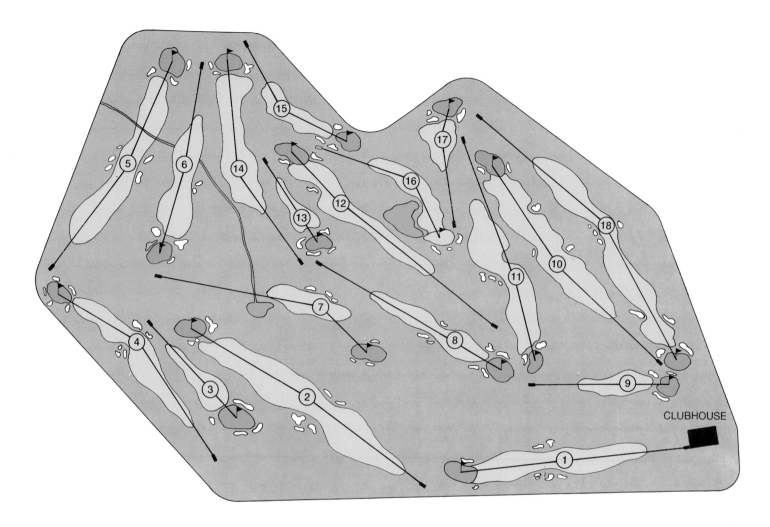

T. C. Chen playing the 5th, a hole he will never forget. In the last round of the 1985 U.S. Open, he was four strokes ahead of the field, but on this chip shot actully struck the ball twice, scoring eight on the hole.

many fiendish par-4 holes, only two of them shorter than 400 yards. It has kept the modern professionals reasonably in check. Gene Littler's Open total in 1961 was 281, the same as Guldahl's 24 years earlier, and little worse than Andy North's 279 in 1985.

Oakland Hills has produced shots of high courage and of low, tragic farce. In the 1972 PGA Championship Gary Player, with three holes to play, was level with Jim Jamieson – the latter already on the 18th. Player's tee shot on 16, a drive and pitch hole, was wildly sliced into rough which had been trampled by spectators. The hole played properly is a drive out to the 250 yards mark (the hole was 408 yards), then a half-right turn to pitch along the length of the green. The putting surface is screened at the front and along the right side by a good-sized lake. Player's drive had left him in the rough 150 yards from the flagstick, with a blind shot which had to clear a copse of willow trees,

travel far enough to cross the lake, then somehow get down onto the green without running into the bunkers immediately behind it – one of them exactly in line with his shot and the flagstick. Player hit a

9-iron. The ball stopped four feet from the flag. He holed the putt, the birdie winning him the championship.

In the U.S. Open of 1985, T.C. Chen of Taiwan, who had led after three rounds, was four strokes ahead of Andy North and eight under par with 14 holes to play. It was surely Chen's championship. At the 5th hole (442 yards) Chen drove into perfect position. Astonishingly, and for no apparent reason, he then hit a 4-iron at least 30 yards off line into heavy rough. Chen's third shot left him a yard or two short of the green, but still in heavy rough. Now came the most bizarre shot imaginable. Chen chopped down on the ball with his wedge. The ball popped up in front of him and the blade of the wedge, in following through, struck the ball for a second time. Penalised, he eventually took eight on the hole and Andy North went on to win the championship. T.C. Chen finished second, one stroke behind.

MUIRFIELD VILLAGE

The course that Jack built should be one of the wonders of the world, for surely no golfer in the world knows more about the playing of great holes and great courses than Jack Nicklaus. His lovely course at Dublin, Ohio, just to the north of Columbus, Jack's home town, was ready for play in 1976, but the concept dates from 1966 when Nicklaus, sitting on the clubhouse verandah at Augusta National, said to a friend, Ivor Young: 'Wouldn't it be great to have something like this in Columbus?'

Nicklaus has never had any qualms about spending vast amounts of money on various projects. He has charged immense fees for his design work, he has never been particularly thrifty, and he has always been his own man. In the 1960s, he was under the management of Mark McCormack and his company. When Jack told Mark about his notion of building a course in the Columbus area, Mark said: 'Forget it'. He took the view that Nicklaus might as well stand on a street corner setting fire to 100 dollar bills. But Nicklaus is a stubborn perfectionist. He went ahead, and after many dramas and disappointments managed to cobble together the finance needed. On 27 May 1974, Nicklaus drove the first ball at the opening ceremony. The costs to that point were four million dollars – 'That would not even get you started today', he said recently. Certainly, 16 years on, you'd have to multiply that sum by, say, a factor of 5.

Muirfield Village, completely dissimilar to the original Muirfield after which it was named, is on steeply rolling land, providing a succession of valleys along which the fairways run. Nicklaus has written: 'From the player's standpoint, everything is well-defined. You know exactly where you have to go and what you have to do. Your short game is tested if you miss a green, but there is not one place on the whole golf course that anyone is going to say is unfair. Golf to me is a game of precision more than power, and I think the course reflects that'.

Nicklaus, with the help of fellow designers Desmond Muirhead and Pete Dye, set out to build a course that would meet three essential requirements. Firstly, it should stretch the abilities of the world's best players in tournament conditions. (Nicklaus' Memorial Tournament is played at Muirfield Village in May.) Secondly it should provide good vantage points to the crowds attending the tournament, and thirdly it should accommodate 'lesser' men, the members of the club that he would form. Since the course opened there have been changes, large and small, nearly 100 in all.

The most extensive changes have taken place at the 11th. Its original design saw a

MUIRFIELD VILLAGE					
Card of the course					
1	446 yards	par 4	10	441 yards	par 4
2	452 yards	par 4	11	538 yards	par 5
3	392 yards	par 4	12	158 yards	par 3
4	204 yards	par 3	13	442 yards	par 4
5	531 yards	par 5	14	363 yards	par 4
6	430 yards	par 4	15	490 yards	par 5
7	549 yards	par 5	16	204 yards	par 3
8	189 yards	par 3	17	430 yards	par 4
9	410 yards	par 4	18	437 yards	par 4
3,603 yards	par 36		3,503 yards	par 36	
Total 7,106 yards par 72					

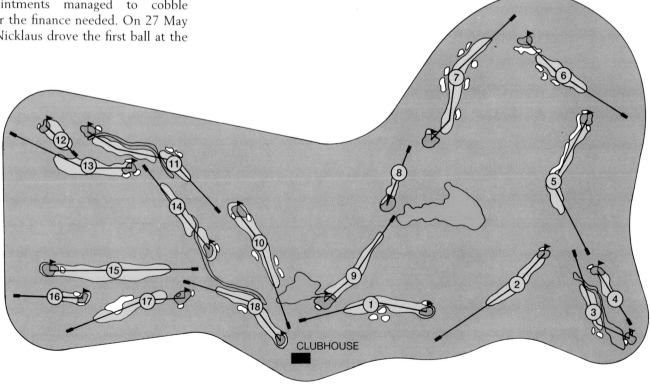

Larry Nelson and Lanny Wadkins against Sandy Lyle and Bernhard Langer in the 1987 Ryder Cup. Nelson hits at the 16th, a par 3 reminiscent of the 16th at Augusta.

stream cutting across the fairway from left to right at about 320 yards from the tee, then running along the right side of the fairway up to the green; it then turned left and fed into a lake, which covered the entire front of the green. When Nicklaus played the hole he realised that from the landing area of the drive, in the fairway, the lake could not be seen. He had it filled and now a narrow stream crosses in front of the green. The cost of that one operation was about $200,000!

On the tenth anniversary of his Memorial Tournament, Nicklaus wrote of golf: 'I believe it is a much better game played downhill than up. You drive from a high tee at the first, second, third, fourth and fifth, on seven you drive over a valley which has the same effect. On seven, eight and nine you drive from elevated tees, on ten you drive over a valley even though you are rising and on eleven, twelve, thirteen and fourteen you hit from a high tee. There is not one tee shot that you are actually hitting uphill. In fact, there are only two second shots on the whole golf course that are uphill'.

There are only 70 bunkers at Muirfield Village, not an excessive number, but it seems that Nicklaus in designing the course succumbed to the obsession that contemporary American designers have with water hazards. Water is in play at no fewer that eleven holes. At the 2nd, a creek crosses the fairway, runs along the right side of it then swings behind the green. At the 3rd, a stream crosses the fairway from the right, then opens out into a lake fronting the entire green. The hole is 392 yards and the green split level. On the 5th hole, a par-5 of 531 yards, a brook runs right up the centre of the second half of the fairway, before passing the green to the left. A stream crosses the sixth fairway and there is a pond in front of the green. Seven and eight are dry holes, but on nine, one of Muirfield's tightest driving holes, all along the right

side of a narrow fairway the ground falls away into woods and once more a stream crosses close to the green. At ten the drive crosses a pond. On the big par-5 11th, as we have seen, again there is water, all along the right side and again crossing in front of the green. The 12th, a par-3 of 158 yards, like the 16th at Augusta National, is over water all the way. And holes 14, 15 and 18 have streams, although they do not come into play as the other water hazards.

Finally, there are three separate tees at each hole, some fifty yards apart – marvellously cosmetic, but surely ruinous on the greenkeeping budget. But that's Nicklaus. Often the members' tee will be fifty yards ahead of the tournament tee. And in providing good vantage points for spectators at his tournament, with little or no expense spared, Nicklaus has done it very well, with mounds and ridges put in place along the fairways, and amphitheatres around the greens. Quite simply Muirfield Village is a magnificent achievement and a great course maintained in mint condition.

AUGUSTA NATIONAL

The Augusta National is the best-known golf course in the world. The Augusta Masters is the best-known golf tournament in the world. Millions of viewers throughout the world, not all of them golfers, see the tournament played on this distinctive course each spring as all the sporting nations of the world link into the American television coverage.

The course is immaculately maintained. Acres of closely-cropped green and luxuriant turf swaddle the property, while magnificent Georgia pines soar 100 feet in the air, forming avenues and backdrops for the holes. The tournament is played in April, in the soft Georgia springtime, and if the weather has behaved and the gardening staff have got their timing right, the entire course will be a flood of flowering shrubs which give names to the golf holes – azalea, dogwood, redbud, camellia, flowering peach, magnolia and so on.

However, the Masters has its critics. They claim that it cannot be called a championship, unless you want to call it a 'closed' championship. Certainly it has a restricted field. Most players qualify to play through established criteria; but many, including up to a dozen amateurs, are invited at the whim of, not a national association but a hugely conservative, often arrogant club. Indeed, Hord Hardin, the present tournament chairman, who could be described as a traditionalist, has been dubbed 'Lord' Hardin by many American journalists. But, in fairness, the Augusta club has never claimed the Masters to be anything other than an invitational tournament.

Bobby Jones's Legacy

When Bobby Jones retired from competitive championship play in 1930, having won the Amateur and Open Championships of both Britain and the United States that year, he had very clear ideas regarding the design of golf holes – ideas which he had amassed in 10 years of play on both sides of the Atlantic. He had often thought of building a course which would incorporate these ideas and he

AUGUSTA NATIONAL Card of the course							
1	Tea Olive	400 yards	par 4	10	Camellia	485 yards	par 4
2	Pink Dogwood	555 yards	par 5	11	White Dogwood	455 yards	par 4
3	Flowering Peach	360 yards	par 4	12	Golden Bell	155 yards	par 3
4	Flowering Crab Apple	205 yards	par 3	13	Azalea	465 yards	par 5
5	Magnolia	435 yards	par 4	14	Chinese Fir	405 yards	par 4
6	Juniper	180 yards	par 3	15	Firethorn	500 yards	par 5
7	Pampas	360 yards	par 4	16	Redbud	170 yards	par 3
8	Yellow Jasmine	535 yards	par 5	17	Nandina	400 yards	par 4
9	Carolina Cherry	435 yards	par 4	18	Holly	405 yards	par 4
		3,465 yards	par 36			3,440 yards	par 36
			Total 6,905 yards par 72				

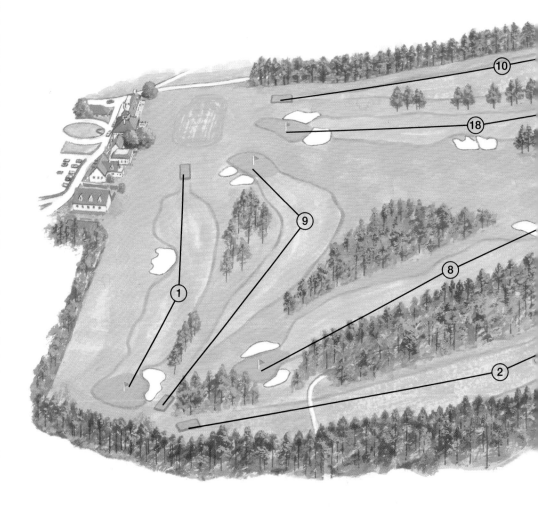

discussed this with a few of his friends.

Jones, from Atlanta, knew the small town of Augusta, 100 miles away – he married an Augusta girl – and often played winter golf there. He also knew Clifford Roberts, a New York merchant banker, who spent time every winter in Augusta. Thus when 'Fruitlands', a famous nursery, came up for sale, Jones and Roberts snapped it up, all 365 acres, at Depression prices. It seemed perfect terrain for the course Jones had in mind. He then had the good sense to retain Dr Alister Mackenzie, a Scot who had emigrated to America and given up medicine in favour of golf-course design, to lay out the course. They proved ideal partners. Jones had been impressed by the size of the double greens at St Andrews, and by the speedy links greens he had found in Scotland and England – sand-based, close-cropped, subtly contoured and fast, very fast. Mackenzie knew them well, and was of the same mind. He had designed Royal Melbourne West in 1926 (see page 186), and Cypress Point in 1928 (see page 52), and was at the height of his powers.

Jones had visualised a club of which his friends, drawn from all over the country, would be members. It would be for winter golf, open only from November to April, and only for golf: there were to be no swimming pools and no tennis courts.

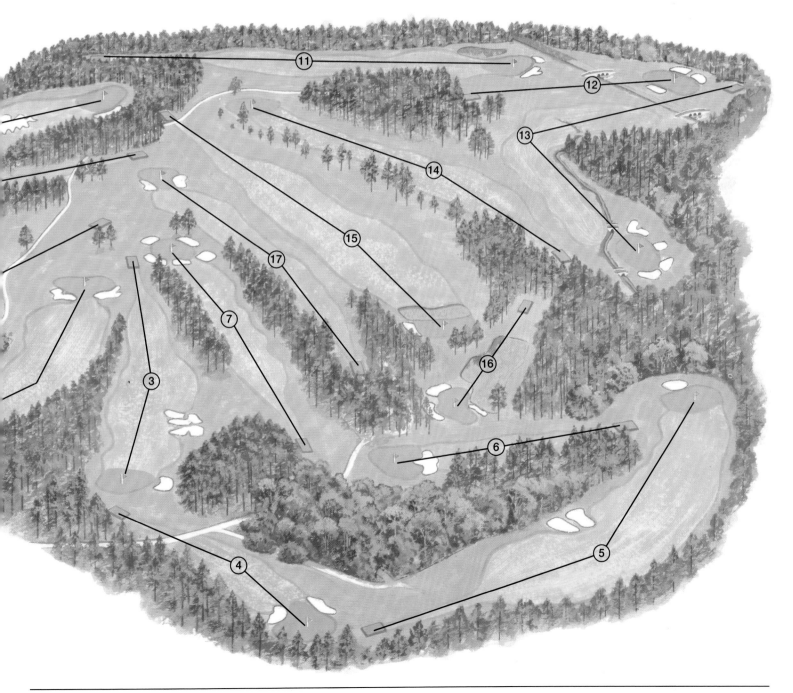

Left: *Part of Amen Corner, the 13th at Augusta National, the beautiful par-5 'Azalea' hole, with its tiara of bunkers behind and the famous Rae's Creek in front.*

Right: *Spain's José-Maria Olazábal hits a tee shot at the short 12th on the first day of the 1989 Masters. The small green is fiercely guarded by bunkers and at front by a creek.*

He made it clear to Mackenzie that he wanted a course which his friends could play and enjoy, yet at the same time one that would test tournament players. The property they had to work with is in the rough shape of a square, with a pleasant but small pre-Civil War mansion serving as the clubhouse on the north side. From there the property falls a good 100 feet down to Rae's Creek, running along the bottom boundary. The downslope is gentle and most of the holes run across rather than up and down the slope. Nowhere do two successive holes run in the same direction, and seldom do they slope excessively from side to side.

When Jones and Mackenzie had finished, they had the 'ultimate' American meadowland course. Nevertheless, its critics have strong reservations about Augusta as a true championship test. There is no rough on the course – at least, no rough as the Scots or Irish or anyone else might know it. Under Augusta's towering pines, there might be a few needles, but little else to inhibit a full recovery shot. Also, the fairways are ridiculously wide, so that sluggers can blast away off the tees to their hearts'

content. And there is an odd absence of bunkers at Augusta – fewer than 50 in all, and only 10 of these in the fairways. Thus far it seems ready made for a careful 15-handicap player!

Lightning-fast Greens
But then there are the greens. Many of them are raised a foot or two and plateaued. All of them are enormous, with extremely steep slopes, and for the Masters they are lightning-fast. It is the greens that hold the key to scoring at

Augusta – more so than almost anywhere else. Its critics say that since putting takes up 50 per cent of the strokes in the theoretical round of golf, it should constitute no more than 50 per cent of any course's challenge. At the Masters, they claim it is much more than that – some would call it 100 per cent of the challenge, since the tee to green requirement is basically little more than that the player should be able to hit the ball a long way.

Many changes have been made over the years to the original design. One of the most important, made by Jones himself, was to switch the two halves of the course, the original outward half now being the inward half. In addition, the 10th, 11th, 13th, 15th, 16th and 18th, in particular have been strengthened.

'Amen Corner'
The inward half of the Augusta National course, as set up for the Masters, merits

The 10th hole. It is here, on the final afternoon of the Masters, that the fun really begins for it is then, on the homeward stretch, that nerves are as much an ally as skill.

The beautifully manicured and fast greens of the par-5 15th with the 16th behind. With water to carry on the second shot this is a formidable hole, but reachable in two for the long hitters.

some study. The 10th hole is a downhill drive. A ridge runs along the centre of the fairway, the hole turning slightly right to left. A drive lined up on the right half will be thrown further right, leaving a second shot of inordinate length to the green. A drive with a line only just left of centre will be thrown forward and down to the left, to a pocket of fairway which will put 20 yards on the shot, give the player a flat and level stance and a clear look at the green. The 11th hole, now 455 yards, has a lake along its left side and part of its front calling for an audacious second shot of great accuracy. Often played defensively.

The 12th is one of the world's great par-3 holes. It measures 155 yards. It plays to a green which is quite wide, but narrow from front to back. Rae's Creek crosses in front, pushing up towards the putting surface. A frontal bunker is squeezed between water and putting surface and there are two bunkers off the

back of the green, with its backcloth of shrubs and tall pines. The pin is often cut on a direct line with front and back bunkers. There may be only a handful of yards between flagstick and water. Behind the green are flowering shrubs and a wall of tall pine trees. And up there, above the green, tree-top high, is wind, the great unknown factor. The player will be hitting a high pitch to this hole, to a really minute target area. If only he could know what the wind will do to his shot, if indeed there is any wind: there's little point in throwing up strands of grass in the air here. So this 12th hole, severe enough in its basic parts, becomes an enigma wrapped in a mystery.

The drive on the 465-yard 13th hole is

like that on the 10th (and unlike many other Augusta tee shots) in that it demands some precision. The hole dog-legs sharply to the left. The perfect drive will be long, with a drawn tail on it, up the left side of the fairway. The creek runs along most of the left side of the hole, crossing in front of the green. The fairway slopes down towards the creek. But if the drive is played precisely, it will carry past the corner and, drawn to the left, will find yet again a pocket of fairway which gives a flat and level lie; on the inside of the angle, this position represents the shortest route to the hole. The second is the gambler's shot. Can he carry that brook and hit the big, two-tiered green and have two comfortable putts for his birdie? Or should he play short and hope to make his birdie with an accurate pitch and a single putt? These three holes are known collectively as Amen Corner, and many of the US Masters tournaments have been won and lost here.

A Tough Finish

The 14th fairway slopes left to right, but the main defences of the hole are the mounds and slopes on the very big green – one of the most difficult on the course. The 15th is a straight par-5 of 500 yards, the drive up to and over a crest, then a second to a crowned green which lies across the shot and is protected by a lake covering its entire front. The second shot is the gamble, of course, like its equivalent on 13. Can the water be carried? Some years back, at the top of the rise on the 15th, some mounds were put in place on the right side to reduce the advantage the long hitters had when their shots would bound on far down the slope. But nowadays the best players will usually be hitting some kind of iron shot to the green. Indeed, the big hitters must beware their approach running through the green and into the lake at the 16th.

The 170-yard 16th, with a fairway consisting almost entirely of water, has

Sandy Lyle's stupendous 7-iron second shot soars out of the fairway bunker on the 72nd hole at Augusta in 1988. It finished 10 feet above the pin and his birdie putt clinched the Masters.

been a turning point in many a Masters. So it was in 1988, when Sandy Lyle won. His victory is best remembered for the epic 7-iron shot he played from the fairway bunker at the very last hole which set up the birdie he needed to win. Yet the birdie he made on the 16th was no less critical. Having lost his lead at Amen Corner, he hit a 7-iron shot some 15 feet above the hole. The fast, downhill putt had a break of a good 18 inches, from left to right, but Lyle rolled it smoothly into the centre of the hole.

The main difficulty on the 17th hole, 400 yards, is in judging distance on the second shot – a pitch to a green slightly above the player – particularly when the pin is behind one of the two front

bunkers. The 18th hole, 405 yards, is uphill all the way, the final drive out of a tunnel of pine trees, the hole turning to the right past fairway bunkers on the left (where Lyle was trapped in 1988), up to the two-level 18th green sloping wickedly towards the player.

The exploits of the great players have highlighted this inward half, some of them scarcely credible: the famous 'double-eagle' of Gene Sarazen in 1935, when he holed his second shot, a 4-wood, at the 15th to tie Craig Wood before winning the play-off; Byron Nelson making up six shots on leader Ralph Guldahl at Amen Corner in 1937 by means of a birdie at the 12th and an eagle at the 13th; Ben Hogan, then 54 years old, coming home in a flawless 30 shots in 1967; Gary Player winning in 1978 with a preposterous last round of 64, including seven birdies; Jack Nicklaus calculating coldly that a final round of 65 might just win him the Masters, and doing it in 1986.

OLYMPIC

Olympic Lakeside is the ultimate American parkland course. So heavily forested is it that the trees must be considered as much a hazard as any bunker or stream. The golfer will find himself playing from tees so over-arched by trees as to be almost claustrophobic, and he will be asked to drive along precise lines down narrow, forbidding chutes between huge stands of pine and cypress, eucalyptus and even some California redwoods, many of them growing to 80 feet. The Olympic fairways are so heavily screened by dense walls of these giants that the golfer seems to be walking along a series of trenches, each hole unvisible from its neighbours. Not surprisingly it can seem an almost spooky place.

The other pronounced characteristic of this formidable course is the sloping fairways – almost all of them tilt from one side to the other, every one is a dog-leg of varying degree, and the slopes throw the ball to the *outside* of the angles. Yet the history of the Lakeside course and the Olympic Club show that it never was a natural parkland. The club made it so.

The Olympic Club of San Francisco originated in the middle of the last century as a gymnastic club, and then developed to embrace almost all sports. The 'Athletic' club in all the major U.S. cities was an American institution. These clubs had, and still have, city premises providing swimming pools, billiards, handball, racquets, fencing, shooting and the like, and of course restaurants. In the golden days of amateurism, before the advent of professionalism and more recently, of televised sport, they would produce teams in football, basketball and ice-hockey which could compete at the highest level; and they produced many Olympic athletes.

The San Francisco club had splendid city headquarters by the time America entered the First World War, but even then a growing demand for golf could be satisfied only when it took over the ailing Lakeside Country CLub. Lakeside's property on the west side of the city, close by the ocean, ran to 365 acres of barren, treeless ground with a ridge running through the property and an existing but indifferent course, laid out early in the century by three immigrant Scottish professionals.

Lakeside and Ocean

Willie Watson, yet another Scot, who had designed the Minikahda club in Minneapolis, was retained to lay out two courses, one on either side of the ridge – one, 'inland', Lakeside; the other, on the seaward side of the ridge, Ocean. Savage storms in 1926 washed out some of the holes, and Sam Whiting, at that time professional and greenkeeper to the club, designed and built two new courses and completely altered the face of the landscape by planting 43,000 trees, three-quarters of them on the Lakeside course. A quarter of a century later they had grown to make Lakeside a forest and every one of its fairways a tree-lined avenue.

The sea mist that rolls in regularly on the prevailing wind from the Pacific Ocean, often covering the entire city,

OLYMPIC Card of the course					
1	530 yards	par 5	10	412 yards	par 4
2	400 yards	par 4	11	427 yards	par 4
3	220 yards	par 3	12	386 yards	par 4
4	428 yards	par 4	13	185 yards	par 3
5	456 yards	par 4	14	417 yards	par 4
6	434 yards	par 4	15	147 yards	par 3
7	288 yards	par 4	16	604 yards	par 5
8	135 yards	par 3	17	517 yards	par 5
9	424 yards	par 4	18	338 yards	par 4
3,315 yards	par 35		3,433 yards	par 36	
Total 6,748 yards par 71					

makes San Francisco a damp town, and Lakeside has, not surprisingly, little difficulty in growing grass. Its problems are in controlling growth, and the Lakeside rough can be dense and tough. The tilted fairways will carry a carelessly-hit ball into the trees and the rough, and recovery from these places often means a scrambling shot out to the nearest point of the fairway – in effect, a shot lost. Ben Hogan experienced just that in the play-off to the 1955 U.S. Open, against Jack Fleck, an unknown touring pro from a public course in Iowa. Just as Hogan finished his fourth round and seemed to have won a record fifth Championship, Fleck tied him with a brilliant last round of 67, scoring two birdies over the four final holes. In the play-off Hogan, one stroke behind, hooked his drive into fierce rough on the 18th hole and scored six on the hole. Fleck was champion.

Lakeside's rough can be unmanageable, as Arnold Palmer found when the Open next came to Olympic in 1966. The 16th is a huge par-5 of more than 600 yards which turns progressively to the left in a crescent shape. Palmer drove into the left rough and, Arnold being Arnold, elected to play a 3-iron out of that jungle. He failed. The hole cost him six. He dropped seven shots over the last nine to Billy Casper, tied the championship and lost the play-off!

Olympic Lakeside is an unrelenting course, even a disquieting course. There is

Ben Hogan, watched by Sam Snead, lines out a drive in practice for the 1955 U.S. Open in San Francisco. Hogan, seeking a record fifth Open win, lost a play-off to club pro Jack Fleck.

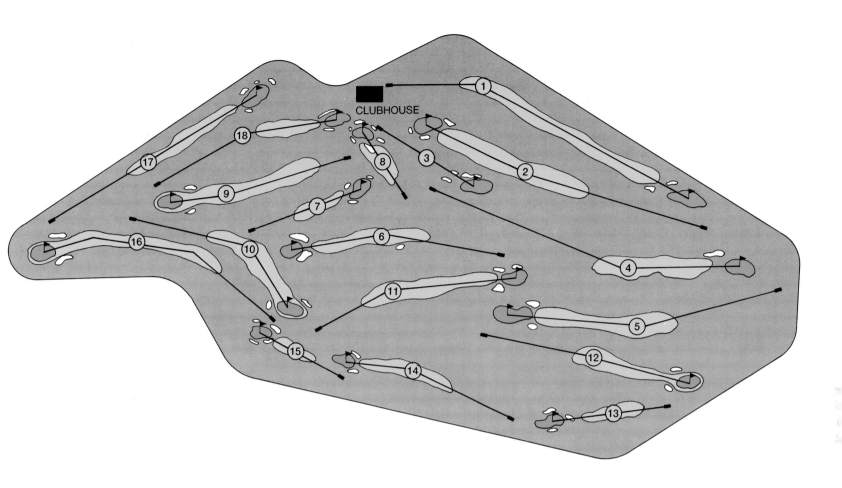

only one fairway bunker, on the 6th, and there is no water hazard. Yet the sloping fairways with the cambers going the wrong way, the severe rough and the small, closely-bunkered greens make it very exacting. The 18th hole somehow personifies the entire course. It is a mere 338 yards, played downhill, perhaps with an iron, to a slight fairway which falls off to the right and has a minute green, totally surrounded by bunkering, with a very narrow entrance.

Yet for all its degree of difficulty and somewhat strange atmosphere, Lakeside is lovely, green and fresh, and although quite different in personality and concept from its California neighbours at Pebble Beach and Cypress Point, it stands beside and equal to them as one of the world's great golf courses.

The approach to the 18th – the shot to the tiny green has to run the gauntlet of four bunkers. Scott Simpson (centre left) strides to the 72nd and victory in the 1987 U.S. Open.

CYPRESS POINT

The Monterey Peninsula contains three great courses: Cypress Point, the somewhat older Pebble Beach, and Robert Trent Jones's 1966 addition, the frighteningly difficult Spyglass Hill. Three courses of such quality side by side brings to mind the Kent coast and its string of three great English links of Prince's, Royal St George's and Royal Cinque Ports – but in what a different landscape!

The Monterey Peninsula is punched out into the Pacific Ocean by the descending thrust of the Santa Lucia mountains on the south side of Monterey Bay, just over 100 miles south of San Francisco. Records of the area date from the middle of the 16th century, but the city of Monterey dates from 1770, when a formal mission was set up. The original Del Monte Hotel dates from 1878, and boasted tennis courts, polo fields, a racecourse, steeplechase track and stables – and from 1897 the golf course, the first 18-hole course in California.

The peninsula is a place of surf booming against high cliffs at high tide, surging among low rocks at low tide. It is a place of quite dazzling beauty, of green forests sweeping down to the shore, of startling silver sandhills, of pine and eucalyptus, of sealions basking on offshore rocks, of deer meandering out of the forests, and of Monterey cypress. Set in this landscape, Cypress Point offers a catalogue of breathcatching delights.

Origins

The club's origins are curiously similar to Pebble Beach's. Its first moving spirit was Marion Hollins, who by the early 'Twenties was a champion amateur golfer selling real estate for the Del Monte company. The lady was obviously a crackerjack personality on and off the course. She had been a beaten finalist in the U.S. National Women's Amateur Championship in 1913, defeated by an English girl, Gladys Ravencroft, the British champion of the previous year, but had come back to win in 1921 when she defeated the famous Alexa Stirling of Atlanta by 5 and 4. Miss Hollins had been very active in promoting the Women's National, a fine 'women-only' course at Glen Head on Long Island. She then discovered California, fell in love with it and moved to Monterey. There she joined Byington Ford, a former mayor of nearby Carmel – then little more than a village – and Roger Lapham, a member of a prominent San Francisco shipping family. The trio paid Del Monte Property Company $150,000 for 175 acres.

The first architect chosen for the work was Seth Raynor, a disciple of Charles Blair Macdonald; but he died unexpectedly, of pneumonia. Marion Hollins wisely, and luckily, was able to appoint Dr Alister Mackenzie to take over the work. Mackenzie had just done some impressive work in Australia, and was to do more, subsequently, at Augusta National in Georgia. The Cypress Point Golf Club opened in August 1928, and had passed the 100 mark in membership commitments when the Depression struck. Not surprisingly there were many withdrawals and the club started up with but 40 members. Plans for a grandiose

Dr Alister Mackenzie – seen here (right) on the 1st fairway at St Andrews – created a masterpiece at Cypress Point. It was here that Bobby Jones asked Mackenzie to design the Augusta National.

Marion Hollins, one of the founders of Cypress Point, is seen here (left) with Alexa Stirling after beating her in the final of the 1921 U.S. Women's Amateur Championship.

clubhouse were scrapped and a more modest building set up. Today, Cypress Point is an exclusive private club of some 250 members, drawn from all over the United States and beyond.

'The Ground Determines the Play'

In the context of golf-course design, Mackenzie produced a work of genius; although, without diminishing his achievement, it can be said that his raw material was quite exceptional. The terrain he was offered included deep pine

CYPRESS POINT				
Card of the course				
1	421 yards par 4		10	480 yards par 5
2	548 yards par 5		11	437 yards par 4
3	162 yards par 3		12	404 yards par 4
4	384 yards par 4		13	365 yards par 4
5	493 yards par 5		14	388 yards par 4
6	518 yards par 5		15	143 yards par 3
7	168 yards par 3		16	231 yards par 3
8	363 yards par 4		17	393 yards par 4
9	292 yards par 4		18	346 yards par 4
	3,349 yards par 37			3,187 yards par 35
Total 6,536 yards par 72				

forests, huge soaring dunes of the whitest sand, crisp turf and a stretch of cliffs which offered him the chance to create spectacular holes right by the ocean. Mackenzie made the most of it. He believed in the aphorism that 'the ground determines the play', and the creed of 'Nipper' Campbell that 'the best golf course is built into the landscape you've got'. Mackenzie immediately recognised that he was never going to improve on this landscape. He could do no more than rejoice in it, and perhaps complement it.

His Cypress Point features two successive par-5 holes and two successive par-3 holes, which has lead to some pedantic criticism, but at the same time the unanswerable: 'But what holes!'. His 16th hole of 231 yards has come to be one of the most photographed of all the world's golf holes. There are students of the game prepared to argue that . of all the thousands of golf holes ever made, this one is simply the best.

The 16th tee is perched on the edge of a cliff. Across a little bay, usually surging with Pacific surf, lies a promontory on the very point of the Monterey Peninsula, where the green is set, guarded by four bunkers. Open fairway skirts round the head of the bay to the left, offering an alternative route. By driving to the left and thus short of the green, the golfer then has to seek his par-3 by pitching or chipping close enough to the flagstick to be able to make a single putt. On such an exposed headland the wind will always be a major calculation, but if ever a single shot favoured the brave it is this one.

The element of strategic design inherent in the 16th is repeated at the 17th. Strategy in design is the simple business of giving the golfer an option, an alternative solution to his problem. It challenges him to make the difficult shot, the dangerous carry over a corner of rough, sand dune, lake or even ocean, as at Cypress or Pebble Beach, with his reward a much

Above: The 16th at Cypress Point. Considered by many as the most beautiful golf hole in the world, it demands a shot of 231 yards across the Pacific Ocean, no less.

Right: The 17th, another clifftop hole illustrating Monterey golf – the cliffs, wind-tilted trees, solitary strategic pins and greens backed by sand, cypresses and ocean.

less taxing, shorter second shot. If he is also given a shorter, easier way, it is liable to be one which makes the next shot longer, or more difficult.

At the 17th hole, a 393-yard dog-leg to the right, the challenge is again in a tee shot driven across a bay to a cliff-top fairway. The second shot is complicated by a cluster of cypress trees growing in the right centre of the fairway. Thus the ideal drive may well be the more conservative one of playing to the left of these trees and trying to fade the ball around them on the left, but not overrunning the fairway. That would give an open route to the green, hard by the cliff top. Driving to the right of these trees gives a much shorter approach shot, but demands a much longer, more dangerous drive which must carry further, over the bay and the cliff and avoiding the ice-plant which lines the top of the cliff and the edge of the fairway.

Thus Mackenzie gave the golfer some

latitude as to where to go and how to get there; rather than facing him with the penal 'This way – or else' attitude that many designers had adopted. And Mackenzie had come to see that the design of greens was of major importance in the overall testing of the player. Varying the pin position, defending the pin position, and making it more inviting meant varying of the type of approach shot required. Careful contouring of the greens had the same effect. So, we find that Mackenzie greens more and more are raised, sloped, tilted, often multi-tiered and carefully 'sized', all in relation to the incoming shot. All of these factors inherent in the Monterey terrain made it quite unnecessary for Cypress to be any longer than its 6,500 yards.

A Fair Test
On the 1st hole, for instance, the green slopes quite sharply. On the 2nd, a par-5 of 548 yards, the drive must carry over a large area of rough on the left and avoid out-of-bounds on the right. The second shot must dodge fairway bunkers, and for a hole of such yardage Mackenzie has quite properly left a fairly large, flat green. The 3rd is a classic par-3 of 162 yards, tee and green on the flat but the front right half and side of the green is closely trapped, permitting some very difficult pin positions near this bunker. On the par-5 5th the green is plateaued

and two-tiered; this is a lovely hole of 491 yards, uphill through the pine forest with a rolling fairway and lovely banks of silver sand. The 6th is a bigger par-5 at 518 yards. Its green, framed by tall, solitary pines and six handsome bunkers, is small, since it will almost certainly be receiving a short pitch, and slopes from right to left.

The 8th green has three levels and, that disposed of, there is a splendid view from the ninth tee of the ocean and over half of the course. The 9th hole at 292 yards, brought out a certain impishness in the good Doctor Mackenzie. It plays downhill with dunes on both sides. The green is long, sloping and set across the fairway. The front left side is closed by a bunker, and there is sand and high grass all around at the back. Again, the architect gives the golfer a choice: go for the green, hoping to sneak on through that narrow gap, or play short and pitch up to the flag.

Holes 10 to 14 work their way through

Right: The 15th, a short hole to rival the 7th at Pebble Beach – at 143 yards it seems a simple pitch along the cliffs and across a rocky inlet, but then the wind comes into play.

Below: The 5th green is approached from a fairway studded with strategically placed bunkers, while the two-tiered green is itself defended at right front and left rear.

open duneland in which almost every green has a backcloth of tall pine trees. The 12th (404 yards) and the 14th (388 yards) are particularly fine holes. The first of these is a dog-leg to the right with a bunker and massed dunes covering the angle of the turn. The 14th green brings us close to the cliffs again and to the remarkable 15th hole, a par-3 of 143 yards. This is a gem which has often had its sparkle taken away, quite unjustly, by the 16th. The hole plays along the cliff tops, crossing an inlet to a little green that is almost overwhelmed by six bunkers, the dreaded Cypress ice-plant, a huge barrier of cypress trees behind, not to mention the Pacific Ocean foaming around below.

Finally, the 18th tee turns its back on the spectacular Pacific coastline and plays back to the pleasant clubhouse over 346 yards away, a drive and pitch for the competent player, but a drive that must thread through a channel of trees, and a pitch that must hold a very fast green.

Cypress Point, a magnificent golf course, basks in a strange anonymity. It has been a supporting course for the old Crosby Pro-Am played at Pebble – Crosby, by the way, had one of the very few holes-in-one made at Cypress's 16th – and staged the 1981 Walker Cup matches, but has otherwise sought no championships and no publicity. To play there is a privilege.

PEBBLE BEACH

In the context of golf, indeed of sport, the Pebble Beach course is a massive achievement. Of all the thousands of golf courses around the world, it would surely be given a place in the top half-dozen in the assessment of knowledgeable and honourable men. Embedded in the same landscape as Cypress Point, only a mile or so away – California is singularly blessed with 36 such holes almost side by side – Pebble Beach is some years older, its history rooted in a different time.

After the transcontinental railway had been established, a spur line was opened in 1880 to serve the Hotel Del Monte and the Monterey peninsula, 100 miles south of San Francisco. The intention was that the hotel would become the core of a resort that would be the Newport of the West, and its expansive Victorian splendours soon attracted the wealthy society from San Francisco and Los Angeles and, increasingly, points further east. The hotel and the land were owned by the Southern Pacific Railroad Company, and the riding trails and carriage drives through the forests of the peninsula were the prime leisure activities. There was also a modest golf course.

Morse and Neville

In 1914 Samuel A. Morse, an Easterner, a Yale man and a nephew of the inventor of the code and the telegraph, came to Monterey to work with the Pacific Improvement Company, a real-estate subsidiary of the Southern Pacific. He was instructed to dispose of all the railroad's real-estate holdings and, very smartly forming the Del Monte Property Company, bought the land, some 7,000 acres, for $1.3 million for himself. Morse had more than a little vision. He decided that a golf course would be critical to the marketing of his development and that the existing course was inadequate. He discovered that one Jack Neville, who was working for Pacific Improvement as a real-estate salesman, was a golfer good enough to have won the California State Championship twice.

Neville was from Oakland, where his father was a member of the Claremont Country Club, at which his brother George and such famous golfing personalities as Macdonald Smith and Jim Barnes all worked at one time. Morse decided to entrust the design and building of the new course to Neville, realising that the young man knew enough about the game to get the work done.

For three weeks Neville walked the property, establishing in his mind the routing of the holes. Then, accompanied by Sam Morse, and starting at the original Del Monte Lodge, he staked out the tees and greens.

The Cliff-edge Masterpiece

The first two holes ran eastward from the lodge, out of sight of the ocean. The 1st was 385 yards, the second a good par-5 of just over 500 yards – two perfectly fine

Jack Neville, many times California State champion, shows some dandy style some 80 years ago, but his chief claim to immortality is as the designer of peerless Pebble Beach.

golf holes, but less than memorable. Then Neville turned towards the sea with another rather routine par-4 of 368 yards curving slightly to the left.

However, the next brings us to the ocean and starts a run of holes along the cliffs to the 10th which make Pebble Beach the greatest 'ocean' course in the world. The holes are simply magnificent. The 4th is only 325 yards, but it gives an inkling of some of the excitements to come. The tee shot is over a cross bunker

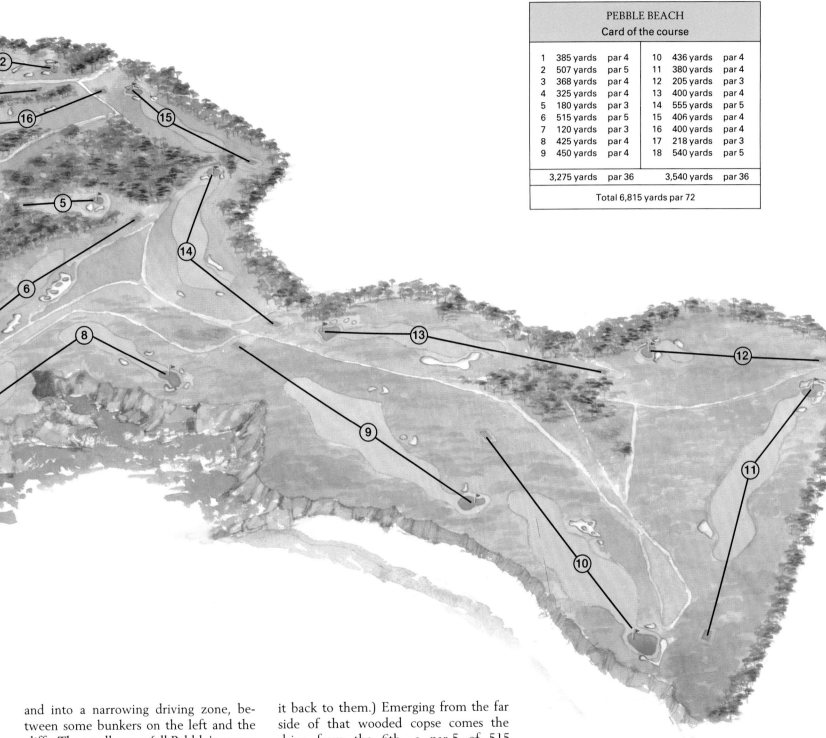

PEBBLE BEACH Card of the course					
1	385 yards	par 4	10	436 yards	par 4
2	507 yards	par 5	11	380 yards	par 4
3	368 yards	par 4	12	205 yards	par 3
4	325 yards	par 4	13	400 yards	par 4
5	180 yards	par 3	14	555 yards	par 5
6	515 yards	par 5	15	406 yards	par 4
7	120 yards	par 3	16	400 yards	par 4
8	425 yards	par 4	17	218 yards	par 3
9	450 yards	par 4	18	540 yards	par 5
3,275 yards par 36			3,540 yards par 36		
Total 6,815 yards par 72					

and into a narrowing driving zone, between some bunkers on the left and the cliffs. The small green (all Pebble's greens are small by modern standards) is surrounded by bunkers and is squeezed close to the cliff tops.

The 5th, a one-shot hole of 180 yards, turns away from the water and runs uphill into a wooded area. (Neville would have preferred to run it along the cliff top, but Morse had sold a critical plot of land there and could not persuade the owner to sell

it back to them.) Emerging from the far side of that wooded copse comes the drive from the 6th, a par-5 of 515 thrilling yards which explodes out to the cliff tops again, above Stillwater Cove, with a second shot that must sweep up to the great plateau on the peninsula spearing out into Carmel Bay, and the green that is placed there. Along the very edge of this stunning promontory, lies the 7th hole, a par-3 of only 120 yards — the shortest hole on any American cham-

pionship course, and none the worse for that. The green, set below the tee, is ringed with a maze of bunkers, an infinitesimal target, a rectangle no more than eight yards across, and subject to all the winds the Pacific can blow.

The 8th, 425 yards, is one of the world's great two-shotters. The course is now returning from that big headland

Above: *The 9th green and, beyond, the 10th fairway. These two magnificent par-4s demand the strictest accuracy in both tee and approach shots.*

Left: *Not for the nervous – the sea-girt chasm that cuts into the direct line between the 8th fairway and the green, in the foreground.*

which houses six and seven and the tee is on the very edge of the cliff. The drive must carry up a slope onto an unseen plateau. It must not be hit too far, as you will discover when you get up there: not far beyond the rise the ocean has carved a huge chunk out of the fairway, which skips around it on the left. The direct shot to the green is over that monstrous chasm, requiring a carry of perhaps 180 yards. In this classic shot (as with the second shot to the 13th at Pine Valley, where a similar carry must be made over sand) lies the brutal challenge of the hole: how much of the angle to cut off, which line dare you take? Too far right, even by the slightest margin, and you will be in the ocean; too far left, and you will be hard pressed to reach the green, which again is small and bunkered on both sides and to the back.

The 9th is a difficult par-4 running downhill, its fairway tilted towards the cliffs. Two high-backed bunkers cover the left side at about 230 yards from the tee, at which point the fairway is no more than 30 yards wide. The 10th hole follows the same pattern, breaking slightly to the right in driving range, where a very long bunker on the left at the top of the fairway compresses it even more than that at the ninth. Three-quarters of the green is bunkered, leaving only a narrow entrance, just short of which is a swale of thick grass. The second shot should carry all the way to the putting surface. These are very severe holes – in the final round of the U.S. Open in 1972, in very windy conditions, Jack Nicklaus at the 10th drove clean over the cliff onto the beach, which was a lateral water hazard. Nicklaus took a drop and penalty, hit his next with a 2-iron and holed out rather thankfully for six.

Pebble's Great Finish

The 10th green is the most distant point from the clubhouse and the course then turns back inland through woodlands of cypress, oak, eucalyptus and Monterey pine, before returning to the ocean at the 17th and 18th holes. The 17th is a compelling one-shot hole of 218 yards. In that same final round of the 1972 U.S. Open, Nicklaus hit a 1-iron into the wind here. The ball took one bounce, hit the flagstick, and flopped down six inches away! But beyond doubt the greatest single shot ever played at this hole was the little wedge shot which Tom Watson holed from off the green in the last round of the 1982 U.S. Open Championship. For the 17th Watson smashed out a 2-iron tee shot which soared high, turned to the left with just a suggestion of a hook in it and finished pin-high but in long grass just off the green. Fortunately it had skipped between two bunkers and the lie was good. As Watson looked it over, his caddie said: 'Get it close'. Watson replied: 'I'm not going to get it close – I'm going to make it'. And he did. He popped-up the ball softly with a sand wedge, it landed on the green and ran straight towards the hole. When it fell in, Watson, seldom a demonstrative fellow, set off on a mad dance around the green. The shot was to win him the U.S. Open Championship.

The 540-yard 18th, one of golf's great finishing holes, curves steadily to the left along the cliff tops. A decision is required as to how much of the angle to cut off with the tee shot. Ultra-greedy players will quickly find themselves on the beach. The ocean is hard along the left side. In the driving zone on the right bunkers and trees menace the fairway; beyond them is out-of-bounds. Trees encroach in the second-shot area around 50 yards short of the green, which is set above the player. Shots over the green are likely also to go over the cliffs. In short, the 18th requires a combination of brute force and fine judgement. In 1982 Watson birdied it with a 3-wood, 7-iron, 9-iron and a superb 20-foot putt.

Pebble Beach Today

Jack Neville's original design has stood up well since the course opened in 1918. True, tees have been extended, bunkers fiddled with. Neville in fact had asked a contemporary, Douglas Grant, who was also good enough to be state champion, to check on his original bunkering. And for the 1929 U.S. Amateur Championship, the first played on the Pacific coast, H. Chandler Egan, a Chicago man who had been U.S. Champion in 1904 and 1905, re-modeled the greens and generally stiffened up the course. This championship was memorable for the fact that, for the only time in his U.S. Amateur career,

Bobby Jones lost a first-round match. He had come all the way from Atlanta – by train of course – only to lose to Johnny Goodman. And Jones was U.S. Open Champion! The press coverage was enormous: it was one of the biggest sports stories of the year, and the publicity did nothing to harm Pebble Beach.

But it was the presentation of the Bing Crosby National Pro-Am tournament, televised, and with Pebble Beach the anchor course and neighbouring Cypress Point and Spyglass Hill the supporting courses, that really established Pebble in the consciousness of world golf. The tournament is played in late January or early February, when the weather can be as capricious as in the west of Scotland, but no one seems to mind. Crosby started his pro-am event in 1936 for charity and so that his Hollywood and other friends might have some fun. In 1947 he moved it from Rancho Santa Fe in Los Angeles up to Monterey. After his death, there was something of a hiatus and, sadly, the Crosby name is no longer in the title. The event is now sponsored by A.T. & T., and the players chase prize-money of the order of $700,000. In a similar way, the world of business did not leave Pebble Beach untouched. It had always been a public course, with privileges for guests of the Del Monte Lodge. After Samuel Morse died in 1969, things were not as they used to be. Del Monte Properties became Pebble Beach Corporation, which was later bought by 20th Century Fox. Maximising the plant became the policy, profit became the key word. Golf cart tracks were laid, more and more players were 'processed' around the course and the $100 green fee loomed ahead. If all of this did little for the condition of the course, it had little impact on Neville's grand design. Pebble Beach remains one of international golf's shrines, and entirely worthy of Robert Louis Stevenson's much-quoted description of the peninsula as 'the most felicitous meeting of land and sea in creation'.

The 18th green. The long scimitar-shaped fairway curving around the bay makes for one of the finest finishing holes in championship golf.

BANFF

If ever a course qualified for greatness on the grounds of beauty and dramatic setting alone, it would be Banff Springs in Alberta, in the foothills of the Rocky Mountains. This is not to say that these are its only qualities. Banff Springs, from the point of view of its design and the pleasures and challenges its varied holes offer the golfer, is by any judgement a great course – but the place, its setting, its whole environment, is breathtaking.

It was built as an adjunct to the huge Banff Springs Hotel, the Canadian Pacific Railway's luxury Shangri-la resort, on the line that presently runs west from Calgary to Lake Louise and threads through the Kicking Horse Pass on the way to Vancouver and the Pacific Coast. The initial course, of nine holes, was constructed in 1911, and a further nine were added during the Great War with the labour of German prisoners of war.

In 1927, Stanley Thompson, the prominent Canadian designer with whom Robert Trent Jones served an apprenticeship, was asked to re-make the course. Thompson was dealing essentially with a wooded strip along the bank of the Bow River, squeezed between the latter and the towering mass of Mount Rumble. He cut down trees by the hundred, blasted tons of rock out of the mountain, imported topsoil from the east and positioned a maze of bunkers on the course – 144 in all. No fewer than 28 of them were in play on the 18th hole! Clumps of bunkers, set into the fairways at critical distances, were a Thompson feature at

The world famous Devil's Cauldron hole is the 8th on the championship course and the 4th on the Rundle. Picturesque and very difficult this 171-yard par-3 has an elevated green and water in abundance.

Banff Springs. In 1989 a further nine holes were added, making three nine-hole courses: Sulphur, Randle and Tunnel (the newest nine).

The course is nicely wooded with conifers, although not oppressively so – save perhaps along the stretch from the 5th to the 10th, where the fairways are simply avenues in isolation. A critical factor when playing this extraordinary course is judgement of distance, and judgement of exactly how far the ball will fly at this altitude, just as it is on the

BANFF					
Card of the Championship course					
1	411 yards	par 4	10	351 yards	par 4
2	394 yards	par 4	11	514 yards	par 5
3	372 yards	par 4	12	138 yards	par 3
4	578 yards	par 5	13	474 yards	par 5
5	414 yards	par 4	14	220 yards	par 3
6	174 yards	par 3	15	398 yards	par 4
7	514 yards	par 5	16	420 yards	par 4
8	171 yards	par 3	17	230 yards	par 3
9	424 yards	par 4	18	429 yards	par 4
3,452 yards		par 36	3,174 yards		par 35
Total 6,626 yards par 71					

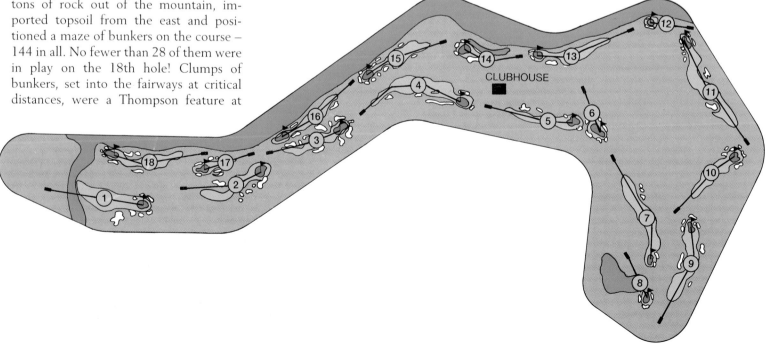

The championship 16th hole (3rd on Sulphur course) is probably the best par-4 on the course. The enormous Banff Springs hotel can be seen in the background.

Alpine courses of Switzerland or the Rand courses in the Transvaal of South Africa. At Banff's 4,000 feet, the light can be sharp and clear, so that there is foreshortening of targets, which can look closer than they really are. On the other hand, in the thin air the ball will fly much further; club selection takes on a whole new dimension in a game at Banff.

The old Banff clubhouse is set close to the confluence of the Bow and the Spray rivers. However, a new clubhouse has been built in the centre of the course and a shuttle bus runs continuously between it and the hotel. In the spring and early summer, when the mountain snows melt, the Bow and Spray can be very lively rivers indeed. And the prospect from the 1st tee (of the championship course) can be daunting. It is set above a minor precipice over the Spray, and the tee shot must carry directly across the river, some 100 yards wide, then into an alleyway of trees and reach or pass a crest at about 200 yards, where a ridge comes in from the right. The first green has a reasonably wide entrance. The 2nd and 3rd holes are reasonable par-4s, splashed all over with Thompson's big, ornate bunkers, but reasonableness ends about here. The 4th

is a very interesting hole, a par-5 which dog-legs to the right – twice. Named 'Windy', it goes 578 yards along a mounded fairway with the left side favoured, the better to see 'round the corner', and into the rather small green. The 7th too is intriguing, in that it is a straight par-5 of 514 yards, pressed in on the right by the cliffs of Mount Rumble with a little kick to the right at the end onto a green well screened by trees.

The most famous hole on the course, renowned far beyond Banff, is the 'Devil's Cauldron', the 8th and a par-3 of 171 yards. It is played from a high tee over a little natural lake, which the Scots might call a 'lochan', to a green embedded in a forest, surrounded by bunkers and raised slightly above a ledge of fairway between its front edges and the lake. To hold the green, a shot must be long and high so that it will flop down vertically to hold the putting surface. The terror intrinsic in the hole is largely environmental – the high tee, the lake, the woodland behind the minute green, and the massive wall of mountain behind it can overwhelm the golfer.

The 12th hole, named 'Papoose' is another par-3 also over water; this time an inlet of the Bow River, but at 138 yards is a very different proposition. The 14th is almost a replica, also over water, but a stronger hole at 220 yards. Banff's finish is a thrilling run along the bank of the Bow which forms the right side boundary of the last four holes. Three stiff par-4s and a single shotter of 230 yards demand some concentration. On the 16th Thompson has put in a fairway bunker with a siting reminiscent of the Principal's Nose bunker on the 16th at St Andrews, tempting the player to line his drive out between it and the river. But concentration on golf, on the swing and on the playing of the game may be difficult at Banff. In the presence of the landscape, the environment and the wild life, the quality of the golf may become secondary and for once, the obsessed golfer will not mind – Banff is a wonderful place.

ROYAL MONTREAL

The Royal Montreal Golf Club is the oldest in North America. It was formed in 1873, fifteen years before the first of the U.S. clubs, St Andrews, in Yonkers, New York. As such, Royal Montreal is appropriately aristocratic and very proud of the substantial contribution it made to Canadian golf during its infant years. It founded the Royal Canadian Golf Association. Its annual match with The Country Club, of Brookline, Mass., was the first international encounter between countries, pre-dating even the England-Scotland amateur match. It inaugurated the first national championship, the womens' amateur of 1901, followed by the mens' amateur in 1902, and it staged the very first Canadian Open Championship in 1904.

The club was formed by 16 wealthy Montrealers, a Scot or two among them. One of the prime movers was Alexander Dennistoun, who presented the club with a medal which is still played for. Rather like Charles Blair Macdonald and the U.S. National Amateur Championship, Dennistoun contrived, perhaps connived, to have his name engraved on the medal as the first winner.

Move to a New Site

A public park, Fletcher's Field on the slopes of Mount Royal, was the club's starting point. But in 1896 a new site was needed, and one was found at Dixie, to the west of the city, which became good enough to stage five Canadian Opens. However, the inevitable growth of Montreal meant that another move was necessary by the 1950s. Fortunately the club found a property at Ile Bizard big enough to provide 45 holes. They first sought the services of Robert Trent Jones, by this time famous for his treatment of Oakland Hills for the U.S. Open of 1951 and for even more grandiose and controversial ventures. Jones at the time was over-committed and declined the invitation. Consequently, the club turned to Dick Wilson, a plain-spoken engineer who had had many design and construction successes, most of them in Florida and other U.S. southern states.

Fortunately for the club, Wilson was a qualified civil engineer: the land had to be cleared of rocks, tree trunks, boulders and dead matter and its swampland drained and channelled off into two lakes, the larger of which was destined to have four

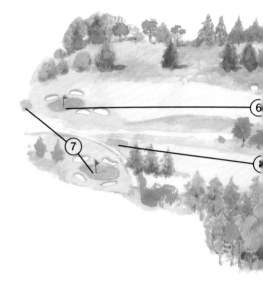

holes played over it. Wilson produced the nine-hole Black course and two of 18: the Red and the championship Blue.

Huge Greens

From a design point of view, Royal Montreal's Blue championship course has two unusual features. There is an absence of fairway bunkering – only 11 in all – and the greens are huge. Wilson was not one for the dramatic excavations or massive landscaping of a Trent Jones. The Blue course is by no means flat, but the ground moves gently, pleasantly contoured; the fairways, nicely aligned, sauntering quietly across a tree-dotted rather than wooded landscape. And Wilson turned his back on length for length's sake – at its championship length the course was no more than 6,738 yards with a par of 70.

In fact Wilson made the size of his greens the penal element in his course design. At around 12,000 square feet they were double the size of the average championship greens, some of them running 40 yards from front to back. They

The 17th is one of the most attractive and shortest holes at Royal Montreal. A tricky 133-yard par-3, it captures the essence of Dick Wilson's design work, with its clever use of sand, trees and water.

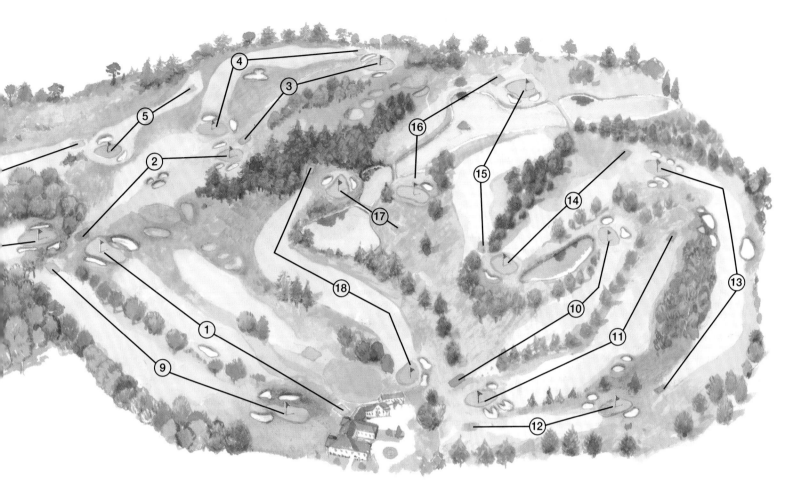

were all closely trapped – he used 48 greenside bunkers in all. They widened out from front to back, but from front to back there was sometimes a two or three club difference. Thus the approach shot and its club selection were the tests – under-clubbing might result in the golfer having to face a putt of 100 feet! The shot into the green was the key shot, and it required the golfer to steel himself to attack and strike boldly, knowing that the shot would be longer than it seemed and that he would have to force the ball, perhaps against his inclination, to the heart of the green and beyond.

Waist Deep in Water

One factor which is inhibiting at Ile Bizard is that over the four final holes, five shots across water are required – the second shot to 15, both drive and second at 16, and drives at 17 and 18. When the wind blows, which it does most of the time at Ile Bizard, these shots can be challenging. Perhaps no man was ever challenged more than Pat Fitzsimons, a young U.S. professional playing in the 1975 Canadian Open, the last played at Royal Montreal. The 16th requires a drive over the spur of a lake which covers the entire left side of the fairway, then a second shot back across the water. The hole is a par-4 of 433 yards and Fitzsimons, seeking to cut off as much of the angle as he could, hooked his drive not into the water but onto a tiny island some 10 yards from the bank. The ball was visible and still in play. So Fitzsimons sent his caddie in to test the water, which was found to be waist deep. An attempt by the caddie to carry him across having failed, Fitzsimons waded across himself, hit a 4-iron from the island to the green and took two putts for his par – perhaps one of the greatest pars in the history of the game! So elated was the dripping Fitzsimons that he birdied the 17th and 18th holes, scored 73 for a 140 total after 36 holes and made the cut.

That '75 Open was won by Tom Weiskopf at the first hole of a play-off with Jack Nicklaus. Testament to the quality of Royal Montreal's course, its world rating and the club's stature in the international game is the fact that the championship was secured with a score of 274, only six strokes under par, and that the ten leading players were: Tom Weiskopf, Jack Nicklaus, Gay Brewer, Arnold Palmer, Bruce Crampton, J.C. Snead, Gary Player, Bob Wynn, Lee Trevino and Ken Still.

ROYAL MONTREAL Card of the course					
1	434 yards	par 4	10	452 yards	par 4
2	375 yards	par 4	11	438 yards	par 4
3	364 yards	par 4	12	193 yards	par 3
4	440 yards	par 4	13	533 yards	par 3
5	179 yards	par 3	14	361 yards	par 4
6	570 yards	par 5	15	420 yards	par 4
7	143 yards	par 3	16	433 yards	par 4
8	397 yards	par 4	17	133 yards	par 3
9	423 yards	par 4	18	450 yards	par 4
	3,325 yards	par 35		3,413 yards	par 35
		Total 6,738 yards par 70			

CLUB DE GOLF MEXICO

Golf architects, most of the time, are ordinary men living in the ordinary world of three-dimensions. But there are times when they are extraordinary men, living in an extraordinary world of four dimensions. The fourth dimension is altitude. It has affected the work of the golf course designer at, for example, the Swiss Alps, where the course at Crans-sur-Sierre is at 5,000 feet, or on the Johannesburg courses of the Rand of Transvaal, at 6,000 feet, or even the central plateau of Mexico, which reaches 7,500 feet in the region of Mexico City. At these altitudes, the golf ball flies and flies, often 20 per cent further than it would at sea level. Thus the yardage of the Club de Golf Mexico, probably Mexico's finest course, is initially frightening: 7,166 yards, is difficult to reconcile with a par of 72.

An Elitist Sport

Yardage and altitude apart, Club de Golf Mexico is a big powerful course, demanding the most careful striking and intense concentration. And despite its yardage, it demands accuracy even more than power. Golf in Mexico, of course, has had an irregular history. As in all Latin American countries, it has been seen as an elitist sport, and certainly social circumstances have made it very much a minority game.

But its aficionados are an influential minority, as the story of the Club de Golf illustrates.

The creation of the club and the course was orchestrated by Percy Clifford, six times amateur champion of Mexico and three times Open champion. With the blessing of Miguel Alemán, the President of Mexico at the time, Clifford found the ground he wanted at Tlalpán, about an hour's drive from Mexico City. It was part of a dense woodland of cedar, pine and cypress. Clifford retained Lawrence Hughes to plan the course – the latter's connection with golf course design running all the way back to the Dornoch of Donald Ross. Clifford, it should be noted, had been to college in England, and had seen the best of the English and Scottish courses. He thus had definite ideas about design and about building courses which would entail a minimum of maintenance expenditure. Similarly, Lawrence Hughes, in his teens, had worked with his

CLUB DE GOLF MEXICO					
Card of the course					
1	431 yards	par 4	10	390 yards	par 4
2	559 yards	par 5	11	569 yards	par 5
3	429 yards	par 4	12	174 yards	par 3
4	384 yards	par 4	13	461 yards	par 4
5	165 yards	par 3	14	222 yards	par 3
6	438 yards	par 4	15	580 yards	par 5
7	220 yards	par 3	16	374 yards	par 4
8	562 yards	par 5	17	412 yards	par 4
9	360 yards	par 4	18	436 yards	par 4
3,548 yards par 36			3,618 yards par 36		
Total 7,166 yards par 72					

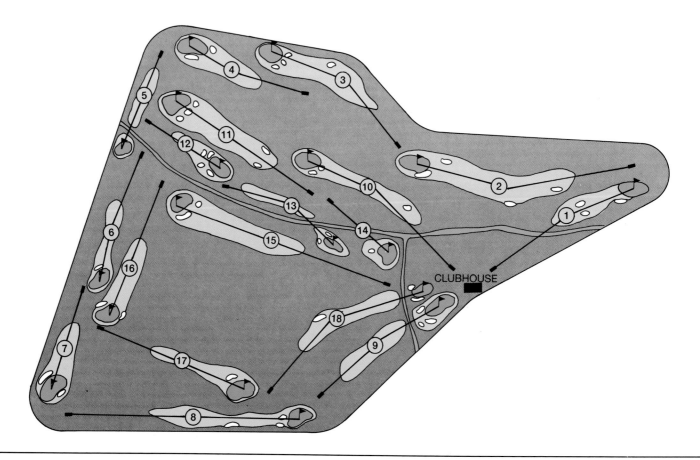

father, a construction supervisor with Ross in his dozens of courses throughout the States. Thus he too had some definite ideas about golf course design.

Shangri-la

In 1946, Hughes met Johnny Dawson, a U.S. Amateur Championship finalist and a Walker Cup player. Dawson was convinced that there were underground springs that would make golf feasible in the Palm Springs desert area, and enlisted Hughes as a designer. Between them they produced the Thunderbird CC in 1947, the first of the post-war golf/property developments in the area. Eldorado and La Quinta were to follow and Palm Springs in time became a golfing Shangri-la. From Palm Springs and work in San Diego, it was a short hop for Hughes to

The 18th green viewed from the creek, which threatens the over-ambitious drive. This is one of seven holes on the course requiring shots over one of the branches of the creek.

get to Mexico, and he and Clifford had produced the Club de Golf by 1951. Significantly, Hughes went on to design a dozen or more courses in Mexico, while by 1980 Clifford had been involved in putting together practically half of the courses in the country.

The course they built at Tlalpán is powerful and in many ways forbidding. It is carved out of a solid forest so that trees become the main hazards, with woodland lining each side of every fairway. There is a creek which winds through the course and is in play on seven holes, although it is

likely to be dry. Only one of the four short holes is less than 200 yards. Of the four par-5 holes, the 15th is 580 yards. There is not too much movement in the ground and, rather surprisingly, almost all the holes are straight, and when they do turn, they turn only slightly. The course is notable for an almost complete absence of fairway bunkering – understandable since a shot off the fairway is in the trees, and is a stroke almost certainly lost.

Evidence of the quality of Club de Golf Mexico came early in its life – the course twice staging the World Cup; Harry Bradshaw and Christy O'Connor winning for Ireland in 1958 and Arnold Palmer and Jack Nicklaus winning for the United States in 1967 – Palmer taking the individual title with an impressive 275, twelve strokes under par.

CAJUILES

Paul 'Pete' Dye was born in Ohio in 1925, and after college became a life-insurance salesman in Indianapolis and a fine amateur golfer, winning the Indiana State Championship in 1958. He also served some time as chairman of the greens committee at the country club of Indianapolis during a complete replanting of the course. Dye was so successful as an insurance salesman that he could afford to leave the business in 1959 and set up as a golf course designer. He worked modestly in the Midwest until 1963, when he and his wife Alice, also a first-rate golfer, toured the championship courses of Scotland. Dye was immensely impressed by the small greens, pot bunkers and sleepers

The 17th green, like others at Cajuiles, is walled with coral on the seaward side. The 18th hole, whose tee is behind the trees fringing the green, involves a drive across the runway.

(railroad ties), which he saw on these Scottish courses.

Although such features were quite out of fashion in contemporary American design, Dye started to apply them to his work. It was work that was to have a significant effect on the whole of golf course architecture. When Hilton Head Island off the coast of South Carolina was beginning to develop as a resort, Dye's Harbour Town course was opened in 1969 – Jack Nicklaus helping out, almost in the role of an apprentice. Harbour Town, and Dye's reputation, was confirmed when Arnold Palmer won the first Heritage Classic tournament, played on the course that year and shown on national television.

Two years later, in 1971, Dye presented to the world one of the most spectacular courses ever built, the Campo de Golf Cajuiles, at La Romana in the

south-east corner of the Dominican Republic. Comparisons with Pebble Beach and Cypress Point are inevitable, since four holes on the outward half and four holes on the inward half are played along, beside, above or over the ocean. Dye had been invited to build a 'special' course by the developer of a luxury resort complex of some 7,000 acres and he saw it as 'the chance of a lifetime' to create a seaside course – few architects get that chance.

Holes 1, 2 and 4, surprisingly, are par-4s of less than 400 yards, and with the trade wind prevailing from the east, are drive and pitch holes. The 5th is a long,

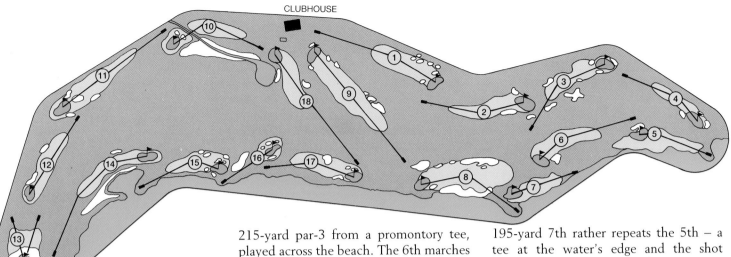

CLUBHOUSE

215-yard par-3 from a promontory tee, played across the beach. The 6th marches parallel with the ocean front, playing over a rise, then down to a small green. The 195-yard 7th rather repeats the 5th – a tee at the water's edge and the shot entirely across sand. The 8th tee is again pushed out into the ocean, and the drive must carry a slice of water over the angle. This 385-yard hole turns left and goes down to a sea-level green behind a huge bunker.

The 9th leaves the shore and the course swings up in a big curve to the 13th, a freakish par-3 to a green literally surrounded by sand and shaded by fur trees. The 14th, the last par-5 at 500 yards, has a bunker along its entire right side, and an ocean inlet screening the green. The 15th and 17th could well be the 17th at Cypress Point – drives across a bay, a dog-leg to the right and the challenge lying in deciding how much of the angle should be cut off. Both greens are heavily protected.

CAJUILES					
Card of the course					
1	380 yards	par 4	10	380 yards	par 4
2	380 yards	par 4	11	548 yards	par 5
3	530 yards	par 5	12	430 yards	par 4
4	320 yards	par 4	13	170 yards	par 3
5	215 yards	par 3	14	500 yards	par 5
6	450 yards	par 4	15	380 yards	par 4
7	195 yards	par 3	16	185 yards	par 3
8	385 yards	par 4	17	435 yards	par 4
9	520 yards	par 5	18	440 yards	par 4
3,375 yards	par 36		3,468 yards	par 36	
Total 6,843 yards par 72					

There is no option but to go for the green at the par-3 7th. Short and to the left is the sea; short and to the right is a gigantic bunker masquerading as a fairway.

MID OCEAN

Bermuda is a coral jewel set in an azure sea. The island is enchanting, and on the grounds of beauty alone its Mid Ocean golf course must rank with the best of them. A member of the British Commonwealth, Bermuda has long been a haunt of the American tourist – New York is only 90 minutes away by air, and Boston is even closer. The Mid Ocean course lies along the southern shore of the island and the lovely property could be described as a parkland course of modest length – 6,547 yards and a par of 71 – moving attractively over a landscape of valleys and crests, through dense woods and flowering shrubs.

Mid Ocean has been compared with Cypress Point and Turnberry, although in truth few of its holes run hard by the ocean as they do at the two other courses. On the other hand, no place in Bermuda is far from the sea, and Charles Blair Macdonald, its designer, took his holes as close to the cliffs above Bermuda's stunning beaches as he dared. Macdonald designed the course in 1924 (he died in

The par-3 13th is the most demanding of Mid Ocean's short holes, not so much in its subtlety but in the powerful shot that it requires, often in ocean breezes.

1928 at the age of 72), and Robert Trent Jones updated it in 1953.

Macdonald was a pioneer of American golf. Having studied at St Andrews as a young man, he had come to love the Scottish approach to the game and to course design, and he preached it incessantly on his return to the States. His greatest work was the National Links of

America (q.v.), at Southampton, L.I., where on a piece of scrubland he built what was the nearest thing to a links in the U.S. at that time. One distinctive characteristic of his design and routing at Mid Ocean, which of course was totally different ground with which to work, was the number of high or elevated tees, which let the player drive down into a valley and often hit his second shot uphill.

The 1st hole, 'Atlantic', is a par-4 of 404 yards running down from the clubhouse and turning left. The 2nd is a dogleg to the left of 465 yards, rated a par-5, and the 3rd is a straightforward one-shotter of 190 yards. Thus Macdonald, noted for his penal attitude to the game – 'if a golfer made mistakes, he should be punished', he said – gave Mid Ocean a friendly start.

MID OCEAN Card of the course					
1	404 yards	par 4	10	404 yards	par 4
2	465 yards	par 5	11	487 yards	par 5
3	190 yards	par 3	12	437 yards	par 4
4	350 yards	par 4	13	238 yards	par 3
5	433 yards	par 4	14	357 yards	par 4
6	360 yards	par 4	15	496 yards	par 5
7	164 yards	par 3	16	376 yards	par 4
8	339 yards	par 4	17	220 yards	par 3
9	406 yards	par 4	18	421 yards	par 4
3,111 yards par 35			3,436 yards par 36		
Total 6,547 yards par 71					

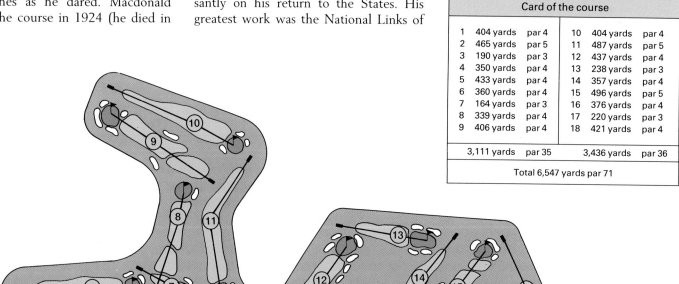

The 5th hole at Mid Ocean and one of the classic design questions which its architect, Charles Blair Macdonald, loved to ask of golfers – how much of the dog-leg to cut off.

The 4th, at 350 yards, is tighter than the yardage might suggest, because of a narrow, mounded fairway and a key bunker to the right. The 5th is beyond any doubt one of the world's great golf holes, using a principle of design that has been repeated with variations on literally hundreds of golf courses throughout the world. From a very high tee, it calls for a drive over Mangrove Lake. The hole then doglegs and runs left to a big, but quite well-guarded green. The trick here is in deciding on the line of the drive, how much of the lake to cut off and then having the confidence to drive along the chosen line. The hole is only 433 yards, yet if the golfer decides on the short carry and plays straight ahead or to the right, he will not reach the green with his second shot. If he goes for the long carry, regardless of what the wind may be doing, he may not succeed in carrying the water. So the tee shot at the 5th hole is a question of optimism or pessimism, fear or courage, judgement and confidence.

On the other hand, the 6th, 7th and 8th are somewhat undemanding – 6 and 8 have raised greens in the old Scottish fashion – and water is in play at the 9th, where the drive must cross a lake. For that matter, the par-3 7th, at 164 yards, is also played over a lake.

Holes number 10, 11, 12, 13 and 15 are the heart of the course, and its most difficult stretch. Numbers 11 and 15 are par-5s and 13 is a par-3 of 238 yards. On each of these holes the drive is very tight, with bunkered dog-leg angles and trees crowding the fairway. And the 14th fairway slopes from right to left, with a cluster of bunkers on the left awaiting a ball that might dribble down towards them. The hole is 357 yards, just a drive and a pitch you might say. But even on its 'easy' holes, Mid Ocean has a sting.

The drive on 16 is uphill. The 17th, par-3 at 220 yards, is named 'Redan' after the North Berwick hole, although the only thing the two have in common is a green set across the line of the shot. The 18th is a fine and fair finishing hole of 421 yards, played from a tee set high above the beach and the cliffs, up towards the huge white clubhouse. For 20 years, this was the place of business and social life of Archie Compston, a rumbustious professional from the West Midlands of England who once tackled Walter Hagen in a 72-holes challenge match at Moor Park, London, and won by 18 and 17.

In conclusion, Mid Ocean is always in prime condition, with Bermuda grass, the strong, sharp, broad-bladed grass, growing in summer and the finer bent grasses thriving during the winter. Its verdant colours are offset by the pink and white houses on the island and the deep blues of the western Atlantic lapping its shores. Quite simply, Mid Ocean is both lovely and unique.

LAGUNITA

The Lagunita Country Club in the suburb of El Hatillo in Caracas, Venezuela, is typical of latter-day South American country clubs – country clubs in the sense that they have very comfortable premises with cocktail bars and restaurants, a variety of sporting facilities with emphasis on the golf course, the essential swimming pool, and the whole complex locked into extensive real estate development. Lagunita dates from 1956, when a group of local businessmen bought rather more than one square mile of land on which to develop some very expensive housing. However, they also retained Louis Sibbett (Dick) Wilson to build a golf course for them on the plot.

Dick Wilson was an almost direct contemporary of Robert Trent Jones and for 15 years throughout the 'Fifties and into the 'Sixties they were the two outstanding architects in America. Unlike Jones, who had made a careful and academic study of all the disciplines involved in the business – landscaping, surveying, agronomy, horticulture, hydraulics and grass – Wilson was proud of his practical background and the fact that he could actually build as well as design a golf course.

A native of Philadelphia, Wilson moved to Florida in the early 'Thirties, made it his base and created an impressive body of work in that state alone. Other than in the Bahamas, he did little work outside the U.S., although what he did was of the highest class – Royal Montreal, Villa Real in Cuba and Lagunita.

Lagunita is a private club with more than 1,000 members. Wilson's course is laid out like a boomerang, with the clubhouse in the centre of the inner

Right: *The 12th is one of the most treacherous holes on the course. The huge green is well defended by a lake which runs right up to the putting surface.*

Far right: *The 18th green has a narrow entrance and is well guarded by bunkers on both sides. It is a straight, uphill hole into the prevailing wind.*

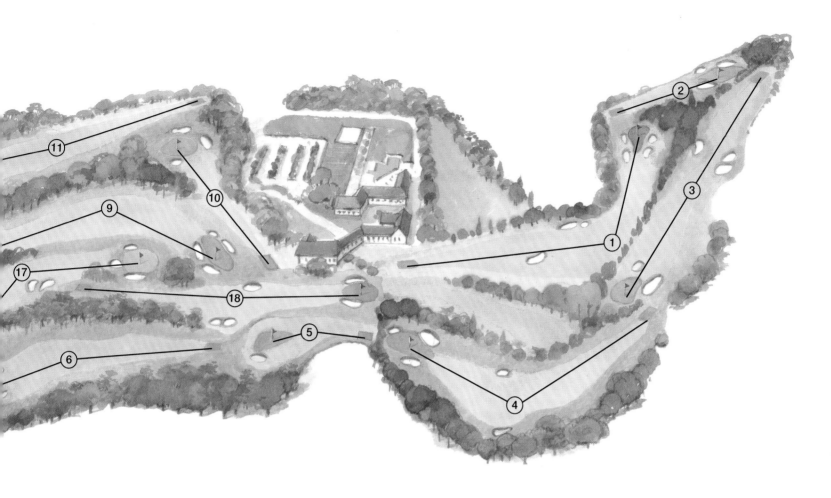

curve. The 1st hole is a big par-5 at 535 yards, with a double turn to the left. There is an out of bounds along the left side into a rather deep quarry, which makes it daring to try to carry over the second angle. Besides, Wilson defended that line with big greenside bunkers.

The 2nd, at 205 yards, is the first of Lagunita's five par-3 holes. The course has only three par-5s, hence a total par of only 70, but the par-3s are long and balance up the overall yardage to 6,895 yards. The 3rd hole, a straight full-length

par-4 of 470 yards, has out of bounds to its left as it turns and starts a swing back round the outer rim of the course to the 8th hole. The 4th hole is rather forbidding. It is 455 yards with a 90 degree turn to the right. A clutch of three bunkers in the angle and trees mean that the corner cannot be cut, and what is left is a long shot to a green with a narrow entrance and bunkered at the sides and rear.

The 8th, the longest short hole at 220 yards, may be almost a little unfair – the front being almost closed off by bunkering. The stretch of holes from 12 to 15, however, is very fine – all strong par-4s beautifully defended; and the 12th green, demanding a most difficult second shot, has a lake at front and right side. The 16th, the shortest hole on the course at 170 yards, has a large green, very fast, with sand at each corner. And the 18th is a good finishing hole of 440 yards. It runs straight uphill to the clubhouse and is well bunkered in the fairway and by the green.

Lagunita is a finely-designed, sharp test of golf for championship players. It is true

and honest, with all hazards visible. When the World Cup of 1974 was played at Lagunita, and won by Bobby Cole and Dale Hayes for South Africa, only three players bettered the 72-hole aggregate. They were Cole, the individual winner, who was also South African Open Champion, Hale Irwin who was U.S. Open Champion, and the leader of the world stroke averages that year, Masishi Ozaki.

LAGUNITA					
Card of the course					
1	535 yards	par 5	10	210 yards	par 3
2	205 yards	par 3	11	510 yards	par 5
3	470 yards	par 4	12	445 yards	par 4
4	455 yards	par 4	13	420 yards	par 4
5	190 yards	par 3	14	435 yards	par 4
6	405 yards	par 4	15	425 yards	par 4
7	380 yards	par 4	16	170 yards	par 3
8	220 yards	par 3	17	390 yards	par 4
9	590 yards	par 5	18	440 yards	par 4
3,450 yards	par 35		3,445 yards	par 35	
Total 6,895 yards par 70					

THE JOCKEY CLUB

Argentina is probably the most powerful golf country in South America, with a hundred or more courses and a history of excellent international golfers, such as Jose Jurado, Tony Cerda, Roberto de Vicenzo and Vicente Fernandez. The game, as so much else, was taken there by the Scots and English who were involved in the management and operation of the railways, the tramways, and the gas, water and power services earlier in the century. But in Argentina, as throughout South America, golf has remained a game for the affluent, and has never begun to rival the great god, football.

For all that, just as the country has produced great players, so it can boast fine courses; and none greater than the Red course of the Jockey Club in Buenos Aires. The club has two courses adjoining its racetrack and polo fields at San Isidro – a suburb on the north side of Buenos Aires, edging the shore of the River Plate and therefore rather flat.

In the early 'Thirties, when they decided to go for 36 holes of golf, the Jockey Club had the good sense to go for the best, and briefed Dr Alister Mackenzie of Royal Melbourne, Cypress Point and Augusta National renown. To get some movement into the land Mackenzie indulged in a good deal of earth-moving, building swales and mounds and raising greens, and called for a programme of planting of trees and shrubs. Across the Rio de la Plata, Mackenzie also at this time built the Golf Club of Uruguay in Montevideo and the Punta del Este Golf Club. Of the Red and Blue courses in Buenos Aires, the Red – the 'Colorado' – was to be the championship course, although at 6,699 yards it was by no means long, even in 1935 when it opened. Sadly, Mackenzie did not see the finished product as he died in 1934.

On two occasions the Jockey Club's Red course has staged the World Cup. In 1962, the American team of Sam Snead and Arnold Palmer won, but the individual title went to Roberto de Vicenzo, on a score of 276. In 1970, the Australian team of Bruce Devlin and David Graham

The elegant clubhouse and part of the two courses of the Jockey Club, in the centre of Buenos Aires. The 1970 World Cup was played on the Red course, with only 19 players breaking par over 72 holes.

won, but the individual title again went to Roberto de Vicenzo, with a 269.

The 1st hole runs straight and directly away from the clubhouse for 437 yards, into an alleyway of trees. The bunkering on the left side of the fairway and the green suggests that this hole should be played entirely along the right. The 2nd is a jinky little 345 yards, and is anything but simple. A large eucalyptus tree on the right, 100 yards out, shuts off half of the target area from the tee. A big bunker on the left at 220 yards tightens it even further, and another bunker covers the front of a small green. The 3rd at 154 yards, has a bunker left front biting into the putting surface – a Road Hole type of bunker. The 4th and 5th run along the edge of the Club's property with an out-of-bounds down the left – a par-5 and a par-4 with ten bunkers between them.

Another of Mackenzie's techniques for compensating for the lack of movement in the ground, and perhaps the lack of yardage available to him, was bunkering and contouring the greens. The par of 72 is well won here!

The inward half is substantially more

severe. The 11th hole, at 518 yards, needs a long drive to get to the turn. Once that is done, bunkers to the left and right of a green which is overhung with trees on the left, make it very difficult to attack the hole. And the 13th hole is probably at the same time the simplest and the most difficult on the course. It is a straight, very narrow 440 yards to an extremely narrow green. The 15th, the last of the par-5s, has an out-of-bounds along the left, turns to the left, is heavily bunkered on the right and plays to a green surrounded by three bunkers! This Red course at the Jockey Club is a course of considerable difficulty. It is also one of distinction – indeed, one of the finest in all of South America.

The 17th green with the 16th in the background. The famous golf architect Alister Mackenzie was employed to give character to a course which was on very flat ground, hence the introduction of mounds and contouring combined with subtle bunkering.

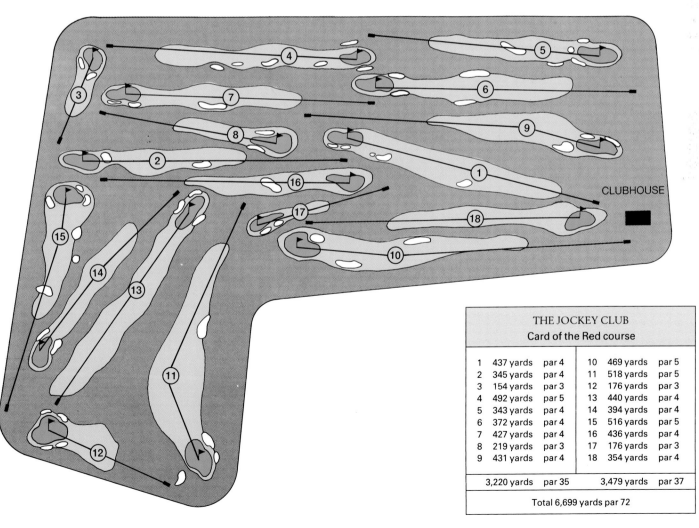

THE JOCKEY CLUB				
Card of the Red course				
1	437 yards par 4		10	469 yards par 5
2	345 yards par 4		11	518 yards par 5
3	154 yards par 3		12	176 yards par 3
4	492 yards par 5		13	440 yards par 4
5	343 yards par 4		14	394 yards par 4
6	372 yards par 4		15	516 yards par 5
7	427 yards par 4		16	436 yards par 4
8	219 yards par 3		17	176 yards par 3
9	431 yards par 4		18	354 yards par 4
3,220 yards par 35			3,479 yards par 37	
Total 6,699 yards par 72				

CLUBHOUSE

EUROPE

Golf in Europe in the Nineties could be compared with the game in America in the Sixties – it is enjoying a second coming. Included in this are the successes of British and/or European teams – men, women, amateurs, professionals – against the Americans. Also there are a complete generation of professionals who have proved themselves outstanding international champions – Severiano Ballesteros of Spain, Bernhard Langer of West Germany, Sandy Lyle of Scotland and Nick Faldo of England – and consequently a massive increase of the media coverage of golf has made it a major sport in Europe as it always has been in the U.K.

In Scotland, the home of golf, and in the British Isles generally, the game remains relatively inexpensive, a game of the people. Its main problem in small, over-crowded Britain has been the shortage of land to meet an incessant demand for new courses.

In continental Europe, the game has always been expensive, aristocratic, even esoteric, but while remaining expensive it has expanded in dramatic fashion. Golf course architects were busy as could be throughout Europe and into the Near East as governments and entrepreneurs alike saw golf as a critical factor in support of tourism, and as in America, of hotel, resort and property development. Thus the coasts and islands of Spain and Portugal had courses galore and became the Florida of Europe. And still to be developed is the growth of the game in Eastern Europe, and dare one say it, in the U.S.S.R.

The 16th green at Turnberry during the 1986 Open Championship. The swales, humps and bumps of this true linksland course are only too evident.

ROYAL ST GEORGE'S

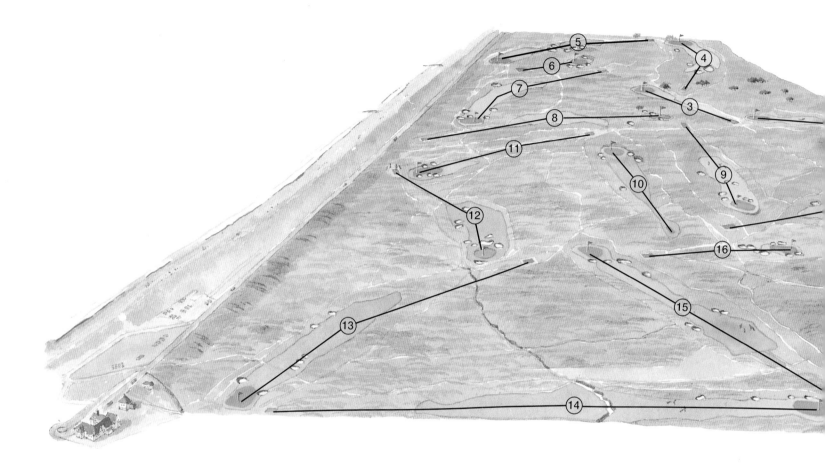

Royal St George's at Sandwich is the classic links course; its immense sand dunes hard by the sea, undulating fairways and severe bunkering give the impression that it is isolated from the world: on no other course in England can a golfer feel so happily abandoned to the game and to an environment which can seem to be a vast wilderness. In still summer sunshine it is a place of beauty and joy. In storms rolling in unimpeded off the North Sea, it can reduce the strongest tournament player to despair.

The origins of the course and the club, as so often in the litany of these great golf courses, can be traced to a single individual – Dr Laidlaw Purves. An Edinburgh man who had played his golf at the old Bruntsfield club there, he became an eye specialist at Guy's Hospital in London. He began playing at Wimbledon,

which like so many other courses in the 1880s was becoming crowded as England enjoyed its first golf boom. Purves and Henry Lamb, the Wimbledon secretary, decided to look further afield. There are various tales of how Purves came upon the huge linksland at Sandwich. One has it that Purves and a couple of friends climbed to the top of the tower of St Clement's church in Sandwich and saw the promised land – a huge expanse of dunes by the sea which in time became three great golf courses side by side: St George's in the centre (1887), Royal Cinque Ports on the southward side, towards Deal (1892), and Prince's to the north, on the Ramsgate side (1904).

Laidlaw Purves and his group leased 320 acres from the Earl of Guildford and promptly laid out their course, named St George's as England's riposte to Scot-

land's St Andrews, in what was an entirely contemporary links style – in those days, course designers were still much addicted to the blind shot over a mountainous sandhill, as at Prestwick, perhaps with a forbidding bunker cut in the face of it and with greens cut into hillsides. There was also a farmhouse on the land which served as a makeshift clubhouse, but much use was made of the Bell Hotel in Sandwich – and is to this day – following the Scottish tradition of golf being associated with inns.

Within five years the Royal and Ancient had noted that this extraordinary new golf course at Sandwich 'might be suitable for big tournaments'. They sent a four-man delegation to look at the course; and in 1894, a mere seven years since the founding of the club, St George's staged the first of its many Open Cham-

ROYAL ST GEORGE'S Card of the course					
1	445 yards	par 4	10	399 yards	par 4
2	376 yards	par 4	11	216 yards	par 3
3	214 yards	par 3	12	362 yards	par 4
4	470 yards	par 4	13	443 yards	par 4
5	422 yards	par 4	14	508 yards	par 5
6	156 yards	par 3	15	467 yards	par 4
7	529 yards	par 5	16	165 yards	par 3
8	415 yards	par 4	17	425 yards	par 4
9	387 yards	par 4	18	458 yards	par 4
3,414 yards		par 35	3,443 yards		par 35
Total 6,857 yards par 70					

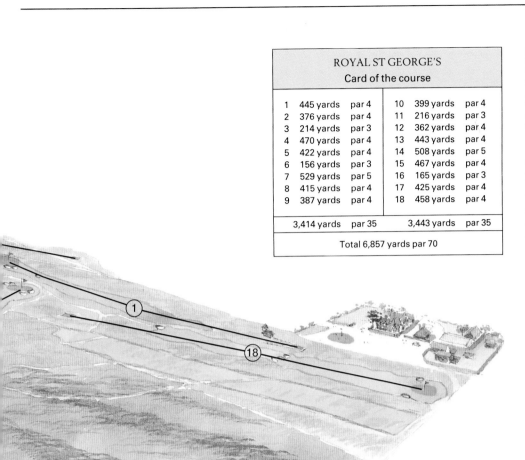

pionships. The first ever played in England, it was won by J.H. Taylor, aged 24, who was to win a total of five championships in all and be confirmed as one of golf's greatest players before the First World War.

Cotton's Triumph

From 1894 to 1949 St George's, often called simply 'Sandwich', staged nine Open championships, with the list of winners showing such illustrious names as Harry Vardon, Walter Hagen, Henry Cotton and Bobby Locke. Perhaps the most significant of these victories was Cotton's in 1934. For 11 years American golfers, in particular Bobby Jones and Hagen, had dominated the championship. At Sandwich Cotton shattered the entire field with opening rounds of 67 and 65. His second round record brought golf the famous 'Dunlop 65' ball. What is often overlooked is that Cotton, in his first qualifying round that week, scored 66, a well-nigh perfect round of golf. He was nine strokes ahead after 36 holes, ten ahead after the third round and finally won by five strokes after a nervous last-round 79. It would be another 12 years before an overseas player won the championship again.

Bobby Locke beat Harry Bradshaw in a play-off in 1949, but the post-war Championship was becoming so large in terms of crowds and cars, so demanding of access and accommodation, that Sandwich fell out of favour. The cramped, narrow streets of the medieval town, with its toll bridge over the river, made the course virtually inaccessible. It was ignored for 32 years, but then, with the highways from London to the coast much improved, Sandwich bypass opened and a back road to Deal modernised with the help of the R. and A., Sandwich came back with a flourish in 1981. The club played host to 114,522 spectators for the week and victory went to a young Texan, Bill Rogers. Architect Frank Pennink had been brought in to bring the course up to

Roger Wethered drives at the 11th at Royal St George's in his Walker Cup match in 1930 against Bobby Jones. Jones, seen on the tee beside the caddie, won 9 and 8 – he never lost a Walker Cup match.

the mark, and he removed most of the blind shots, re-positioned a green or two, stretched some tees and checked on St George's bunkers – not many more than 100, but all of them in prime positions.

A Muirfield of the South

Royal St George's is not so much a St Andrews as a Muirfield of the south, although it is even more rugged. They share a quality of spaciousness, of being not in any way overlooked, of being adrift in an immense and ancient landscape.

Perhaps the triangle of holes 13, 14 and 15 contains the very essence of this course, requiring play in three 'different' winds. The 13th is the first of four big par-4 holes over the final six. It is 443 yards long and turns slightly to the left. There are bunkers on the right at the outside of the turn, at 240 and 265 yards. The drive to the left of them must cross a diagonal line of rough country and small

Above: *Sandy Lyle in one of St George's man-deep bunkers. Lyle won the Open Championship of 1985 at the Sandwich links, the first 'home' winner since Tony Jacklin in 1969.*

Left: *The monstrous sand trap at the 4th hole at Royal St George's, one of the most intimidating courses on the Open Championship rota.*

sandhills. The line is desperately important. An over-ambitious shot, too far to the left, can find disaster in that ground.

At 508 yards, the 14th hole is the last par-5. It runs straight, with an out-of-bounds fence hard along the right side (Prince's Golf Club is beyond the fence) and a broad stream, known as the 'Suez Canal', running across the fairway at 320 yards from the back tee. There is very rough ground to the left of this fairway and bunkers string along the left-hand

side forward to the green, which is extremely flat and almost an extension of the fairway.

In winning the 1975 PGA Championship over this course, Arnold Palmer played one of the greatest rounds of his life – a 71 in a freezing gale on the last day. He played that 14th hole with a drive, a 3-iron shot under the wind, and one short putt.

Sandy Lyle, in the last round of his Open in 1985, played it rather differently. He drove into heavy rough on the left. His recovery shot advanced him a mere 80 yards. He then hit a 2-iron shot a fulminating 220 yards to the green and holed the putt of 45 feet. And when he hit a lovely 6-iron second to the 15th – one of the classic par-4 holes in British golf – he 'suddenly realised I had a real chance of winning'. He did, and was the first Scot to win the Open since Tommy Armour in 1931.

ROYAL LYTHAM AND ST ANNES

Visually, the Royal Lytham and St Annes course is the most modest, you might almost say, of all the British championship courses; yet it is linksland at its best. Its environment is urban. There are no massive sand dunes as at Birkdale or St George's; no panoramas of island and estuary, as at the West of Scotland courses, Troon and Turnberry; no grand sweep of bay as at St Andrews.

In fact, the course is a mile or so from the sea, with the Lytham-Blackpool railway line defining the seaward side of the course. Its other boundaries are overlooked by private properties, which has the golfing purist shuddering, but which

may well be considered a pleasure by the owners. Above all, Lytham calls for courage, nerve, confidence and accuracy from the tees and it has in abundance the one absolute quality that distinguishes links golf from any other – its greens will receive the running approach shot.

The St Annes-on-Sea Land and Building Company was formed in 1874 by a group of Lancashire businessmen with the simple but imaginative intention of building a new resort town between Lytham and Blackpool's south shore. They did it. And they persuaded the railway company to build them a fine station, and after some teething troubles,

St Annes prospered – the present town having grown out of the square mile of land which the company leased in 1874.

The initiative in getting the golf club started came from Alexander Doleman, a Musselburgh schoolmaster, who had opened a school in Blackpool. He was a golfer talented enough to play in the 1870 Open at Prestwick, with the Morrises and

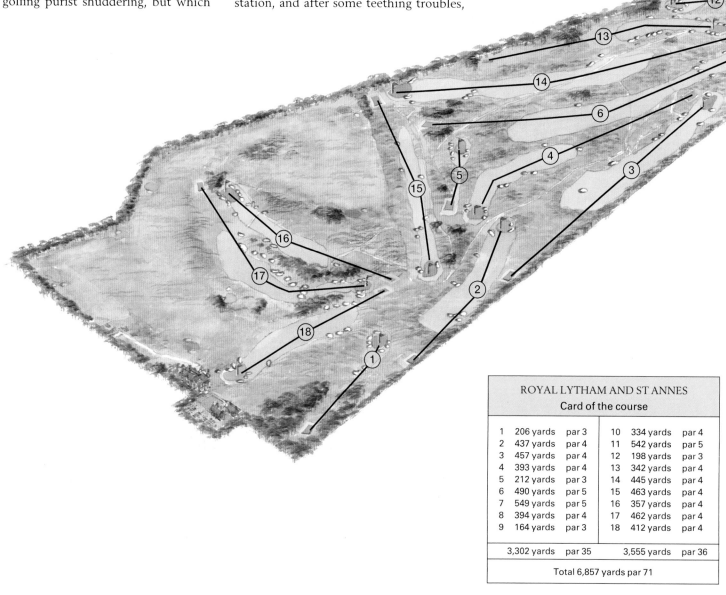

ROYAL LYTHAM AND ST ANNES					
Card of the course					
1	206 yards	par 3	10	334 yards	par 4
2	437 yards	par 4	11	542 yards	par 5
3	457 yards	par 4	12	198 yards	par 3
4	393 yards	par 4	13	342 yards	par 4
5	212 yards	par 3	14	445 yards	par 4
6	490 yards	par 5	15	463 yards	par 4
7	549 yards	par 5	16	357 yards	par 4
8	394 yards	par 4	17	462 yards	par 4
9	164 yards	par 3	18	412 yards	par 4
	3,302 yards	par 35		3,555 yards	par 36
Total 6,857 yards par 71					

Right: *The lovely rhythm of Tony Jacklin brought him the Open title of 1969, his purple patch caught here in his crucial tee shot at the 72nd at Royal Lytham. The following year he won the U.S. Open by seven shots.*

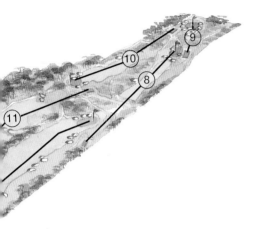

Below: *Peter Thomson, the urbane, five-times Open Champion, plays a bunker shot at Fairhaven, qualifying for the 1958 Open, which he won after a playoff with David Thomas.*

Straths of the time, and in the first Amateur Championship played at Hoylake in 1885. Although the club quickly laid out 18 holes, and indeed had a separate nine for the ladies, there were problems with the St Annes-on-Sea Land and Building Company, who were not very interested in extending what was a

rather short initial lease. Thus by 1891, with the club in a healthy state and a membership of around 400, it was decided that it was time to find a more permanent site. In 1897, the club moved to its present location and into a splendid clubhouse, reported to have cost £8,000 – an impressive sum at the time. The 1897 course cost £2,500 to build and is generally thought to be the work of George Lowe, who came from Hoylake in 1888 to be the club's first professional. Subsequently, such famous architects as Herbert Fowler, Harry Colt and G.K. Cotton made changes to firm up and 'modernise' the course.

Lytham has stood up well to the modern game and its list of Open Champions could not be more impressive: Bobby Jones in 1926, Bobby Locke in 1952, Peter Thomson 1958, Bob Charles 1963, Tony Jacklin 1969, Gary Player 1974 and Severiano Ballesteros in 1979 and 1988. All of them might well have agreed that on this course, the foundation of the round would have to be built on

the outward half, and any birdies made there would have to be protected on the inward half – for the last half dozen holes represent perhaps the toughest sustained finish in championship golf.

An Opening Par-3

A Lytham oddity is that the first hole is a par-3 of 206 yards. It is played out of a grove of trees, so judging the wind is difficult on this opening shot. The 2nd and 3rd holes are strong par-4s. The railway running hard down the right side is an intimidating factor. These three holes run straight out, but the 4th turns back on them and together with the short 5th and long 6th, 'triangulates' back towards the railway line. The 4th is 393 yards, but turns to the left and is likely to be into wind. The 5th is a long one-shotter of 212 yards from a raised tee to a mounded green – a difficult tee shot this, especially in wind.

Now we have another Lytham oddity: successive par-5s, of 490 yards and 549 yards, both considered prime birdie holes. The 8th, at 394 yards, takes us nearer to the end of the course and the one area of Lytham which has some rolling, if modest, sand hills; while the 9th, 164 yards, is a pitch down from a plateau to a bowl green ringed by 10 bunkers. The 10th, at 334 yards, is only a drive and pitch hole – although the drive is into a narrow, broken fairway.

The Long Road Home

The 11th is really the start of a long and grinding road home. It is 542 yards, dog-leg left, with two deep bunkers in the angle at 256 yards out. A drive over these bunkers gives the player some hope of being on the green in two. To the right of them, the second shot becomes longer and longer. The short 12th is rather like the first hole in that it is 198 yards and played out of a spinney of trees, which again make the wind difficult to assess. The green is set across the shot, and there is a road and an out-of-bounds uncomfortably close to it. The 13th is something of a catch-your-breath hole of 342 yards, but now we are into the king-sized finish.

All the finishing holes, without exception, feature very narrow fairways with vigorous bunkering and set the sternest

Above: *The 16th at Royal Lytham, 356 yards and a blind tee shot, is known as the 'car park' hole. In the 1979 championship, Severiano Ballesteros drove far to the right amongst parked cars, was allowed a free drop, pitched to the green and holed for a birdie!*

Left: *Severiano Ballesteros exults in his chip shot from the back left of the last green, on the last round of the 1988 championship at Royal Lytham. The ball nudged the hole, stopped a few inches away, and made his victory certain.*

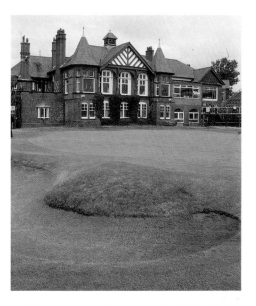

This enormous bunker protects the left-hand side of the 18th green; in the background the fine Royal Lytham clubhouse.

examination of driving patterns and angles. The 15th, at 468 yards and as often as not into the wind, is one of the most demanding par-4 holes in championship golf. The 16th, at 356 yards, is more manageable, but needs a blind drive over tumbling ground, while the green and its approaches feature no fewer than 11 bunkers. It was at this hole in 1979 that Ballesteros drove into a car park on the right, dropped clear without penalty, pitched to the green and holed the putt for a wonderfully preposterous birdie.

Jones's Historic Mashie Shot

The 17th hole, of 462 yards, is a marvellous golf hole, intrinsically and because of its place in the Lytham sequence. It dog-legs to the left some 300 yards from the tee. All along the left side are bunkers. At the 300 yards mark, a broad swathe of rough crosses the fairway, containing another rash of bunkers. The green is quite large by Lytham standards. It was on this hole in 1926 that Bobby Jones, in winning the first of his three Open Championships, hit one of golf's most famous shots. Trapped in a shallow bunker on the left, 175 yards from the green, he found a clean lie. Jones picked the ball off the sand cleanly and found the green with his mashie to secure a par-4. Al Watrous, playing with Jones and level with him for the Championship, was so unnerved that he three-putted, and finished second. To this day, a plaque marks the bunker from which Jones played the shot.

The last hole at Lytham seems to be a microcosm of the whole golf course. At first glance it seems almost nondescript, running on to a flat green which runs right under the clubhouse windows. At 412 yards, it was lengthened by some 25 yards for the 1988 Championship, but can be considered short for a finishing hole. However, it is in fact a superb driving hole. Across the fairway in the driving zone are two diagonals of bunkers; there are clumps of bushes in the right rough, so that the landing area for the tee shot is terribly confined. It demands a drive that is long, finely calculated and straight, and no champion has ever played it better than did Tony Jacklin in winning his Open Championship in 1969.

ROYAL BIRKDALE

If ever a piece of land seemed designed exclusively for the hand of the golf architect, it was surely the coast of Lancashire running north from Liverpool along Liverpool Bay and the Irish Sea to the town of Southport. Tumbling sand dunes, heather, pine forest, willow scrub; and the railway tracks, which seem almost mandatory for British links courses, marking the boundaries of some holes, and serving a litany of famous courses – all of this has given us West Lancs., Formby, Southport & Ainsdale, Hillside and Royal Birkdale. And the greatest of these is Royal Birkdale.

The course is laid out through a great wasteland of sand dunes, the design following the valleys between them. The original course, dating from 1889, is generally thought to have been the work of George Lowe; but problems arose with the renewal of the lease and in 1897 the founding fathers moved to the present site. In 1931 Southport Corporation bought the land and leased it to the club for 99 years. The present clubhouse was then built, and Fred Hawtree and J.H. Taylor re-modeled the course. Royal Birkdale was now ready for the modern age of steel shafts.

In 29 years from 1954, it staged six Open Championships and two Ryder Cup matches. It has also presented the Curtis Cup match, the Walker Cup match, British and English championships and several major professional tournaments. And its Open champions form a distinguished hierarchy: Peter Thomson

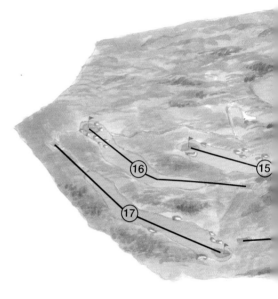

Arnold Palmer, wearing his storm gear on the 2nd tee during the first round of the 1961 Open at Royal Birkdale, the first of his successive wins which did much to rejuvenate the championship.

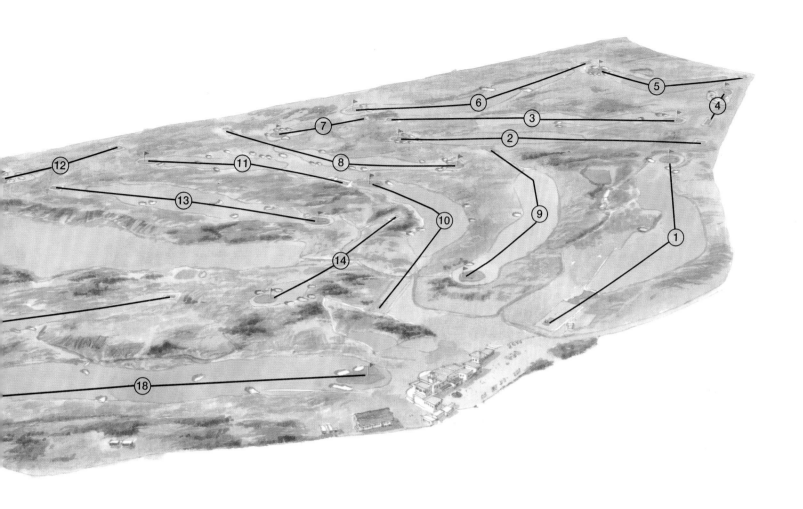

(twice), Arnold Palmer, Lee Trevino, Johnny Miller and Tom Watson.

While the Birkdale fairways, rising and falling, have a good deal of movement in them, there is an absence of those small mounds and pimples such as we find at St Andrews or Troon or St George's, which can make a lottery of the bounce of the ball. The sand dunes are huge, giving both shelter to the fairways and splendid vantage points for spectators. One particular feature of the course has been the siting of the greens and their defences. There are no blind shots at Birkdale. But the greens in general have been planted tightly into the dunes. All of them have impish little slopes running off the putting surfaces, all of them are closely bunkered and many of them – the 2nd, 6th, 15th and 17th, for example – are all but surrounded by plantations of willow scrub. Thus missing the green at Birkdale, even by a few feet, can bring retribution most foul!

In championship trim, Royal Birkdale

ROYAL BIRKDALE			
Card of the course			
1	448 yards par 4	10	395 yards par 4
2	417 yards par 4	11	409 yards par 4
3	409 yards par 4	12	184 yards par 3
4	203 yards par 3	13	506 yards par 5
5	346 yards par 4	14	199 yards par 3
6	490 yards par 5	15	543 yards par 5
7	154 yards par 3	16	414 yards par 4
8	458 yards par 4	17	525 yards par 5
9	414 yards par 4	18	472 yards par 4
3,339 yards par 35		3,647 yards par 37	
Total 6,986 yards par 72			

runs to just under 7,000 yards with a par of 72. On the outward half the course has two par-3 holes and no par-5. On the inward half, it has four par-5s packed into the final six holes, ready made for high drama and deeds of derring-do in tight championship finishes. Two such were shots to the last green, 200 yards away,

finding the narrow entrance between the flanking bunkers. Peter Thomson did it in 1965 and Tom Watson did it in 1983, each man winning his fifth championship. Each played a 2-iron, and Thomson won by two strokes, Watson by one. Watson said afterwards that it was the best 2-iron shot he had ever played.

Palmer's Heroics

Birkdale is man-sized on the outward half: six of its par-4 holes are 400 yards or better. Yet it always seems to produce better than man-sized champions. In the Open of 1961 a gale flattened Birkdale on the second day; tented areas were devastated, and fairways were in part under water. But Arnold Palmer gave an astonishing display of power and control in keeping the ball under the wind, hitting 1-iron shots that never rose more than six feet off the ground. He was three under par after five holes and eventually finished with a remarkable 73.

At the 15th hole (now the 16th) of the last round, Palmer hit a shot that is immortalised by a plaque marking the spot. The hole is 414 yards and Palmer drove off the fairway into the heavy right rough in the elbow of the fairway. The green, raised on a plateau, has two bunkers on either side and four short of the green. Palmer would have to extract his ball from the rough and advance it by a good 150 yards through the air to reach the putting surface. He gave the ball the most immense smash with a 6-iron, and from this awful rough it flew all the way, finishing 15 feet from the flagstick. He won the championship by a stroke from Dai Rees.

The most interesting (and difficult) hole on the outward half is the 6th, a big, 490-yard par-5 which turns to the right. At the angle, a long, mounded bunker crosses most of the fairway, leaving a gap of only a few yards on the left, while rough closes out the right end of the bunker. Playing safely short of it leaves a very long second shot to a large but raised green, bunkered and backed by willow scrub. On the other hand, to carry the bunker means a giant shot, and even in perfect conditions few will manage it. Similarly, trying to sneak past the left end of the bunker will require a drive of impressive length and accuracy.

Of the par-5s, the 13th at 506 yards is perhaps the most open. From a high tee the hole plays straight along a fairly flat fairway, with a ditch on the left. The pretty green is in a little canyon, with high dunes and willow scrub on three sides. The 15th is an immense hole: at 543 yards, it demands a very long drive to give the player any chance of carrying a screen of eight bunkers with his second shot to get anywhere near a green which has a closely trapped entrance. The 17th, at 525 yards, is almost as forbidding. The drive must find a rather narrow fairway set between huge sand ridges. The green is long and rather narrow; it will receive a running shot, but it gives the impression

This tranquil shot of the 13th hole, taken during an early round of the British Ladies' Championship of 1986, illustrates Royal Birkdale's ranging sand dunes and valley fairways, not to mention its famous willow scrub.

Johnny Miller holes out to win the 1976 Open at Royal Birkdale with a closing 66. An inspirational player, Miller had also scored a final low round, a record 63, in winning the 1973 U.S. Open Championship at Oakmont.

that it is slightly sunken, and it too has willow scrub pressing close.

Enter Ballesteros

In one sense, the Royal Birkdale championship of 1976, won by Johnny Miller, was a portent of things to come. It was a year of heatwave – part of the course had caught fire during the second day – and playing conditions were perfect. It was also the year that Severiano Ballesteros, 19 years old, played his first Open. He played the first 36 holes in 69, 69 with all the brio of a man enjoying Sunday morning golf. He went into the last round leading the championship by two strokes from Miller. They were paired together on that last round, and Miller, hardened championship player that he was, was not about to let this young Spaniard take any liberties with him. Playing relentlessly attacking golf, Miller was out in 33, round in 66, and took the championship by six strokes from Ballesteros and Jack Nicklaus. But for many the moment of the championship came at the 13th hole in the final round, when Miller chipped in from off the green and Seve Ballesteros skipped across the green and smilingly shook his hand.

FORMBY

The course of the Formby Golf Club is a lovely, unsung link in that necklace of courses that runs from the northern fringes of Liverpool to Southport. But Formby, even if it is more unassuming than most, is second to none of them. The club dates from 1881, making it one of the oldest of Lancashire clubs, and it could scarcely have had a more modest beginning. The minutes of the original meeting remain and show that ten 'gentlemen' met at the Rev. Lonsdale Formby's Reading Room on the 11th of December 1884. Mr William McIver, who was to become the first captain of the club, took the chair. They resolved to call it the Formby Golf Club, the number of members being restricted to 25. Subscription was one guinea and the 'Links should be open for play on 1st October, closing on the Saturday nearest 15th April following'. So it was winter golf they had in mind, in spite of the fact that, at that moment, they did not have a course – they thought they would rent Mr William Halewood's 'Warren' as their links at a rental of £10 per season, but only £5 'for the unexpired portion of this season'!

The Warren was rough grazing land, with sandhills and scrub, in the general area of the present first and second holes, adjoining the railway line, and the 18th. McIver had shooting rights over it – the area was infested with rabbits. Formby's start was certainly primitive! Nine holes were knocked out, with greens no more than extensions of the fairways, and with little more than a year gone, it was agreed that membership could rise to 40, and a wooden shanty was raised as a 'clubhouse' (built by a member for less than £3). The most significant fact of that first year came when Formby was asked to support the initiative of the Royal Liverpool Club, which had suggested to the Royal and Ancient that an Amateur Championship should be established. Two delegates from each of the supporting clubs, including Formby, met to organise the event, played for the first time that year, 1885,

Formby is a classic links course of charm and elegance. This natural bowl around the 10th hole provides spectators with a superb vantage point to watch the play.

at Hoylake. Formby contributed their guinea to pay for a championship trophy. This put a stamp on the personality of the club. Formby perhaps took on an air of the amateur establishment which it has never quite lost. Not only the merchants of Manchester and Liverpool but the Lancashire county set made it their club. It prospered steadily, and had the flavour of Muirfield or Royal St George's.

Willie Park, Jr and Harry Colt
In the 1890s, the course was extended to 18 holes of just under 6,000 yards, but all of them were in the same compass, packed into the area in front of the clubhouse. But early in the new century, additional land to the north and west was taken over and the course was able to march into an area of sandhills and towards the sea. In 1907 Willie Park, Jr designed 18 holes, many of them still in place after Harry Colt reviewed them in the 'Twenties. Thus Formby has been touched by two of the greatest golf architects. Park, a perfectionist and probably the first golf champion to make a professional study of course design, laid

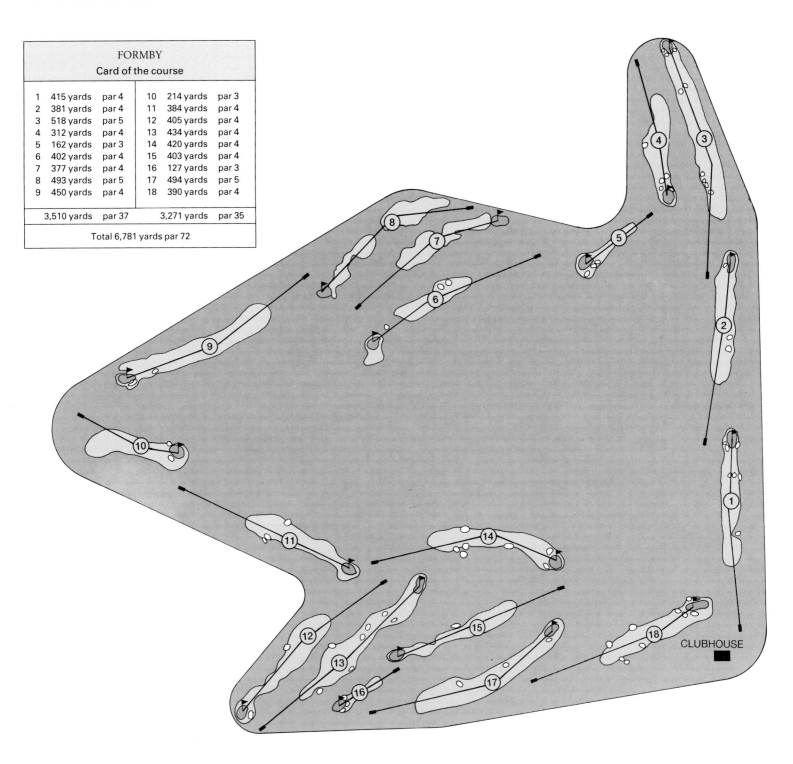

FORMBY					
Card of the course					
1	415 yards	par 4	10	214 yards	par 3
2	381 yards	par 4	11	384 yards	par 4
3	518 yards	par 5	12	405 yards	par 4
4	312 yards	par 4	13	434 yards	par 4
5	162 yards	par 3	14	420 yards	par 4
6	402 yards	par 4	15	403 yards	par 4
7	377 yards	par 4	16	127 yards	par 3
8	493 yards	par 5	17	494 yards	par 5
9	450 yards	par 4	18	390 yards	par 4
3,510 yards	par 37		3,271 yards	par 35	
Total 6,781 yards par 72					

out some 70 courses in the United States, and others in Canada, Austria, Belgium and France as well as Britain.

Frank Pennink

The first three holes of the Park/Colt course at Formby run hard by the Liverpool-Southport railway line, and are reminiscent of the start at Royal Lytham. Two strong par-4s and a big 518 yards par-5 run north across fairly flat ground. The course then turns westward into a range of rising duneland garlanded with pine woods planted by the club. Like Ballybunion and Portrush, Formby has had erosion problems, but fortunately had enough spare land to allow Frank Pennink to replace a couple of holes. The last half dozen holes play every which way, giving differing wind problems and creating an extremely difficult finish.

Formby is a classic links course of charm and elegance and stillness. It does have some iron in its soul, since it can now muster 6,781 yards and a par of 72. It has offered the warmest of welcomes to amateur championships – it has staged all of them, mens' and women's, boys' and girls' – but it has been just a little indifferent to professional events.

GANTON

Glorious Ganton in North Yorkshire is nine miles from the sea, yet it has all the qualities of a typical links course. It is certainly one of the finest inland courses in Britain, and boasts a sandy sub-soil which makes it quick-draining, crisp turf, enormous banks of gorse (which have become its signature) and cavernous, links-type bunkers. The course lies snugly in the Vale of Pickering, which runs from Pickering in the west to the coast at Scarborough and in recent geological times was under sea water; this explains why, to this day, the Ganton ground staff turn up sea shells when digging new drains or bunkers.

Ganton is a beautiful golf course and, if not long at 6,720 yards, offers a keen examination for the best players, having staged Amateur Championships and a Ryder Cup match. This is hardly surprising: since it was formed in 1891, the club has been advised by Tom Sherrin, Tom Dunn, Harry Vardon, Harold Hilton, James Braid, Harry Colt, Herbert Fowler,

Harry Vardon in his prime. Six-times winner of the Open Championship, winner of the U.S. Open, he is one of the three or four most influential players in the history of golf.

Major Hutchinson, C.K. Cotton and Frank Pennink – a veritable galaxy of golfing and design talent.

In 1891 Scarborough was the premier resort in the north of England and had been a spa for more than 200 years. With the golfing explosion in England in the last quarter of the 19th century, some prominent citizens resolved that the town needed a golf course, and formed the Scarborough Golf Club. They chose a site which was part of the Ganton estate, owned by one of their number, Sir Charles Legard. It was very rough, uneven ground, covered with gorse and bushes, and had been used only for rough shooting. But it was only nine miles by road from Scarborough and only 300 yards from Ganton station on the North-Eastern railway line from York to Scarborough – an important factor in the age before motoring.

In the 1920s Dr Alistair Mackenzie was employed to redesign the greens. The result is one of his specialities: tiered

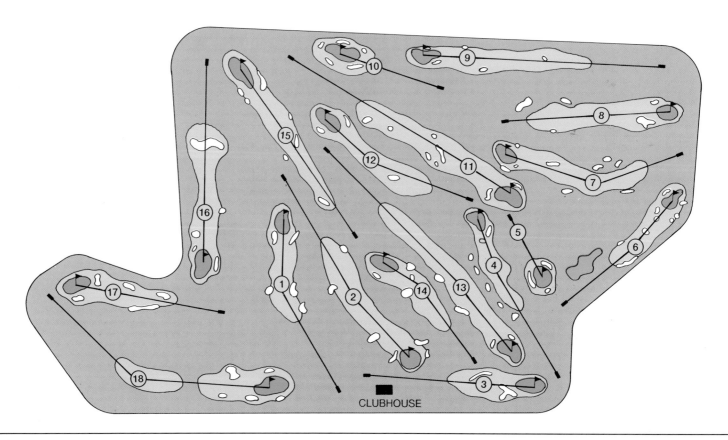

CLUBHOUSE

greens, as at the 3rd and 7th and 9th. Ken Cotton was then brought in to strengthen the course for the Ryder Cup matches of 1949 and lengthened many holes by building new tees. This was the Ryder Cup match in which Ben Hogan, the American non-playing captain, created something of a scandal by claiming that some of the British clubs were illegal, because their iron-club faces were too deeply punched.

Bernard Darwin, the venerable correspondent of *The Times* newspaper, was asked to resolve it and did so by suggesting diplomatically that there was nothing 'a little judicious filing could not put right'. This in fact was no more than a little tit-for-tat by Hogan – Henry Cotton, British captain in the previous match at Portland, Oregon, had said the same about the American clubs then.

Over the years Ganton's gorse has been allowed to grow considerably, but under control, and is now an outstanding feature of the course. Extensive planting of Scots and Corsican pine has added to the Ganton woodland, but in recent years

GANTON					
Card of the course					
1	373 yards	par 4	10	168 yards	par 3
2	418 yards	par 4	11	417 yards	par 4
3	334 yards	par 4	12	363 yards	par 4
4	406 yards	par 4	13	524 yards	par 5
5	157 yards	par 3	14	282 yards	par 4
6	449 yards	par 4	15	461 yards	par 4
7	431 yards	par 4	16	448 yards	par 4
8	414 yards	par 4	17	252 yards	par 4
9	494 yards	par 5	18	434 yards	par 4
3,476 yards	par 36		3,349 yards	par 36	
Total 6,825 yards par 72					

two elm trees, important to the play, were stricken by Dutch elm disease. One was on the right of the 282-yard 14th, a potential one-shot hole for the powerful hitter; the tree and a bunker had crucially narrowed the gap into the green. Fortunately it shows some sign of life and has been retained. The other tree, on the left of the 448-yard 16th, squeezed the line of the second shot. It had to be replaced by a flowering chestnut, 18 feet high.

The 13th hole at Ganton, a par 5 of 524 yards, demands a drive over a sierra of gorse to a none-too-wide fairway.

There are only two short holes and two par-5s on the course – neither of the latter being excessively long. Accuracy and careful driving at Ganton are more important than power – only six of the two-shot holes are more than 400 yards. Its large, bungalow-type clubhouse included, Ganton is a place of pleasure, and not of confrontation – even if you were J.H. Taylor facing the 'unknown' Harry Vardon in 1896. Vardon was professional of the club at the time. Taylor, the reigning Open Champion, wrote later: 'Little did I guess when playing him at Ganton that I was playing with a man who was to make golfing history and develop into what is in my solemn and considered judgement the finest and most finished golfer that the game has ever known'. Taylor was beaten 8 and 6.

SUNNINGDALE

When the Royal and Ancient Golf Club of St Andrews decided to award the staging of the 1987 Walker Cup match to the Sunningdale club, it was the first time that this famous match between the amateurs of Great Britain & Ireland and the United States of America had been played on an inland rather than a seaside links course. And the compliment was no more than an acknowledgement of the Sunningdale Old Course's quality, its charm and its subtleties, and of the contribution that the club and its members have made to golf, both in play and in council.

Sunningdale Old is one of the loveliest of golf courses. Only 25 miles south-west of London, it plays through heather and woodland of pine and birch and on a sandy sub-soil which gives quick drainage, encourages crisp lies in the seaside manner and allows year-round play. It is a quite splendid heathland course in which the fairways are ample, the hazards clearly seen, the greens true and the vistas stunning. And if the course, even at a modest 6,500 yards, is quite testing for all but the best tournament pros, it never quite seems so. The joy of Sunningdale is the total experience of the round, and not

the challenge of one hole more than another. The place has a certain elegance. It is altogether superior, and it knows it.

When Bobby Jones played the course in the Southern Qualifying Competition for the Open Championship of 1926, he scored what has come to be considered the perfect round of golf. His 66 had 33 shots and 33 putts. Every hole was scored in three or four. He missed only one green, the 13th, by a few feet, but chipped close for his par. In his second qualifying round, he scored 68, this time including one five and one two. He said later: 'I wish I could take this golf course home with me'. Sunningdale is that kind of place.

The end of the last century was an intriguing time for golf in the London area. Heathland was discovered to be entirely suitable for golf, and sand belts to the south and south-west of the capital quickly accommodated such fine courses as Woking in 1893 and Walton Heath in 1904. Sunningdale dates from 1901.

The golf course land was owned, and still is, by St John's College, Cambridge. It had formed part of the Benedictine nunnery of Broomhall, suppressed by Henry VIII, but John Fisher, Bishop of

Rochester, was able to possess it for the College in 1524. The founding father of the golf club, T.A. Roberts had built a house in 1898 close to what is now the entrance to the club. He approached the College for a lease to allow him to build a golf course and some housing. A committee was formed of his interested friends, and Willie Park, Jr, twice Open Champion and a pioneer of golf architecture, was approached to lay out and build the course. His price was £3,800.

The ground at that time was almost entirely open, quite bare of trees, and the lovely woodlands of Sunningdale are an illustration of the hand of man improving on nature. Later, Harry Colt made some changes to the course to protect it against the longer flight of the Haskell ball. (Colt was secretary of Sunningdale for 17 years and designed the New Course, which dates from 1922.) His work now means that almost every hole treads its own pathway in some privacy, if not in complete isolation, and there is a splendid variation in the holes. No two are in any way alike.

Views over London

One of Sunningdale's most intriguing sequence of holes is 10, 11 and 12. The 10th tee is the highest point on the course, with compelling views over the forest towards London. The drive is downhill into a broad valley, with bunkers on

SUNNINGDALE Card of the course					
1	494 yards	par 5	10	478 yards	par 5
2	484 yards	par 5	11	325 yards	par 4
3	296 yards	par 4	12	451 yards	par 4
4	161 yards	par 3	13	185 yards	par 3
5	410 yards	par 4	14	509 yards	par 5
6	415 yards	par 4	15	226 yards	par 3
7	402 yards	par 4	16	438 yards	par 4
8	172 yards	par 3	17	421 yards	par 4
9	267 yards	par 4	18	432 yards	par 4
3,101 yards	par 36		3,465 yards	par 36	
Total 6,566 yards par 72					

The view from the 5th tee, with the pond at centre-right in the fairway and beyond it the green bunkered at left and front right. All the trees in the picture are a product of Harry Colt's planting programme.

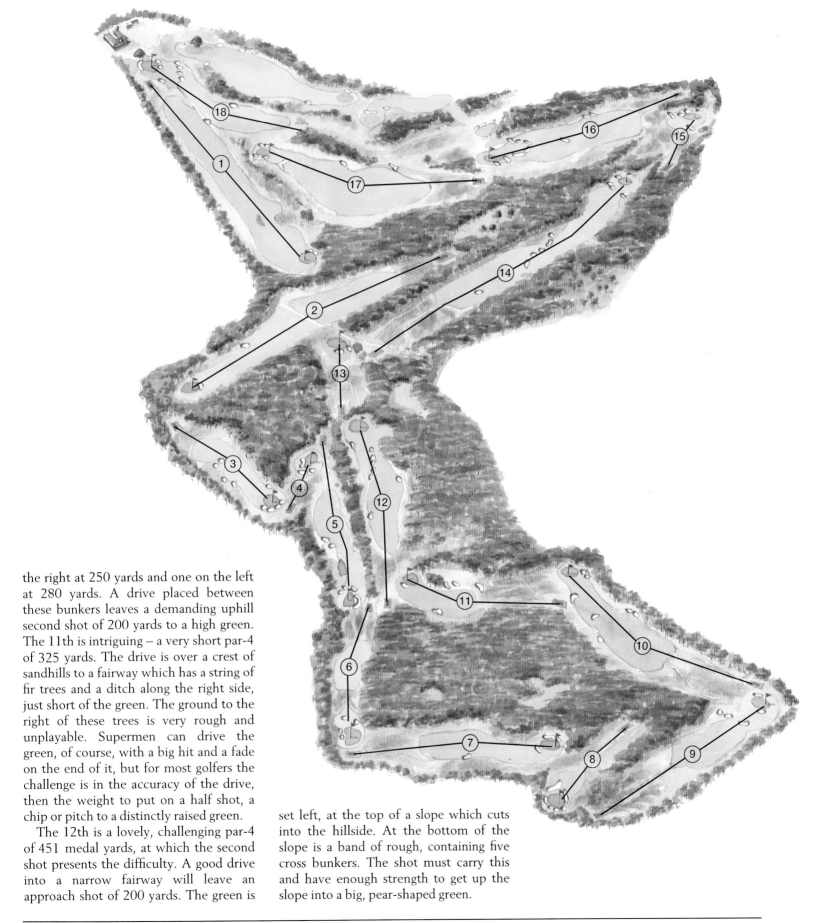

the right at 250 yards and one on the left at 280 yards. A drive placed between these bunkers leaves a demanding uphill second shot of 200 yards to a high green. The 11th is intriguing – a very short par-4 of 325 yards. The drive is over a crest of sandhills to a fairway which has a string of fir trees and a ditch along the right side, just short of the green. The ground to the right of these trees is very rough and unplayable. Supermen can drive the green, of course, with a big hit and a fade on the end of it, but for most golfers the challenge is in the accuracy of the drive, then the weight to put on a half shot, a chip or pitch to a distinctly raised green.

The 12th is a lovely, challenging par-4 of 451 medal yards, at which the second shot presents the difficulty. A good drive into a narrow fairway will leave an approach shot of 200 yards. The green is set left, at the top of a slope which cuts into the hillside. At the bottom of the slope is a band of rough, containing five cross bunkers. The shot must carry this and have enough strength to get up the slope into a big, pear-shaped green.

WALTON HEATH

Walton Heath was once common-land of the manor of Walton-on-the-Hill, owned since feudal times by lords of the manor. At the end of the 19th century it was a vast wasteland of heather and gorse. Nowadays the Walton Heath Golf Club, less than 20 miles from London, is the owner of two courses which offer the finest heathland golf to be found anywhere in the world. The golfing area of the heath is huge, some 500 acres in all, and at over 600 feet it is as high as Gleneagles. Exposed to the elements, it is a place of big skies, fine, dry, crisp turf and a wonderful feeling of spaciousness.

A man of many parts was largely responsible for the creation of the club and the courses. Cosmo Bonsor was among many things a director of the Bank of England, a Justice of the Peace and Deputy Lieutenant for Surrey, a Member of Parliament for Wimbledon from 1885 until 1900 and chairman of the South Eastern Railway Company. In this last capacity he had brought the railway to Kingswood and Tadworth, near Walton, and he was convinced that a golf course would supplement the railway in developing the area.

A second marriage for Bonsor brought William Herbert Fowler as a brother-in-law. Fowler, like Bonsor, was larger than

WALTON HEATH Card of the Championship course					
1	410 yards	par 4	10	341 yards	par 4
2	513 yards	par 5	11	521 yards	par 5
3	391 yards	par 4	12	462 yards	par 4
4	422 yards	par 4	13	470 yards	par 4
5	174 yards	par 3	14	465 yards	par 4
6	489 yards	par 5	15	404 yards	par 4
7	390 yards	par 4	16	475 yards	par 4
8	395 yards	par 4	17	165 yards	par 3
9	189 yards	par 3	18	432 yards	par 4
3,373 yards	par 36		3,735 yards	par 36	
Total 7,108 yards par 72					

The par-5, 16th hole on Walton Heath's Old Course illustrates some of Herbert Fowler's design principles: raised green, deep greenside bunkering, the use of heather, and a reasonable width to the fairway.

life. A talented cricketer for Essex, Somerset and MCC, he took up golf only when he was 35 but quickly became scratch. As a member of the R & A and the Honourable Company, he won medals at St

Andrews, St George's, Westward Ho! and Walton, and played international golf for England. He was also enchanted by St Andrews, studied the Old Course carefully, and made it very clear to Bonsor that he had ambitions as a golf-course designer. Bonsor and his eldest son Malcolm and their friends made it possible: they purchased the land, formed a company, and turned Fowler loose on the heath in August 1902.

He settled on a design, the course was seeded in August 1903 (rabbits were a problem and miles of expensive mesh fencing had to be laid), and by the spring of 1904 it was ready for play. In January of that year Fowler, who became secretary of the club, a shareholder and eventually managing director, signed a con-

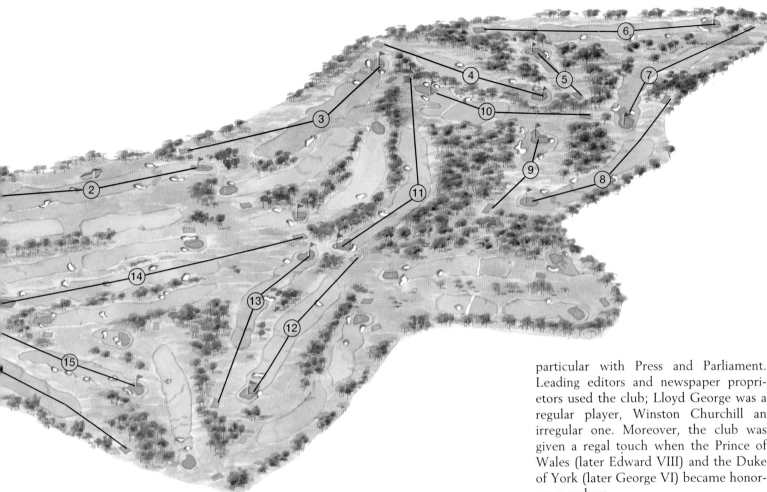

tract with the great James Braid to be professional to the club. It was an association that lasted 45 years, until Braid's death in 1950 at the age of 80.

Herbert Fowler was a big, powerful man who was a powerful striker of the golf ball. He designed his courses on the grand scale, no doubt with other powerful strikers in mind. His first course at Walton ran to 6,300 yards and has been little changed, save in length, over the years. The success of Walton took him on to other projects. He worked on Saunton East and The Berkshire, and with Tom Simpson at Cruden Bay. James Braid too had an extraordinary career as a golf architect, designing dozens of courses throughout the British Isles and Ireland, travelling everywhere by train.

An additional nine-hole course was opened in 1907 and extended to 18 in 1913, by which time the club had almost 500 members. It had been an outstanding success, and quickly became associated in

Johnny Miller ponders the destination of a drive in the 1981 Ryder Cup match. He and his partner Tom Kite (with eyeshade) halved their fourball match with Howard Clark (in white) and Sam Torrance.

particular with Press and Parliament. Leading editors and newspaper proprietors used the club; Lloyd George was a regular player, Winston Churchill an irregular one. Moreover, the club was given a regal touch when the Prince of Wales (later Edward VIII) and the Duke of York (later George VI) became honorary members.

The original course, which became the 'Old' only with the opening of the 'New', shared many characteristics with the Old at St Andrews. Fowler designed greens that would take the running approach shot. They are often raised, with ridges compromising to some extent the area in front; many have little depressions or downslopes at the sides, and feature deep greenside bunkers. But, as a principle, Fowler held that they should have reasonable entrances. He maintained the heather, the fiercest rough in the game of golf, but on the other hand did not design brutally narrow fairways — at Walton there is almost always wind, and the golfer needs room to cope with it!

Walton has had its share of the major events in golf; none more so than the Ryder Cup match of 1981, when a composite course of 'Old' and 'New' holes were played, and when the United States won by 17 to 8 with one of the strongest teams ever to play in the event.

WENTWORTH

The Wentworth Estate of 1,750 acres, 21 miles south-west of London, was one of the earliest British developments that sought to make golf the core of a major property development – as is widespread in the United States, and now the rest of the world. Wentworth House dates from 1802 and was once the home of the Duke of Wellington's sister; it now forms part of the clubhouse. The property was acquired in the 1850s by Ramón Cabrera, an exiled Spanish count, and on his death his English widow, the Countess de Morella, bought up most of the adjoining land to encompass today's acreage. In 1923 development rights and planning permissions were given. The Wentworth development was to be of large houses, each set in at least an acre of land, adjoining or very close to the golf courses.

Harry Colt of Sunningdale, only four miles away, was commissioned to design first the East Course and then the West – the 'big' course which opened in 1924; in

Nick Faldo makes the winning putt on the 18th green at Wentworth's West Course in the 1989 final of the Suntory World Match Play Championship against fellow Ryder Cup player Ian Woosnam.

addition there was a much shorter nine-hole course. Colt had the classic heathland elements with which to work: heather, pine, silver birch, a sandy, fast-draining soil and, in later years, enormous banks of rhododendron. He made the most of this, producing two lovely courses which were as testing as any golfer might imagine. The East Course, at 6,176 yards, is considered quite a few shots easier than the West. It staged the very first Curtis Cup matches in 1932. The West Course, at 6,945 yards, is an entirely different proposition. It, too, was early on the international scene: in 1925 the professionals of Great Britain and the United States played an informal match here, forerunner of the Ryder Cup matches.

Sandy subsoil, more than almost anything else, and rolling woodland give a golf architect a head start, and in the West Course, Colt created one of the finest inland courses in Britain. Significantly, his design has remained unchanged.

Colt's design demands, above all, long and accurate driving. The 13th and the 17th, quite different golf holes, illustrate this requirement. The 13th hole, playing slightly uphill at 441 yards, and turning slightly to the left, demands a drive of 250

WENTWORTH Card of the West course				
1	471 yards par 4		10	186 yards par 3
2	155 yards par 3		11	376 yards par 4
3	452 yards par 4		12	483 yards par 5
4	501 yards par 5		13	441 yards par 4
5	191 yards par 3		14	179 yards par 3
6	344 yards par 4		15	466 yards par 4
7	399 yards par 4		16	380 yards par 4
8	398 yards par 4		17	571 yards par 5
9	450 yards par 4		18	502 yards par 5
3,361 yards par 35			3,584 yards par 37	
Total 6,945 yards par 72				

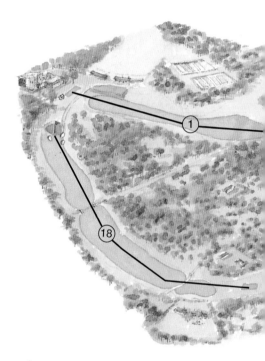

yards or more to 'see round the corner' to the small green, which lies further uphill and in a hollow. And 17 is one of the great par-5s, the great driving holes, of British golf. It is a monster of 571 yards, downhill from the tee for almost 300 yards, where it turns to the left and runs uphill to a crest, then downhill to a middle-sized green. All along the left side are private gardens which are out-of-bounds. The fairway in the drive landing zone is tilted sharply from left to right, falling away towards the outside of the turn. To have any chance of reaching the green, the player must drive long, into the left centre of the fairway To get there, he simply

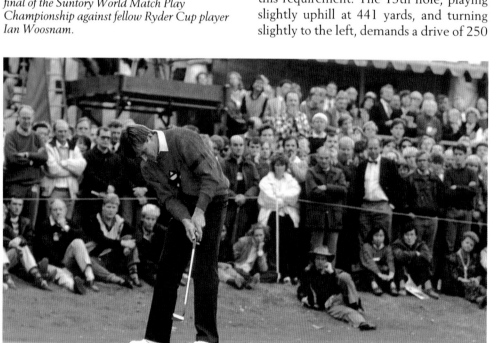

must drive on the tightest possible line along the left, flirting with the out-of-bounds, and with draw to counter the tendency of the ball to bounce right. Time and time again, this hole has become the climax of matches in the World Match-Play Championship, that marvellous tournament which started in 1964.

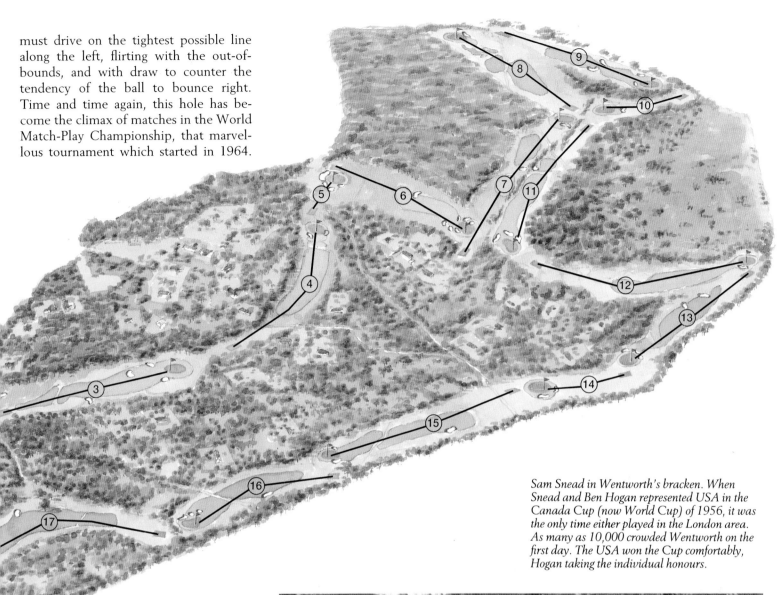

Sam Snead in Wentworth's bracken. When Snead and Ben Hogan represented USA in the Canada Cup (now World Cup) of 1956, it was the only time either played in the London area. As many as 10,000 crowded Wentworth on the first day. The USA won the Cup comfortably, Hogan taking the individual honours.

In the 1989 event, in beating Ian Woosnam at the 36th hole in a pulsating final, Nick Faldo scored a 'nominal' 64, on the second 18, including an eagle at the last. So much (or, rather, so little) for the constraints of length on today's stars when conditions are favourable.

The course staged the Ryder Cup in 1953, when the U.S. won by one slender point, and the World Cup (then the Canada Cup) of 1956, when the winning U.S. team was Sam Snead and Ben Hogan. Wentworth has also had famous professionals in George Duncan, Archie Compston, Jimmy Adams, Tom Haliburton and Bernard Gallacher. The property company that now owns Wentworth has plans for a new 18-hole course designed by Gary Player and John Jacobs.

ST ANDREWS

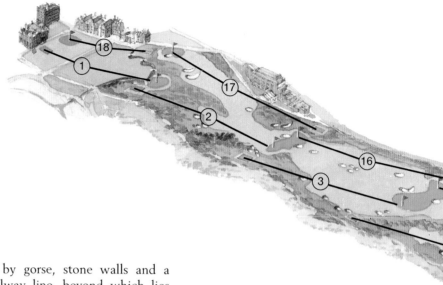

Golf has been played on the links at St Andrews since medieval times, and for better than 400 years on the turf of the present Old Course, which has 'evolved' to its present state without much interference from the hand of man. It is the most famous golf course in the world, and as such, like it or not – and many keen students of the game for one reason or the other do not care for this golf course – it must be maintained and preserved.

The course is unique. It is a links course, yet somehow it is different from all other links courses. The 1st hole runs more or less to the west. The course then turns almost at right angles and goes straight out to the 7th in a northerly direction. Holes 8, 9, 10, and 11 form a loop, and holes 12 to 17 run back more or less southwards, side by side with the outbound holes; the 18th turns to the east to form a common fairway with the first. The right side of the course on the way out is screened by banks of gorse bushes which separate the Old Course from the parallel and adjoining New Course. The right side of the course on the inward half is defined by gorse, stone walls and a disused railway line, beyond which lies the Eden Course.

The Double Greens

The course is liberally sprinkled with bunkers, some large, some small, some visible, some not, but all carefully charted. The greens are huge, in several cases one green serving one out and one in hole. And by and large the out and in fairways are shared. The course is generally flat in the sense that there is very little elevation – there are no huge sand dunes such as one would find at Birkdale or Ballybunion – but the fairways are a swelling sea of ripples and ridges, dips, swales and mounds which can turn and throw the ball in completely unexpected and incalculable directions. The bunkering and the double greens are Old Course characteristics, but the very essence of the course and its challenge is this movement in the ground. A player new to the course may well drive his ball along the perfect line to what he believes to be the required place, only to find on arrival that the ball is on a side and a down slope, and he will do well to find a proper stance for his next shot, much less hit it perfectly. To that extent, the course is unfair; or, to be strictly accurate, it can be played confidently only by those who know it well. For any apparent unfairness is counterbalanced by the other major characteristic of the Old Course: the remarkable facility its holes provide for giving the golfer alternative routes, alternative distances and alternative shots. When Bobby Jones first played the course in 1921, he was so bemused by it that he tore up his card in the middle of a round. Six years later he

Harry Vardon gets set on the first tee at St Andrews in the 1900 Open. Sandy Herd, hands behind back, is on the right, and 'Old Tom' Morris, in the big cloak, and beard, is on the left. Vardon, who had won the Open in the two preceding years, missed his hat-trick.

won the Open Championship on the Old Course and nine years later took the Amateur Championship. When in 1958 he was given the freedom of St Andrews, Jones said of the course: 'The more you study it, the more you love it, and the more you love it, the more you study it', and, to the delight of his audience, he added: 'I could take out of my life everything except my experiences at St Andrews, and I would still have a rich, full life'. It is, in short the very essence of 'strategic' design.

A St Andrews Primer

Within the variety of its strategic options a few general principles stand out. For safety, especially on the outward half, play to the left; for gorse and hidden bunkers menace the right side. If you get into a bunker, get out first time, even if it means playing backwards.

Nowhere is there an easier start to a championship course than here: a vast flat, lawn-like fairway, shared by the 1st and 18th holes. Your only peril is the possibility of a slice out-of-bounds over the fence on the right. The only hazard at this hole is the Swilcan Burn, which crosses directly in front of the green, then turns back towards the tee for 30 yards.

The 411-yard 2nd is the perfect example of the St Andrews golf hole – a telling introduction to the variety of hazards and optional routes that these holes contain. A long line of gorse marches up the right side. There is a bunker 130 yards out on the right, with two little pots backing it. On the left, between the 2nd and 17th fairways, perhaps some 250 yards out, is Cheape's Bunker. A good driving line would be slightly to the right of this. Now we face the first of St Andrews' big double greens, the second sharing with the 16th a putting surface all of 55 yards across. The flag position will govern the

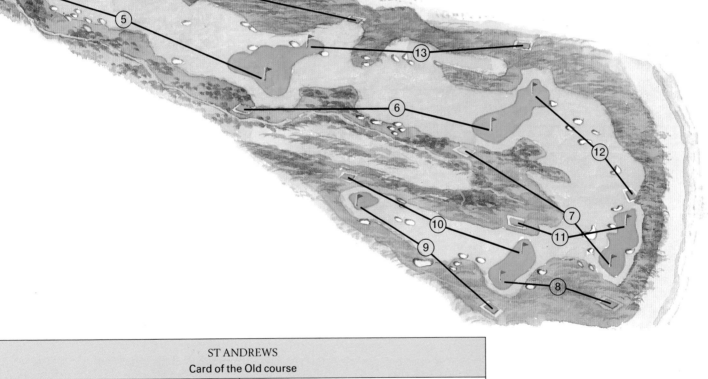

ST ANDREWS							
Card of the Old course							
1	Burn	370 yards	par 4	10	Bobby Jones	342 yards	par 4
2	Dyke	411 yards	par 4	11	High (in)	172 yards	par 3
3	Cartgate (out)	371 yards	par 4	12	Heathery (in)	316 yards	par 4
4	Ginger Beer	463 yards	par 4	13	Hole o'Cross (in)	425 yards	par 4
5	Hole o'Cross (out)	564 yards	par 5	14	Long	567 yards	par 5
6	Heathery (out)	416 yards	par 4	15	Cartgate (in)	413 yards	par 4
7	High (out)	372 yards	par 4	16	Corner of the Dyke	382 yards	par 4
8	Short	178 yards	par 3	17	Road	461 yards	par 4
9	End	356 yards	par 4	18	Tom Morris	354 yards	par 4
		3,501 yards	par 36			3,432 yards	par 36
		Total 6,933 yards par 72					

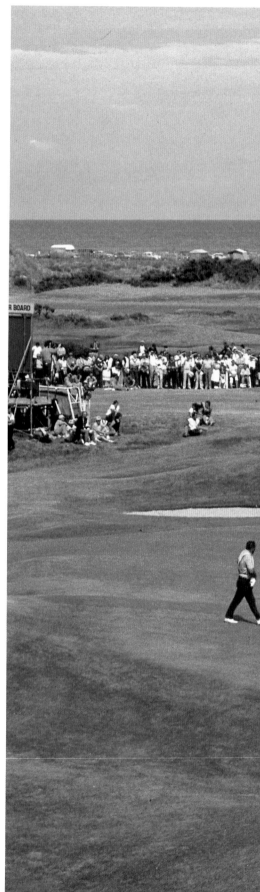

playing of this hole. There is a ridge across the front of the right half of the green, the part we are concerned with.

There is also a front bunker which 'separates' the 2nd green from the 16th; and the green dips from front to centre, then rises slightly to the back, where Wig Bunker helps to give it a hollow effect.

A second shot from the centre of the fairway must find a way of coping with the ridge, the left-hand bunker and the contours of the green, while getting the ball close to the hole. The second hole is obviously better played from the right side of the fairway, which gives a much better entrance to the green. The question is: will the golfer dare to tackle that tight right-hand line on the drive, what with gorse and bunkers and broken ground and a left-to-right prevailing wind? This is the kind of dilemma which this old course will impose upon the golfer over and over again.

Perhaps the most celebrated short hole in the world, and certainly one of the most difficult, is the 11th of 172 yards, the 'High Hole In'. The green is built on a ridge above the River Eden and slopes fiercely from back to front. At the front left, is the very large, very deep Hill Bunker. At the front right, there is Strath Bunker – small, circular, deep and deadly. The flow of the ground in front of the green, even the scontouring of the first part of the putting surface, gathers shots

Above: Huge, deep, one of golf's most insidious hazards, Hell Bunker on the 14th hole of the Old Course has ensnared hundreds of golfers, among them Gene Sarazen, Bobby Locke and Peter Thomson in Open Championship play.

Right: Play in the 1984 Open Championship at St Andrews showing the huge expanse of the combined 4th and 14th greens. Putts of as much as 80 feet have to be tackled on these rolling lawns.

into these bunkers. Gene Sarazen once scored six on this hole, with three shots in Hill Bunker. This is perhaps the one penal tee shot on the entire course – the only place to be on this hole is on the green, below the pin. There is almost always wind at the 11th. The green is wholly exposed and almost always lightning fast. It is well nigh impossible to stop downhill putts.

The 'Long Hole In', the 14th, at 567 yards, is fascinating in the various options it offers. A stone wall edges into the fairway from the right, then drifts back out again, marking the out-of-bounds line. The first major hazards on the hole, and a key factor in its strategy, are the Beardies in the centre of the driving line – one large and three small bunkers extending from about 160 yards to 200 yards from the medal tee. Between them and the stone wall is a rather narrow gap. Forward from the Beardies, for about 150 yards or so, stretch the Elysian Fields,

reasonably flat, uncluttered fairway, at the end of which is the huge Hell Bunker. A string of other bunkers runs up the centre and left side between the Beardies and Hell – Crescent, Kitchen and others – and on the left beyond Hell, which is 80 yards from the green, are the invisible Grave and Ginger Beer Bunkers.

On the tee, depending on wind and weather conditions, the golfer has choices to make. He can drive on either side of

Mark James calculates what is needed to face down the challenge of the Road Hole bunker at the 17th green of the Old Course at St Andrews, one of golf's most demanding shots.

the Beardies, or over them if he thinks he is capable of it. Depending on the success of his drive, he may then elect a direct line to the green, which is right over Hell – but he'll be facing a carry of some 200

yards. Or he can simply advance the ball along the Elysian Fields, staying short of Hell Bunker and take a third shot to the green. Or he can try to pass Hell on the right, but there are other bunkers and badly broken ground there. What may be his best option is to play about as far as he can to the left, onto the 5th fairway, from where he will have a fine view of, and good approach to, the green. But the 14th hole has not finished with him. There is a

architects all over the world. The hole is a very powerful par-4 of 461 yards, which doglegs to the right around the Old Course Hotel. The hotel stands on what was formerly the site of some black railway sheds, over the corner of which the golfer used to drive. Thus we have the shot across the angle and the judgement of how much or how little to cut off – a shot that has been repeated over sand, rough, rivers, lakes and the ocean, at Pebble Beach, Pine Valley and dozens of courses all over the world.

Having driven across the corner and into the fairway, the golfer faces a long second shot to a single green – the most feared in golf. It is raised on a plateau, three or four feet above the fairway. It is long from left to right, very narrow from front to back, and set diagonally to the fairway. At the front left-centre of the green is the small, steep-sided abyss called the Road Hole Bunker, biting into the green so severely that there are putting surfaces on either side of it. Players of championship class have putted into this bunker. In the 1978 Open Tommy Nakajima of Japan hit two lovely shots to the front of the green, and then putted into the bunker, took four strokes there and eventually scored 10.

Over the back of this green is a pathway, then a metal road, then a stone wall; all in bounds and all in play. Thus over the back of the green is absolutely the one place the golfer does not wish to be. As so often at St Andrews, the tactic for the second shot depends on wind and weather conditions, and the state of the competition. In the 1984 Open Championship, the Road Hole had a critical role to play. The Championship was between Tom Watson and Severiano Ballesteros, Watson playing directly behind Ballesteros in the last pairing of the event. At 17, Ballesteros hit an enormous drive right over the fairway into the left rough. From there he hit an immense shot with a six iron which reached the front edge of the green. His first putt, from long range, ran up six inches from the hole, and he had his par. When Watson came to the hole, he hit a perfect drive into the centre of the fairway but was not absolutely certain of his clubbing for the approach. He decided on the 2-iron. How odd it is:

whenever a golfer, even a great champion, is not absolutely convinced that he has the right club in his hand, the swing is affected. Watson pushed the shot slightly and the ball flew over the green, over the pathway, over the road and finished snug against the stone wall. He scuffled the ball back to the green, took two putts, and at almost the same moment Severiano Ballesteros holed a putt for a birdie on the 18th green.

Watson against the wall which became a wailing wall. With little room for a backswing, Tom Watson chips back at the 17th at St. Andrews after his second shot went over the green in the last round in 1984. He lost to Severiano Ballesteros.

These holes, these shots, this land, puts a man to the test. But the Old Course gives the thinking golfer a chance, and there is always a way to travel from point A to point B in safety. All that he needs to do is negotiate that minefield of bunkers and gorse and humps and hollows and huge greens. And the thing to do is play it, not talk about it; play it as often as possible over and over again, since every day on the Old Course seems different to the one before. Do that and you will come to agree with Bobby Jones that in all the world the Old Course is 'the most favoured meeting ground possible for an important contest'.

dip in front of the green which rises abruptly to form a bank at the front; the green then falling away, towards the back! Not surprisingly, in Open Championship play, Bobby Locke scored eight on this hole, Peter Thomson seven.

The Road Hole

The 17th hole, the Road Hole, is the most famous single hole in golf. It has features that have been used and copied by golf

MUIRFIELD

Muirfield is a patrician among golf courses, which is as it should be, since it is the home of a patrician golf club. The Honourable Company of Edinburgh Golfers, which plays its golf over the Muirfield course, came into existence in 1744 at Leith, when 'several Gentlemen of Honour skilful in the ancient and healthful exercise of Golf', petitioned the Edinburgh city council to donate a silver club for their annual competition. The council obliged, and has done so ever since – maintaining a tradition which saw them donate a fourth such club in 1980. The Honourable Company thus predates the Royal and Ancient Golf Club of St

Andrews by 10 years, and in fact is the oldest golf club in the world, with continuous records to prove that claim. It drew up golf's first set of rules – the famous 'Thirteen Rules' – and these were by and large adopted by the R & A.

The club first played on the links of Leith (Edinburgh's port on the Firth of Forth). But the public land was used by the local citizens for various purposes and occasionally by the military for drill, and by 1836 the golfers were squeezed out. They moved six miles eastward along the coast to Musselburgh and remained there for 50 years. The course was shared with the Musselburgh Golf Club (and anyone

else who cared to play on it). Initially the club used the racecourse grandstand there as their premises, but by 1868 had their own clubhouse. These early golf clubs were as much dinner clubs, and the Honourable Company's golf was match play between members.

The links at Musselburgh in turn became more and more crowded and less to the liking of the gentlemen of the Honourable Company, and another eastward move was planned for the 1890s – this time far from the clamour of the city, to Muirfield, near Gullane. The new course was opened for play in 1891 on a rainy 3rd of May, and a year later was staging

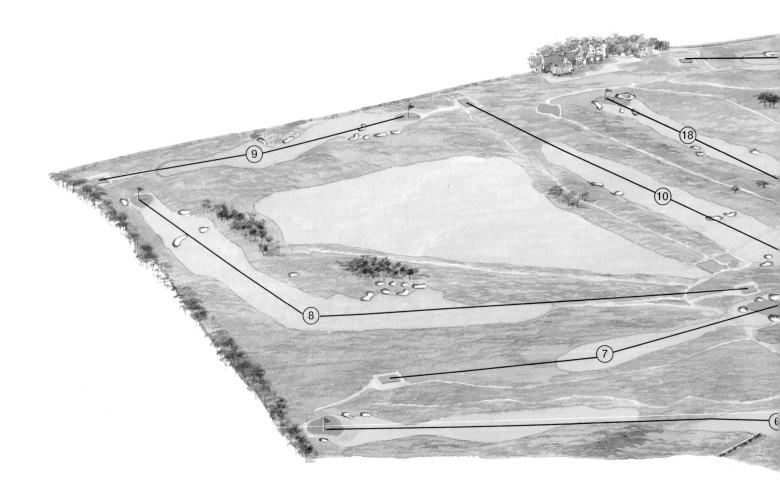

MUIRFIELD Card of the course				
1	447 yards par 4	10	475 yards	par 4
2	351 yards par 4	11	385 yards	par 4
3	379 yards par 4	12	381 yards	par 4
4	180 yards par 3	13	152 yards	par 3
5	559 yards par 5	14	449 yards	par 4
6	469 yards par 4	15	417 yards	par 4
7	185 yards par 3	16	188 yards	par 3
8	444 yards par 4	17	550 yards	par 5
9	504 yards par 5	18	448 yards	par 4
3,518 yards par 36		3,445 yards	par 35	
Total 6,963 yards par 71				

the Open Championship – won by an Englishman, and an amateur to boot: Harold Hilton of Hoylake (his club-mate John Ball was equal second).

Looking over the 12th green with the Forth estuary behind and beyond the hills of Fife. Arnold Palmer putts out, playing with Guy Wolstenholme, in the 1966 Open; Jack Nicklaus won the championship.

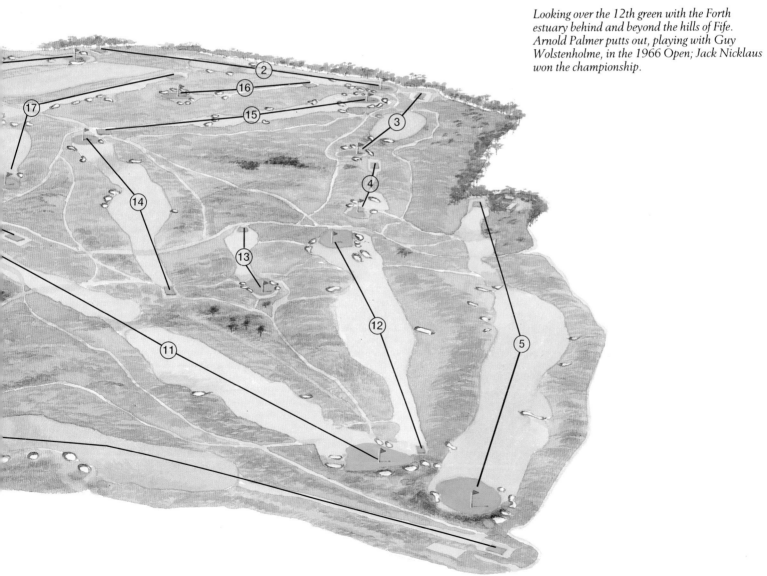

Morris, Colt and Simpson

The original course was built by hand and horse to a design by Old Tom Morris. Sixteen holes had been opened in May, two more in December of the same year, and the entire construction was completed rather casually. Not for some years did the club see any need for a greenkeeper (and to this day they see no need for a professional). Four more Open championships were held at Muirfield up to 1914 and several changes were made to the holes, but it was not until 1925, after Harry Colt, of Sunningdale fame, and Tom Simpson had been brought in that Muirfield became the magnificent course that is recognisable to us today.

One hundred yards or so down a quiet driveway off the North Berwick road, to the east of Gullane village, a majestic vista unfolds. The entire golf course can be taken in within a single compass: uninterrupted, spacious, strangely private and still, the land moving along gently, with few abrupt slopes; to the north, beyond the sand dunes, are the waters of the Forth estuary and, beyond, the hills of Fife. On its three other sides, the course is enclosed by a low stone wall. Beyond that, to the east, lies Archerfield Wood; to the west is Gullane Hill, and beyond that, on a clear day, Edinburgh and the Forth bridges are visible; to the south lies the rolling farmland of East Lothian.

The course is maintained in quite immaculate condition: the club makes sure that it is not overplayed. If there is one outstanding visual feature of Muirfield, it is the bunkering – deep, steep walls of revetted turf, as though a talented bricklayer had built them, often with surrounds that reach out and 'persuade' a ball into them. Any shot that finds a fairway bunker at Muirfield is a shot lost. It will not be possible to reach the green from any of them. Indeed the club might be offended that anyone should suggest such a possibility; after all, 'this is not Florida, old boy'.

Unlike many of the older links courses

A time of immortality. Nick Faldo on the 72nd green of the 1987 Open Championship at Muirfield, a championship which he won with 18 relentless pars on that final soggy Sunday.

which run out to a distant point then run back again, Muirfield was one of the earliest courses in the world (with Portmarnock, 1893) to consist of two loops of nine holes – the 9th returning to the clubhouse – that run contrary to each other. Muirfield's first nine run clockwise around the outer edge of the course; its second nine run anti-clockwise inside the first nine. Only three holes, the 3rd, 4th and 5th, run in the same direction and, of these, the 4th is a short hole.

A Beautifully Balanced Course

There are no ridiculous carrys, no trees and no water hazards on the course. Muirfield's exceptional reputation is based on the fact that it is fair, honest and beautifully balanced. On the entire course there are no more than two blind shots. All its perils are open for the player to see – notably the most demanding opening and closing holes of any course on the Open Championship rota.

The 1st hole is a par-4 of 447 yards (the Honourable Company with its tradition of matchplay 'between Gentlemen', has no need of 'par' or 'bogey', neither of which appear on the club scorecard) and runs to the west along a flat and narrow fairway. There is a very large C-shaped bunker on the left side of the fairway at 200–230 yards; only part of it can be seen from the tee. The line of the drive should be just to the right of this bunker. There are twin bunkers in the left rough not quite 100 yards from the green, and a central bunker just short of the green screening off its right side. Greenside bunkers are placed right centre and left back, so that the way in to this green should preferably be from the left side of the fairway. This is a very demanding opening hole, especially into the wind.

The 18th is strikingly similar in both length (448 yards) and design. The second half of the hole runs slightly uphill. There is a big bunker on the right, 190 yards out from the medal tee. On the other side of a very narrow fairway are two bunkers at 210–250 yards. The drive, to the right of these two bunkers, is critical. Further up the fairway, in its left half, are two separate bunkers – one 40 yards short of the putting surface, the other 20 yards short. A very long greenside bunker covers the left side of the green, and a comparable one, with an island of turf in it, the right side. With a strong, prevailing wind, right to left, this hole takes a good deal of playing. In 1948, on this the 72nd hole, Henry Cotton had two shots in that right bunker, scored 5, but still won the championship. In 1959, Gary Player had three putts, scored six, and still won the championship. While in 1972, Lee Trevino, leading by a stroke, was so supercharged and hit such an enormous drive that it left him an 8-iron to the green.

Glorious Par–5s

The par-5 holes at Muirfield are superb. The 5th hole (559 yards) runs west to east along the northern side of the course on the edge of dune land. It turns slightly to the right through its entire length and that side of the fairway is massively defended by bunkers and strong rough. There is a bunker placed on the left edge of the fairway 240 yards out, with a support bunker 25 yards further along, and the small green is ringed by half a dozen deep traps. The drive is quite critical here. In the 1972 Open Championship Johnny Miller hit a perfect drive of almost 300 yards into prime position in the fairway. From there, he hit a 3-wood shot which pitched short of the green, ran on and fell into the hole for an albatross!

The 9th hole, the second of Muirfield's long holes, at 504 yards, poses different but no less searching problems. The hole runs back towards the Greywalls Hotel and the spacious Muirfield clubhouse. A low, greystone wall, the boundary wall, runs straight as an arrow along the left side of the hole. About 200 yards out, a great eruption of rough streams into the fairway from the left, narrowing it down to little more than 15 yards across. On the edge of this rough, facing back towards the tee, is a very large cross bunker and about 60 yards beyond that, also on the edge of this rough, is another big bunker. On the second section of the 9th, the rough on the left vanishes and the fairway runs clear across to the wall. A ridge along the fairway leaves this left side higher than the right, and reasonably open and undefended. However, the ridge tends to throw the ball off to the right, where a

The green of the 5th hole at Muirfield, a monstrous par 5 of 559 yards which runs along the north side of the course, and a view of Muirfield's famous, carefully-revetted bunkering.

The power of the modern golfer. Johnny Miller, Open Champion on both sides of the Atlantic, almost airborne at a full drive shows how to keep the head anchored at Muirfield in 1972.

string of bunkers some 70 yards long waits to gobble the careless approach; there is also a solitary central bunker – Simpson's bunker, named after the architect who put it there – some 50 yards short of the green. Thus the whole thrust of the hole is that the drive must keep to the right, playing into the narrowest part of the fairway; the second shot must play to the left, finding the higher side of the fairway, but always under threat from the out-of-bounds wall. Peter Thomson, in the Open Championship of 1959, hooked a second shot over that wall, and Arnold Palmer, in 1966, going for a big drive, failed to find that narrow gap.

However, when conditions are right the 9th is reachable in two. In the 1972 championship, when Lee Trevino and Tony Jacklin were locked together in the last round, they each scored eagles on this hole. Jacklin drove into the left rough, between the bunkers; Trevino into the right rough. Yet they were both able to hit iron shots, they both reached the green, and they both holed their putts!

But it was the 17th hole, the 71st, the last of Muirfield's par-5s that was to settle that thrilling Championship in '72. The hole runs from west to east and therefore is usually played down the prevailing wind. It is 550 yards long and at 250 yards

doglegs to the left. There are no bunkers on the outside, the right side, of this fairway, but in the angle of the turn there is much rough, heaving ground, containing five major bunkers. Also there are fairly prominent sandhills along the left side of the hole and an unusual strip of ground extends across the entire fairway about 100 yards short of the green – perhaps 25 yards from front to back, it contain's three of Muirfield's largest and most frightening bunkers.

In the 1972 championship, Trevino drove into the first bunker on the left, knocked the ball out and up the fairway, hooked his third shot into the left rough and hit his fourth shot over the green into more rough. Jacklin, on the other hand, had hit a solid drive in the fairway, a second shot just short of the green and had chipped on. Trevino hurried to his ball, chopped it out of the rough, in resignation it seemed, and saw the ball speed into the hole for a par-5! Jacklin was so unnerved that he three-putted and lost the Championship. And the 1987 Championship also turned on that hole when Paul Azinger drove into a bunker and took 5 instead of the 4 he needed to hold off the winner, Nick Faldo. At the equivalent hole of the 1966 Open, Jack Nicklaus drove with a 3-iron and reached the green with a 5-iron!

The short holes at Muirfield are just as magnificent as the par-5s: mounded greens with fringing bunkers as deep as a man is tall, and exposed to wind and weather. And the quality of its par-4s, ranging from the 349 yards of the 2nd to the 475 yards of the 10th – one of the truly great par-4s in world golf – is just as compelling.

But perhaps the one overwhelming demand that Muirfield makes on the golfer is the tee shot. It is said that when Henry Cotton won the Open in 1948, he missed only four fairways in 72 holes. When Jack Nicklaus won in 1966, he owed his victory above all to his marvellous long-iron play in the final round.

Tom Watson, five times winner of the Open Championship, chipping at Muirfield in 1980 for his third victory. His aggregate of 271 was a record for Muirfield Opens and included a third-round 64.

ROYAL DORNOCH

Royal Dornoch is the least-known, least-played of all the great links courses. It may well be the finest natural golf course in the world; in the words of Tom Watson, five times Open Champion, it is '...at least one of the great courses of the five continents. I have played none finer, a natural masterpiece'. The village of Dornoch, of rather less than one thousand souls, lies some 60 miles north of Inverness on the east coast of Sutherland, more than 200 miles from the populous central belt of Scotland and 600 miles from London.

Records show that golf was being played there as early as 1616. Dornoch's claim to antiquity, which places it behind only St Andrews and Leith, was confirmed by the publication in 1630 of Sir Robert Gordon's *History of Sutherland*. Gordon was tutor to the house of Sutherland and had been educated at St Andrews University. He wrote: 'About this toun there are the fairest and largest links of any pairt of Scotland, fit for archery, Golfing, Ryding and all other exercise; they do surpass the fields of Montrose or St Andrews'.

Common Land
A golf club as such, however, was not formed until 1877. The two men responsible for calling a meeting and launching the Dornoch Golf Club were the local Chief Constable, Alex McHardy, a Fifer, and local man Dr Hugh Gunn, who was a St Andrews graduate, and no doubt

Roger Wethered, with his wife Joyce, the famous amateur golfer who lost the 1921 Open Championship at St Andrews in a playoff was instrumental in promoting Royal Dornoch in its early days.

learned some of his golf there. In 1883 came an event of the greatest importance for the fledgling club: John Sutherland was appointed secretary, a post he was to hold for more than 50 years. Sutherland was an estate agent and factor in the town and as such a pillar of the community – which was important to the club, since the golf course ground was owned by the town, and Sutherland was obliged to consult with the townsmen in any changes he wanted. In his early years, for example, cattle and sheep were free to roam the course, it being common land.

Sutherland was a golfing pioneer. He was a first-class player and administrator, planned several northern courses and studied greenkeeping and maintenance, with particular emphasis on the making and maintaining of greens. He added an additional nine holes to the course, and he and J. H. Taylor, who became a fairly regular summer visitor, made a number of revisions. Sutherland also wrote a weekly golf article for the London *Daily News* from 1902 for more than 20 years.

By 1903, the railway and an overnight sleeping-car service from London had

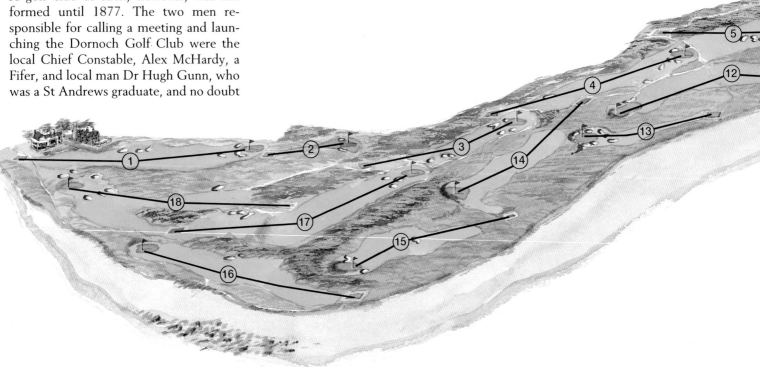

reached Dornoch, and for the next ten years the town grew and prospered as a summer resort. It would never be a Cannes, but increasingly it attracted wealthy and influential amateur golfers from the south: Roger and Joyce Wethered, Ernest Holderness and others, whose families would take a house there for the summer and who could be said to have 'learned' their golf on Dornoch's magnificent links.

Donald Ross

The year 1898 is now seen as of great significance for the future of the world game. In that year Donald James Ross emigrated to America. Ross was born in Dornoch in 1873, in a house in St Gilbert Street. He became a very good player and was apprenticed to a carpenter. But John Sutherland, noting his interest in the game, arranged for him to go to St Andrews as an 'apprentice' to Tom Morris, who had laid out Dornoch's second nine in the 1880s. Ross went there at the age of 20 but in 1895 came back to Dornoch to serve as professional and

The 17th hole at Dornoch, known as Valley. The narrow green is well guarded with three pot bunkers. The magnificent sweep of Embo Bay can be seen in the background.

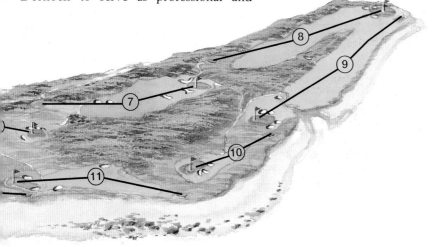

greenkeeper. Then in 1898 he was persuaded by an American visitor that he could make his fortune as a teacher and course designer in the United States. There he became the most celebrated golf architect of his day. He had a hand in the design of at least 600 courses all over the country, including Pinehurst No. 2 (probably his masterpiece – see page 30), Oak Hill (page 16), Oakland Hills (page 40) and Scioto.

Ross courses were characterised by many of the features he had known at Dornoch. These were: a sense of 'naturalness', and meticulous attention to detail, particularly in the siting and contouring of greens and the siting and shaping of bunkers. Ross sought to combine beauty, subtlety and strategic alternatives in his holes. His greens were often raised, as were the Dornoch greens, with slopes running off them and seldom with bunkers biting directly into the putting surfaces – so that chipping as well as that staple of the links game, the bump-and-run with a medium iron, could be profitably employed.

ROYAL DORNOCH							
Card of the course							
1	First	336 yards	par 4	10	Fuaran	148 yards	par 3
2	Ord	179 yards	par 3	11	A'chlach	445 yards	par 4
3	Earl's Cross	414 yards	par 4	12	Sutherland	504 yards	par 5
4	Achinchanter	418 yards	par 4	13	Bents	168 yards	par 3
5	Hilton	361 yards	par 4	14	Foxy	448 yards	par 4
6	Whinny Brae	165 yards	par 3	15	Stulaig	322 yards	par 4
7	Pier	465 yards	par 4	16	High Hole	405 yards	par 4
8	Dunrobin	437 yards	par 4	17	Valley	406 yards	par 4
9	Craiglaith	499 yards	par 5	18	Home	457 yards	par 4
		3,274 yards	par 35			3,303 yards	par 35
Total 6,577 yards par 70							

'Guid gear goes into sma' bulk'

In the final analysis the course of his boyhood, the magnificent course that runs along Embo Bay, was responsible for Ross's success. The first two holes do not reveal the character of Dornoch, but from the 3rd tee the course unfolds, running through gorse on a shelf above the beach holes to the eighth; then turning and running alongside the great curve of the beach all the way back, along the most perfect links ground imagineable. Among many fine holes on the back nine, the superlative 14th, a par-4 of 448 yards, ranks with any in Scotland. Virtually a double dog-leg, its fairway bears left at about 230 yards, then continues straight for some 170 yards before turning right into the green. As a two-shotter, then, the hole requires a longish drive with controlled draw off the tee, followed by an equally finely controlled fade with a medium or long iron to the green.

Donoch measures only 6,577 yards,

Left: *The Royal Golf Hotel at Dornoch, by the 18th green. The gabled building with clocktower to its left is the 'new' clubhouse, opened in 1909.*

Below: *Another view of the 17th green with the 15th tee and green in the background. Dornoch is famous for its wild beauty and the natural feel of its links.*

which is a classic confirmation of the Scottish saying that 'guid gear goes into sma' bulk'. While Dornoch is a long way from anywhere, Britain's Amateur Championship of 1985 was played there and was an outstanding success. Not surprisingly, to everyone who made the journey it was deemed well worth while and a memorable experience.

Perhaps only Turnberry can rival Dornoch in the beauty of its surroundings, for at Dornoch the vistas of sea and sand and mountain are stunning. To the north of the course are the seven miles of golden sandy beach to Littleferry and Loch Fleet. Beyond, past Dunrobin Castle (and the fine courses at Golspie and Brora) is the Ord of Caithness, and from there a breathtaking panoramic view of the immense and ancient mountains of Sutherland and Wester Ross, Tain and Tarbat-Ness, the sands of Whiteness and, on a clear day, Nairn, the Moray coast and the hills of Aberdeenshire.

All of this poses the question as to how important the surroundings may be when we pass judgement on the quality of a golf course. No doubt a subjective element in the judgement is unavoidable. Golf courses have been laid out on barren deserts, hacked out of rain forests and placed in humdrum suburbs. However, Royal Dornoch may be one of the few places in the world where the scenery is matched by the majesty of the course.

CARNOUSTIE

Stark, evil, gigantic, brutal, monstrous – these words and worse have been used to describe the championship course at Carnoustie. At 7,101 yards, it can be crushingly long. It is without a weakness. It is unrelenting. It is flat and exposed (its two or three little spinneys of trees have no bearing on the play). It is hard by the sea, but the sea is never seen. Never does it have more than two holes running in the same direction. Walter Hagen declared it to be the best course in Britain; one of the three best in the world. It is a municipally owned course, and it may be one of the wonders of the golfing world.

Golf has been played along the Angus coast for centuries, as it has on the links of the Moray Firth, and Aberdeen and Fife and East Lothian. There are parish records of 'gouff' being played on Barry Links, adjoining Carnoustie, in 1560. The Carnoustie Golf Club's date of found-ation is given variously as 1839 and 1842, but certainly at this time 10 holes were laid out by Allan Robertson of St Andrews, the first of the great early professionals. In 1857, the course was extended to 18 holes by Tom Morris; and that same year his son 'Young Tom', just 16 years old, beat all comers in a tournament there.

Carnoustie and the Open

Carnoustie and the Burnside course which it encloses are public courses and are played over by six clubs, each of which has a clubhouse adjoining the links. Thus there is nothing palatial about golf at Carnoustie; no grand and dominating clubhouse as at Troon or Muirfield or St Andrews. The game, and little else, is the thing here. But a wider world crept up on Carnoustie. In 1926 James Braid revamped and modernised the course to such good effect that in 1931 it staged the Open Championship for the first time, and rejoiced in the victory of a Scot, Tommy Armour, albeit a Scot who had defected to the United States!

In the 1930s a Dundee chartered accountant, James Wright, became chairman of the Carnoustie Golf Courses Committee, administered the courses and set about improving the big course to bring it properly into the age of the steel shaft. Wright was a man of the world, with extensive land and farming interests in the United States, and he had ambitions for the course. He produced a flexible Carnoustie which could be played

Tom Watson chips to the 16th green in the last round of the 1975 Open. One of the most formidable par-3s in championship golf, the 248-yard 16th denied winner Watson a par in any of his rounds.

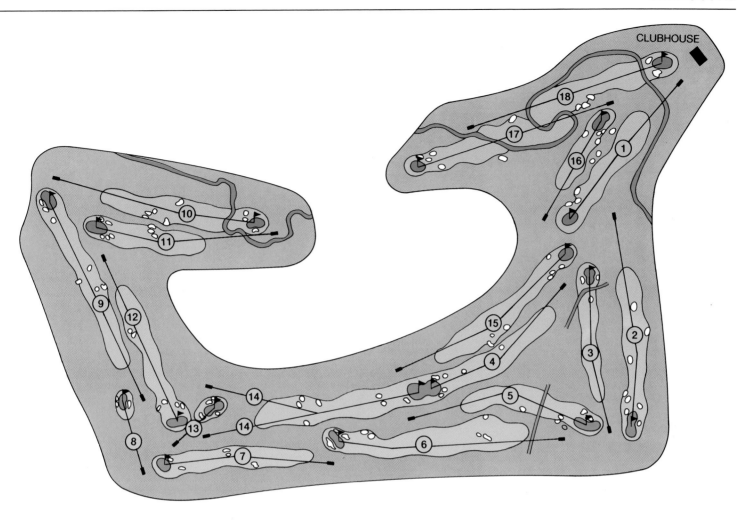

at various yardages. His creed: 'We do not attach much importance to length …quality, rather than pure length has been our objective'.

His altered course was ready for another Championship in 1937. It was won by Henry Cotton against a field which included the entire United States Ryder Cup team, including Densmore Shute, Byron Nelson, Sam Snead. On a final day of torrential rain, Cotton scored 71 – one of the greatest rounds of his career – and won by two shots from Reg Whitcombe.

No reference to Carnoustie and Open Championships can be made without mentioning Ben Hogan. The great American champion made a detailed study of the course and how it should be played with the small ball in practice in 1953, then applied himself quite surgically to dominating the course with rounds of 73, 71, 70 and 68. He won by four strokes. It was a performance beyond criticism, so much so that there did not seem to be one stroke more important than any other.

CARNOUSTIE					
Card of the course					
1	416 yards	par 4	10	452 yards	par 4
2	460 yards	par 4	11	358 yards	par 4
3	347 yards	par 4	12	475 yards	par 4
4	434 yards	par 4	13	168 yards	par 3
5	393 yards	par 4	14	488 yards	par 5
6	575 yards	par 5	15	461 yards	par 4
7	397 yards	par 4	16	250 yards	par 3
8	174 yards	par 3	17	455 yards	par 4
9	474 yards	par 4	18	486 yards	par 5
	3,670 yards	par 36		3,593 yards	par 36
	Total 7,263 yards par 72				

But in the championship of 1968, that was certainly not the case. Gary Player produced the one critical shot. Paired with Jack Nicklaus in the last round, and battling him stroke for stroke, Player hit a 3-wood second shot on the 482 yards 14th hole over the 'Spectacle' bunkers. The ball finished three feet from the flagstick, giving the South African an eagle three and a two-shot margin with

which he won the Open Championship.

Carnoustie's finish puts the seal on the course's hostility. The 16th is a 250 yard par-3 to an elevated, undulating green surrounded by six bunkers. Into the wind, it can take a massive hit. The 17th is the Island hole, so called because the Barry Burn crosses the fairway twice in a big oxbow, at 180 yards then again at 300 yards – the entire hole stretching 455 yards. And the 18th in the reverse direction sees the same burn crossing the fairway 130 yards out from the tee, then passing across the face of the green just 20 yards short of the putting surface.

Carnoustie has made a huge contribution to the game of golf, not least in the hundreds of its citizens who have gone abroad to every corner of the golfing world as fine players and teachers of the game. A lack of local hotel and other facilities kept Carnoustie off the Open Championship rota in the 1980s. It's to be hoped this great shaggy monster of a course will soon have the chance to put the current superstars to the test.

ROYAL TROON

The Glasgow to Ayr railway, running through Troon and Prestwick, was opened in 1840. Earlier, in 1811, one of the first railways in Scotland connected Kilmarnock with Troon and helped to make the latter an important harbour on the Firth of Clyde. For the citizens of Glasgow, Paisley and Kilmarnock a beguiling stretch of the Ayrshire coast was opened up, with miles of golden sandy beaches backed by one of the longest stretches of duneland imaginable. It was ready-made for golf, and came to produce a line of magnificent links courses: Irvine, Glasgow Gailes, Western Gailes, Barassie, Troon and Prestwick. They form an almost continuous file: Troon and Prestwick, for instance, are separated only by the Pow Burn.

On Saturday, 16 March 1878 at '4 o'clock pm' in the Portland Arms Hotel, Troon, 'a Number of Gentlemen belonging to Troon and the neighbourhood, resolved to form themselves into a golf club'. The instigator of the meeting was one James Dickie of Paisley, who had a summer house on the south beach at Troon village. Dickie had arranged with the fifth Duke of Portland, who owned the land, to have the use of links lying between Craigend Burn and Gyaws Burn. Craigend Burn is now piped under the road in front of the clubhouse, while Gyaws Burn is very much part of the present course, crossing the 3rd and 15th holes. The Duke of Portland was a re-

The 'Postage Stamp', Troon's famous 8th hole, at 126 yards the shortest of all Open Championship holes in Britain. It has seen many holes in one, none more lauded than that of Gene Sarazen in 1979, 50 years after he had first played at Troon.

cluse. However, he was succeeded by a cousin who was an entirely different personality and who gave the club permission to use the land all the way out to the Pow Burn. Within a decade Troon had 18 holes of golf.

A Formidable Examination

Over the years, Willie Fernie, James Braid, Dr Alister Mackenzie, Frank Pennink and Charles Lawrie amended the course and now Troon is as frightening a Championship test as any on the roster. It is a course of long carrys, narrow, heaving fairways, very strong rough, a couple of blind shots, and greens that are almost always immaculately conditioned. If the wind blows it offers formidable examination of the finest players.

The course features the longest hole in Open championship golf – the 6th at 577

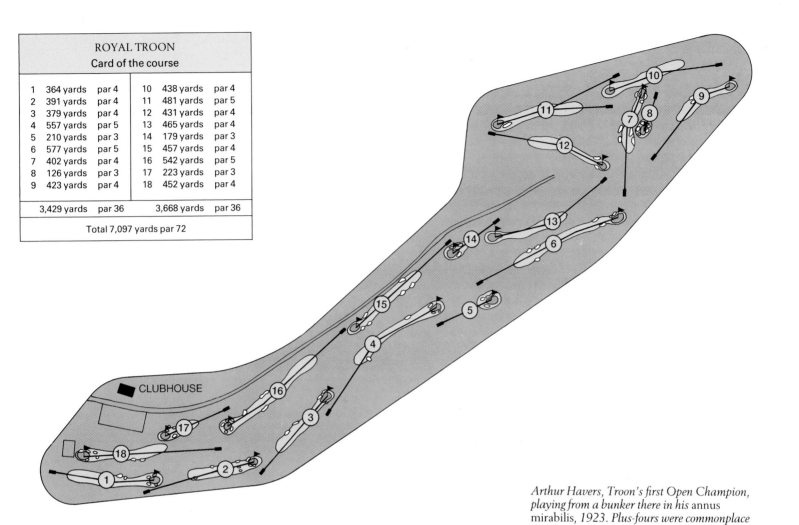

| ROYAL TROON | | | | | |
Card of the course					
1	364 yards	par 4	10	438 yards	par 4
2	391 yards	par 4	11	481 yards	par 5
3	379 yards	par 4	12	431 yards	par 4
4	557 yards	par 5	13	465 yards	par 4
5	210 yards	par 3	14	179 yards	par 3
6	577 yards	par 5	15	457 yards	par 4
7	402 yards	par 4	16	542 yards	par 5
8	126 yards	par 3	17	223 yards	par 3
9	423 yards	par 4	18	452 yards	par 4
	3,429 yards	par 36		3,668 yards	par 36
		Total 7,097 yards par 72			

Arthur Havers, Troon's first Open Champion, playing from a bunker there in his annus mirabilis, 1923. *Plus-fours were commonplace then, and ladies* and *gentlemen wore hats.*

yards – and the shortest – the 8th at 126 yards (the famous 'Postage Stamp'). The 6th hole runs to the south; and since Brian Anderson, the club's experienced senior professional, insists that Troon's prevailing wind is from the north-west and not the south-west, it may be slightly across, from right to left, on this hole. The fairway is narrow, and there is a carry of at least 150 yards to reach it. There is a bunker on the right at about 230 yards and another pair on the left at about the same distance. The drive must be just to the right of these left-hand bunkers. There is another bunker in the left rough some 80 yards short of the green, a very deep bunker on the right 30 yards short of the green, and two very deep greenside bunkers to the left.

The next five holes, 7 to 11 inclusive, plunge into and through a huge range of sandhills containing, of course, the 8th – the Postage Stamp. This green is cut into

Arnold Palmer, with wife and son, practices for the 1962 Open Championship at Royal Troon. He went on to win the tournament, his second in a row (the first being at Royal Birkdale).

a sandhill on the left. There is a very large bunker covering the front of the green, with two more on either side. All are very deep, with steep faces – those on the right being also much lower than the green. The shot is down from a high tee to this very narrow green, and the only alternative it offers to being on the putting surface is to be over the green, where there is a modest area of security.

A Famous Hole-in-One

The hole is rich in history. In the 1950 Open Championship, Herman Tissies, a German amateur, scored 15 on the hole, yet took only one putt! There have been many holes-in-one, none more widely acclaimed than that of Gene Sarazen in 1973. Sarazen, in his time a winner of all golf's major championships, had played in the Troon Open of 1923, aged 22, and, caught in a gale, scored 75, 85 and failed to qualify for the championship proper. He was U.S. Open Champion at the time. Fifty years on, now aged 72, he made a

sentimental journey back to Troon for the 1973 Open. On the eve of the championship, Sir Ian Stewart, captain of the R & A, presented inscribed silver cigarette boxes to Sarazen and to Arthur Havers, the winner of that 1923 Championship. The next day Sarazen, playing honorary rounds with former champions Fred Daly (1947 at Hoylake) and Max Faulkner (1951 at Portrush), made his hole in one at the Postage Stamp. Into a slight breeze, he hit a punchy 5-iron shot which pitched short of the flag and rolled in. The next day he bunkered his tee shot at the same hole – then with his recovery shot from the sand he holed out for a two! Sarazen presented the 5-iron he had used on both days to the R & A.

Troon's finish, especially when it is into wind, is as harrowing as any in golf. The 465-yard 13th and the 457-yard 15th are very serious two-shot holes, played into wickedly uneven, narrow fairways bordered by intense rough. The carry to the fairway of the 16th, the last par-5 at 542 yards, is at least 150 yards and the Gyaws Burn crosses the fairway at 300 yards. The fairway is reasonably friendly by Troon standards and the green is rather flat, but is ringed around by five bunkers.

The 17th hole may well be the most severe par-3 in all of championship golf, and is certainly comparable to Carnoustie's 16th. The raised green falls away on all sides. Two bunkers, short and left of the green, must be carried. The prevailing wind left to right, making the three bunkers to the right very dangerous indeed. At 223 yards, this is really a par-3.5 hole. The 18th hole was stretched to 452 yards for the 1989 championship, giving a carry to the fairway of 225 yards. The green is flat, well-guarded and slopes up to a path in front of the clubhouse – the path being out-of-bounds. The hole will never see a finer shot than the second played by winner Mark Calcavecchia in the play-off in 1989 – a soaring long-iron from the right rough that finished seven feet from the flag to set up a birdie.

Mark Calcavecchia hits an inspired 5-iron shot to Troon's 18th green in the play-off to the 1989 Open. The ball finished a few feet from the hole giving the American a birdie and victory over Greg Norman and Wayne Grady.

TURNBERRY

The Ailsa Course of the Turnberry Hotel in Ayrshire, Scotland, is the course that died twice but is now enjoying its third, magnificent, incarnation. It is one of the most spectacular seaside courses in the world and rivals Pebble Beach and Cypress Point in California in being an outstanding championship course that is also stunningly beautiful.

The Turnberry Hotel, sited on a wooded slope, overlooks a fine spread of links that includes two courses, the Ailsa and the Arran; the latter is less famous but only marginally behind the Ailsa in quality. The Ailsa's run of holes from the 4th to the 11th, by the waters of the Firth of Clyde, and the landscape they inhabit, have made the course world famous.

Across the water to the north-west stands the island of Arran with its towering mountains; behind it and to the west is the long peninsula of Kintyre; to the south-west the massive volcanic outcrop of Ailsa Craig rears out of the sea; and to the east is the ripe farmland of Ayrshire. Turnberry is an enchanting place of long Scottish twilights, sea mists and blinding summer sunsets.

The Ailsa's 4th hole, aptly named 'Woe-be-Tide', is an intriguing par-3 of 167 yards. It plays from sea level across a little inlet to a green cut high into the top of a sandhill – the beginning of a long ridge which runs above the sands of Turnberry Bay and contains the valley in which holes 5, 6 and 7 run. At the 8th

green the course bursts out onto rocky cliffs and runs by the water to the 11th tee, past the famous Turnberry lighthouse.

The First Hotel/Golf Complex

The origins of Turnberry – the hotel and the golf courses – are tied, as are so many other courses, to the spread and development of the railways. The third Marquis of Ailsa was a keen golfer (in 1899 he was captain of Prestwick) and at the turn of the century he leased land at Turnberry to the Glasgow & South Western Railway Company. The Marquis commissioned Willie Fernie, professional at Troon, to design 13 holes of golf for his private course. By 1905, Fernie had designed a

	TURNBERRY						
	Card of the Ailsa course						
1	Ailsa Craig	350 yards	par 4	10	Dinna Fouter	452 yards	par 4
2	Mak Siccar	428 yards	par 4	11	Maidens	177 yards	par 3
3	Blaw Wearie	462 yards	par 4	12	Monument	448 yards	par 4
4	Woe-be-Tide	167 yards	par 3	13	Tickly Tap	411 yards	par 4
5	Fin' me oot	441 yards	par 4	14	Risk-an-Hope	440 yards	par 4
6	Tappie Toorie	222 yards	par 3	15	Ca Canny	209 yards	par 3
7	Roon the Ben	528 yards	par 5	16	Wee Burn	409 yards	par 4
8	Goat Fell	427 yards	par 4	17	Lang Whang	500 yards	par 5
9	Brice's Castle	455 yards	par 4	18	Ailsa Hame	431 yards	par 4
		3,480 yards	par 35			3,477 yards	par 35
		Total 6,957 yards par 70					

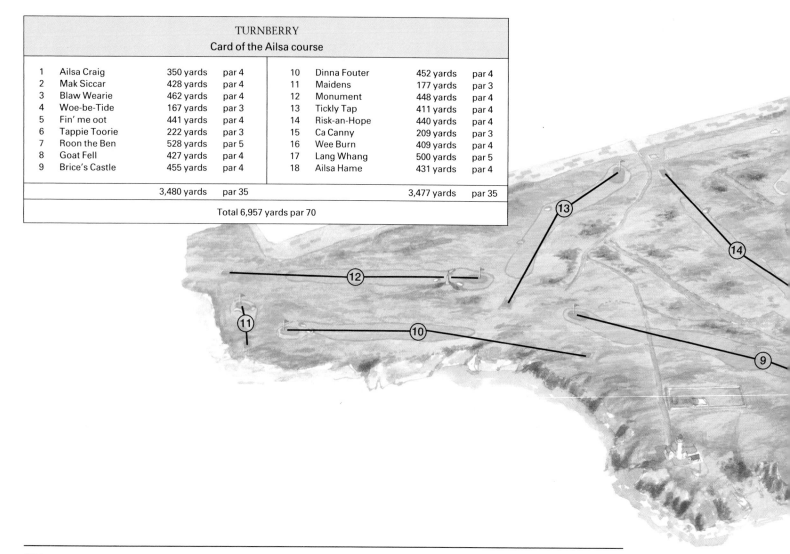

second, separate 13, and in 1907, with the hotel completed, all golfing facilities were taken over by the railway company. Willie Fernie's son Tom became the first Turnberry professional at what may have been the very first hotel-golf complex anywhere in the world.

A Triumph of Survival

The early courses offered pleasant resort golf but were badly compromised by the coming of the First World War, when the Royal Flying Corps built a training airfield on them. After that war, the Ailsa, named after the Marquis, was destined to be-

The defences around the green of the 222-yard 6th hole demand a shot of great accuracy – but the length of the hole and the prevailing wind often call for the use of a driver from the tee.

come the principal course. Major C.K. Hutchinson, who had worked with James Braid at Gleneagles, was retained to remove some blind holes and put some length into it; the course was shaping up to championship standard when the Second World War came along. This time, the Royal Air Force set up a training airfield and devastated the place with three runways with deep foundations and several inches of concrete on top, as well as buildings.

Knowledgeable folk were convinced that the Turnberry courses had gone beyond recall. But happily Frank Hole, managing director of British Transport Hotels, a British Rail subsidiary (the four

railway companies had been nationalised in 1948), did not. In a post-war campaign that lasted several years, Hole nagged the RAF and the government for the compensation he felt entitled to, and he eventually got it. Hole was an exceptional man. With the funds in place, his next triumph was to select Philip Mackenzie Ross to re-design and re-build the courses. Ross was a Musselburgh man who died in London in 1974 at the age of 83, when his credits included Royal Guernsey, Southerness, and Las Palmas in the Canary Islands; and in collaboration with the eccentric Tom Simpson, Royal Antwerp and Spa in Belgium and Deauville and Hardelot in France. With the help of Jimmy Alexander, the hotel company's superintendent of grounds and golf courses, and with Suttons of Reading as contractors, Ross created a masterpiece at Turnberry.

The courses were completed in the summer of 1951 and over the next two decades the reputation of the Ailsa was consolidated: it staged the Amateur Championship, two PGA Match Play Championships, the amateur international matches, a Walker Cup match and many professional tournaments. By 1977 it was ready to hold its first Open

Championship, which proved to be as sensational as any Open had ever been. Jack Nicklaus and Tom Watson played three identical rounds of 68, 70 and 66. It had been a summer of drought, Turnberry's rough was meagre and playing conditions were perfect, but this was startling scoring. And paired together in the final round, they again played quite brilliantly – Nicklaus with a 66 and Watson with a 65, making Tom Open Champion for the second time. The winning total of 268, a record, was 12 under par. Only one other player, Hubert Green from the United States, was under par at 279, 11 shots behind Watson. Green quipped: 'Tom won the Open – I won the tournament the rest of us were playing'.

The Ailsa is a fine, honest, open golf course with a splendid selection of two-shot holes. One of the major drawbacks to playing well there is the distraction of its beauty. A more serious criticism is that is does not have one big, honest-to-God, under-any-conditions par-5 hole. The 7th is 528 yards at championship length, but

Top: *Turnberry's 'Wee Burn' 16th hole, at 409 yards, may be a comfortable drive and pitch for the expert, but the depth and width of Wilson's burn can be a frightening hazard for the club golfer.*

Above: *Tommy Nakajima of Japan and Greg Norman of Australia, the eventual winner, on the photographic 9th tee of Turnberry's Ailsa Course in the 1986 Open.*

Opposite: *The shot from the championship tee at the 9th, atop a 50-foot-high promontory, involves a carry of 200 yards across a rocky inlet.*

it runs approximately down the prevailing south-west wind. It calls for a drive from a tee high above the beach across broken ground and high dunes to a valley fairway running off to the left. There is a saddle in the dunes giving access to this valley. The carry is perhaps 200 yards over a perfectly positioned bunker. Watson, in his last championship round in 1977, drove over the corner, then hit a magnificent shot with his driver again, off the fairway to reach the green for his birdie. The 17th, at 500 yards, goes in quite the opposite direction. It is called 'Lang Whang', meaning a good strong crack at the ball. Into a strong prevailing wind, the best of them will need just that.

And finally, the most photographed of all Ailsa's delights is the 9th tee, perched out on a rocky promontory of cliffs, with sheer falls of 50 feet or more, and a drive that must carry a good 200 yards over an inlet in the cliffs. Rather than putting the nerves to the test with that tee shot, better to watch Turnberry's famous diving gannets.

GLENEAGLES

The King's Course at the Gleneagles Hotel is one of the best-known courses in Britain, largely because of the power of television. More tournaments and other golfing promotions have been televised from the King's than from any other course – with good reason. It is one of the most beautiful inland courses in the world. The fact that its international reputation, like that of the Augusta National course in Georgia, has been immensely enhanced by television exposure should not detract from its quality, which is of the highest order.

The King's, like the Queen's, the Prince's and the Glendevon – the other Gleneagles courses – is laid out on a wooded moorland plateau in Perthshire, a property of some 700 acres at an altitude of 600 feet. The turf is crisp, the fairways wide and smooth, the hazards in the main clearly defined and the course is immaculately groomed. There are banks of golden gorse and purple heather, stands of tall pines and the views in all directions are superb – the Ochil Hills to the east and south, with the valley of Glendevon reaching through to Fife; to the north lie the Grampians, to the west the Trossachs.

The hotel, built in the French Empire style, is the most luxurious in Scotland and has an interesting history. It was originally a railway hotel owned by the Caledonian Railway Company and was conceived by Donald Matheson, the company's general manager, just before the First World War. The truth of the matter may have been that Matheson could not tolerate the existence and success of the Turnberry Hotel, then owned by the Glasgow and South Western Railway Company, and he resolved to outdo it. Construction of Gleneagles was halted by the war, but Matheson had already engaged the great James Braid to design its courses. Braid, in collaboration with

The typically immaculate greens of the short 16th and (beyond it) the 15th. The King's course offers an enjoyable challenge to every calibre of golfer amid spectacularly beautiful scenery.

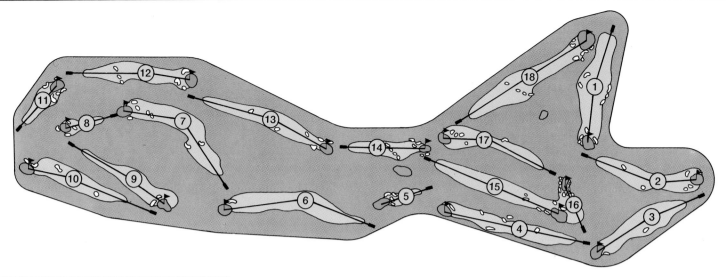

GLENEAGLES			
Card of the King's course			
1	362 yards par 4	10	447 yards par 4
2	405 yards par 4	11	230 yards par 3
3	374 yards par 4	12	395 yards par 4
4	466 yards par 4	13	448 yards par 4
5	161 yards par 3	14	260 yards par 4
6	476 yards par 5	15	459 yards par 4
7	439 yards par 4	16	135 yards par 3
8	158 yards par 3	17	377 yards par 4
9	354 yards par 4	18	525 yards par 5
3,195 yards par 35		3,276 yards par 35	
Total 6,471 yards par 70			

Major C.K. Hutchinson, designed the King's Course and nine holes for the Queen's. A second nine was added to the Queen's, and when the hotel opened in 1924, golf was very much in place.

Braid's Moorland Masterpiece

Braid's brief for the King's Course had been: 'Make it spectacular, make it look difficult, but make it easy to get round'. That might sound like an invitation to cheat, but Braid by and large filled the client's bill. The basic feature of the site was a long ridge that ran through the entire property. The holes then follow patterns which seem to have been inflicted on the design by the ridge. Braid has a tee on the ridge, playing down into a valley. He has a green set on top of the ridge, demanding an uphill approach. On occasion, he has a blind shot over the ridge. (The blind shots may persuade some that the course is slightly old-fashioned; but the fact is that in design terms the blind shot was not frowned

upon in the first decade of this century.)

In terms of his brief, Braid certainly made it spectacular; made it look difficult. Whether or not it is easy to get round depends entirely on the talent and the wit of the golfer. There are some holes that must be difficult even for a first-class player. The 3rd hole, 374 yards, for instance, plays uphill into a valley full of heaving mounds and devious hollows. There is then that huge ridge, with a very big bunker in its face. The entire green is beyond the ridge, so that the second shot is completely blind.

The most famous hole is no doubt the 13th, 'Braid's Brawest' (it was his favourite), again with the ridge running all along the right side. A lesser ridge with a bunker in its face crosses the fairway at about 200 yards and must be carried. At 448 yards, this is a challenging two-

Philomena Garvey of Ireland in the final of the 1957 British Ladies' Championship in which she beat Mrs Valentine ('Wee Jessie' to her Scottish fans) by 4 and 3. The Gleneagles trees have grown considerably since then.

shotter. The second shot is to a plateau green above the player. It slopes from right to left, down into a dip at the front, then up towards the back. The fairway narrows as it nears the green, which is adroitly bunkered – a fine hole. The pleasures of Gleneagles are many, and go beyond the playing of the shots. Depending on the season, you may hear the call of wild geese, or grouse or pheasant or partridge or duck among the woods.

And looking to the future, there are plans for a championship course in the 1990s to be designed by Jack Nicklaus – his first major commission in Scotland.

ROYAL PORTHCAWL

Wales has much to be proud of in the range and variety of its golf courses. It boasts a good hundred of them, ranging from links to mountain courses and running the gamut of seaside, parkland, meadowland, heathland and moorland. Particularly noteworthy are Aberdovey, Ashburton, Caernarvonshire and Royal St David's – those courses that crowd along the north coast of Wales from Prestatyn to Llandudno.

The game came to Wales, as it came to England, with the great Scottish emigration of golfers and architects (often one and the same) in the last quarter of the 19th century. One of the oldest of Welsh clubs is at Tenby and dates from 1888. Clubs established in 1890 included Rhyl and Glamorganshire at Penarth, and the greatest of Welsh courses, Royal Porthcawl, dates from 1891.

Lock's Common

Early in 1891 a group of Cardiff businessmen, mainly, as you would expect, from the shipping and coal trades, resolved to start a golf club at Porthcawl, and by April of that year had arranged permission to cut nine holes for play on Lock's Common – a dense and tangled undergrowth of gorse, whin and bracken – and the rest of the year was spent in clearing it. Early in 1892, Charles Gibson, the professional at Westward Ho!, was invited to lay out an original nine-holes course. Within three years, the club was ready for an extra nine, and before the turn of the century the original nine were abandoned and the present 18 established. These were to be revised regularly by impressive names from the ranks of golf architects – James Braid in 1910, Harry Colt in 1913, Tom Simpson and possibly Fred Hawtree between the wars, Ken Cotton in 1950 and Donald Steel in 1986.

The fruit of their labours is an outstanding course. Royal Porthcawl has a magnificent setting on the Glamorgan coast 25 miles west of Cardiff, 14 miles east of Swansea. The property slopes towards the west and also south towards the Bristol Channel; and should probably

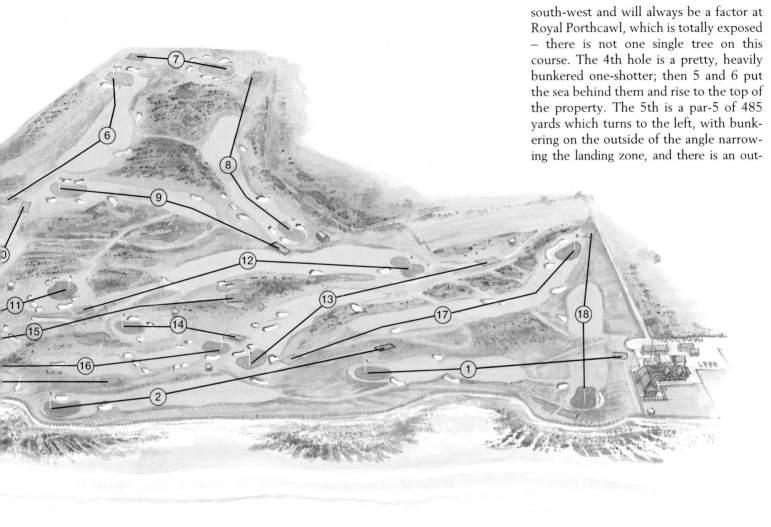

south-west and will always be a factor at Royal Porthcawl, which is totally exposed – there is not one single tree on this course. The 4th hole is a pretty, heavily bunkered one-shotter; then 5 and 6 put the sea behind them and rise to the top of the property. The 5th is a par-5 of 485 yards which turns to the left, with bunkering on the outside of the angle narrowing the landing zone, and there is an out-

be described as a seaside, rather than a links course because of the absence of dunes. However, spreading banks of gorse and broom are colourful substitutes and there is no shortage of movement in the ground. The course also provides arresting views: to the west Swansea and the Gower Peninsula; to the south, the coast of Somerset.

The Wind Factor
The first three holes are a delight, running to the west along the shore. The 1st hole, at 326 yards, is a drive (crossing the 18th fairway, by the way) into a small valley, then a pitch to a small green. The 2nd and

Royal Porthcawl's first three holes and the 18th run along the Cardigan coast looking out to the Bristol Channel. The natural humps and bumps of a linksland course are very evident here.

ROYAL PORTHCAWL
Card of the course

1	326 yards	par 4	10	337 yards	par 4
2	447 yards	par 4	11	187 yards	par 3
3	420 yards	par 4	12	476 yards	par 5
4	197 yards	par 3	13	443 yards	par 4
5	485 yards	par 5	14	152 yards	par 3
6	394 yards	par 4	15	447 yards	par 4
7	116 yards	par 3	16	434 yards	par 4
8	490 yards	par 5	17	508 yards	par 5
9	371 yards	par 4	18	413 yards	par 4
	3,246 yards	par 36		3,397 yards	par 36
		Total 6,643 yards par 72			

3rd holes are very fine par-4s, bunkered artfully in driving range and asking for long seconds down to greens placed closer to the shore than is comfortable for most golfers. These holes will normally have the wind against, since it prevails from the

of-bounds all the way up the left. The 6th is a par-4 of 394 yards, it too turning to the left with a bunker on the outside of the angle and out-of-bounds along the left.

The 7th is a pop of a hole, at 116 yards shorter even than Royal Troon's 'Postage Stamp' and surely the shortest hole on any championship course anywhere. In truth, it may be altogether too short, bordering on the comic. The 8th, on the other hand, is a lovely hole, turning to the left, this time with a fairway bunker on the inside of the angle, then an uphill second which must carry over cross-bunkers some 40 yards short of the green. A score of five is hard-won over its 490 yards.

Sea Views
One of the special features of Porthcawl is that there are views of the sea from almost every point on the course. This is true in spite of the fact that the remaining

holes seem to run in an almost arbitrary fashion, every which way. Nowhere is the view more striking than from the crest of the 13th fairway. The second part of the hole (a par-4 of 443 yards) falls down to the green with the sea spreading beyond. Most of the golf course can be seen from this point.

Holes 15 and 16 are powerful par-4s, at 447 and 434 yards respectively, and the 17th is a real tester. It is a double dog-leg, first to the right, then left into the green. The drive must carry a swathe of rough ground, then negotiate the turns and 508 yards of precisely bunkered fairway, running uphill to a green which is long and tightly trapped on both sides. The 18th hole plays straight downhill at 413 yards, crossing in front of the first tee and playing to a green perched perilously close to the rocky beach. This is a challenging finish to a course that measures no more than 6,643 yards, yet has never been overwhelmed by any player.

International Tournaments

The merits of Porthcawl are demonstrated by the fact that it has staged all the great events of the game with the exception of the Open Championship. It has seen five Amateur Championships, the European Amateur Team Championships of 1989 and the men's Home Internation-

Above: The crowd gathers by the green of Porthcawl's 485 yards, uphill par-5 5th hole, at the Amateur Championship final of 1988, when Christian Hardin of Sweden beat Ben Fouchee of South Africa in a 'foreign' final.

Right: The flavour of Porthcawl – beyond the 17th tee is the 2nd green, hard by the shore and the wide sweep of the Bristol Channel.

al Championships eight times. It has presented three Ladies's Amateur Championships, a Curtis Cup match, a Vagliano Trophy match between the ladies of Great Britain and Ireland and the Continent of Europe, the ladies' Home International matches four times, and many professional events.

The scoring of the professionals over the years is a good indication of the quality of the course and how true a test it remains. Gordon Brand, Jr scored 273, fifteen under par, in winning the 1982 Coral Classic tournament. Yet 50 years earlier, Percy Alliss had won a Penfold Tournament with 278, only five strokes adrift of Brand despite half a century of improvement in clubs and balls. And Peter Thomson, at the height of his career in 1961, had to play quite brilliantly through a stiff wind to score 284 in winning the Dunlop Masters.

ROYAL COUNTY DOWN

Royal County Down is one of the world's greatest seaside courses. It is set on a quite magnificent piece of golfing ground along the shore of Dundrum Bay, by the town of Newcastle on the east coast of Ireland, 30 miles from Belfast. It is an area of striking beauty, dominated by the mass of Slieve Donard and the Mountains of Mourne to the south of the town. The course plays through a piece of ground, in the old days known as The Warren, surely destined for nothing but a golf course. Emerald green fairways cut channels through oceans of gorse-covered dunes, ridges and swelling rises in a stunning linksland that has its own entirely distinctive character.

Royal County Down is not really comparable to any other links course. Its sand dunes don't quite tumble with the sharpness of those of Ballybunion or Lahinch. It

is not as stern as Portmarnock or Portrush. Its first three holes run north-east, hard along the beach and then the course turns inland, putting the sea behind it, leaving the golfer in wondrous admiration and isolation on the most beautiful of golf courses.

The club was formed in 1889, one of the oldest in Ulster (Royal Belfast, the oldest, 1881; Royal Portrush in 1888). Newcastle was a summer resort for Belfast businessmen then, and perhaps encouraged by the success of the Belfast club and by the fact that The Warren was an obvious site for golf, a meeting was called on 23 March 1889 in 'the hall of Mr Lawrence's Dining Rooms, Newcastle. Lord Annersley presided and over 70 ladies and gentlemen were present'.

Old Tom Morris

A provisional committee meeting decided to invite 'Tom Morris of St Andrews to lay out the course at an expense not to exceed £4'. Nine holes were already in existence. Old Tom came over and played the existing holes on 16th and 17th July and left recommendations for an 18-hole

course which was quickly laid out. Tees and greens would be the priority in those times – there was no sophisticated equipment in use and this was still very much in the time of the gutty ball, when 200 yards was a good hit. Golf course architecture was a simple, infant business – Horace Hutchinson, the 1887 Amateur Champion who came over to play these 18 holes, wrote ten years later: 'The laying out of a golf course is a wonderfully easy business, needing very little training'.

By 1890, the club felt able to appoint its first professional, Alex Day, and soon afterwards its first greenkeeper. One of the founder members, George Combe, contributed greatly to the evolution of the course. Captain in 1895–6, he spent many years as chairman of the greens committee and was largely responsible for changing the design to two loops of nine holes, with the ninth returning to the clubhouse area in the Muirfield fashion.

In 1898, the club was sufficiently confident and well-founded to put up 100 guineas for its first professional tournament. It attracted Harry Vardon, J.H. Taylor, Ben Sayers, Sandy Herd, Andrew

ROYAL COUNTY DOWN					
Card of the course					
1	506 yards	par 5	10	200 yards	par 3
2	424 yards	par 4	11	440 yards	par 4
3	473 yards	par 4	12	501 yards	par 5
4	217 yards	par 3	13	445 yards	par 4
5	440 yards	par 4	14	213 yards	par 3
6	396 yards	par 4	15	445 yards	par 4
7	145 yards	par 3	16	265 yards	par 4
8	427 yards	par 4	17	400 yards	par 4
9	486 yards	par 5	18	545 yards	par 5
3,514 yards	par 36		3,454 yards	par 36	
Total 6,968 yards par 72					

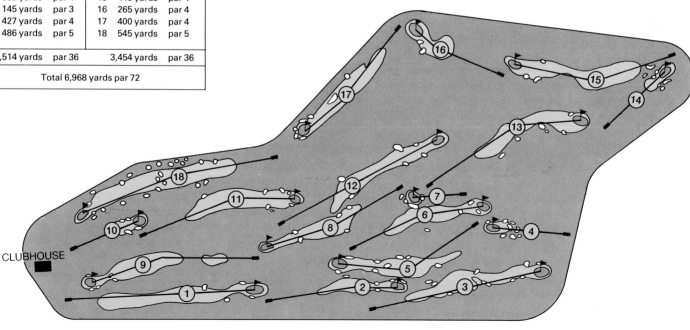

Three of Royal County Down's short holes are 200 yards or better. This is the 10th, running exactly 200 yards to the north away from the clubhouse, over broken ground to a green only 27 yards long.

Kirkaldy and Willie Fernie. Harry Vardon beat Taylor by a staggering 12 and 11 in the final.

The Amateur Championship

In 1897 the club had opened a new clubhouse – it had previously used facilities at the nearby railway station, and early in the new century, there was an arrangement with the Belfast and County Down Railway Company to provide special trains, soon dubbed the 'Golfers' Express', leaving Belfast at 10.10am and returning from Newcastle at 5.35pm. By 1902, the course was at 5,760 yards and becoming well-known throughout Britain. And the club had such a conceit of

itself that in the same year it sent a delegation to the Amateur Championship Committee – comprising representatives of the Royal and Ancient, Honourable Company, Royal St George's, Royal Liverpool and Prestwick – petitioning to have the Amateur Championship at Royal County Down. It was rejected. An indignant article in the *Northern Whig* pointed out that the local scenery 'is more to be desired than the flat lands of St

Andrews or the morass of Muirfield'. However, Royal County Down did get the Amateur Championship – 58 years later, when Michael Bonallack won his fifth championship, his third in successive years.

In 1904 Seymour Dunn, professional for a couple of years, suggested some course changes, and Harry Vardon, who was back in 1908, suggested others. The club then had good times and bad, the two World Wars being particularly difficult times, as they were for almost every golf club. By 1923, the course measured 6,451 yards, but it was not until Harry Colt had run his eye over it in 1926, and his recommended changes were put into

Above: *Royal County Down's 9th is one of the most testing holes in golf at its championship length of 486 yards, demanding a long drive, then a second shot over cross bunkers, uphill to a small, raised green.*

Left: *Rolling panorama of Royal County Down, with the formidable short 4th and its fiercely defended green in the foreground, framed in the distance by the Mourne Mountains.*

practice, that it took on its present magnificent form.

A Flawed Masterpiece

Now, at its championship length of 6,968 yards with a par of 72, it is a test for the best. The 1st hole, a par-5 of 506 yards, plays down into a long, slender valley with sandhills on either side and the five miles strand of Dundrum Bay parallel to the right. Behind lies the massive back-drop of the Mourne Mountains, and ahead, running northward, golden gorse in blossom, fierce heathery rough, restless fairways and swelling dunes. It is a magnificent place. But some have it that County Down is a flawed masterpiece, because of its blind shots.

The 'blind' holes hit the golfer so quickly that as early as the second tee he will be mumbling about the advantages of local knowledge. The drive there is blind, as it is at the 5th, over a ridge. The drive

on the 6th is blind, and part of the short 7th's green is hidden from the tee. The drive at the 9th is across a mass of sandhills and the second to the 13th is blind. All told there are five tee shots at Newcastle which are shots into the unknown, and this course definitely needs to be known! But blind shots are still featured to a greater (at Prestwick) or lesser (at Royal St George's) degree in the modern game.

The par-3 holes are outstanding. The 4th is a 217 yards carry over gorse to a long green with ten (!) bunkers. The 14th at 213 yards is a very similar hole, but downhill, and has only six greenside bunkers. The 10th, at 200 yards, is played from a raised tee down to a closely trapped green. Some golfers know how to cope with such holes. In the final of the Irish Open Amateur Championship of 1933, Eric Fiddian, playing against Jack McLean, holed his tee shot at the 7th during the morning round, and repeated the feat at the 14th of the afternoon round. It was unprecedented in such a final, but McLean nevertheless, won. But, win or lose, any golfer who plays Royal County Down can only rejoice in the splendour of its scenery, in the quality of the shotmaking it requires and in the delights and damnations of its design. Royal County Down is a golf experience second to none.

ROYAL PORTRUSH

The Antrim coast road, running along the northern cliffs of Northern Ireland, is a dramatic passage, by Ballycastle Bay, White Park Bay and Benbane Head, with the boomerang shape of Rathlin Island offshore. Past the Giant's Causeway and Portballintrae it goes, and when it turns just past the ruined Dunluce Castle, there is a panorama to make the heart of any golfer skip. The entire spread of the Royal Portrush courses are laid out before him. Not ridges or mounds, but hills, minor mountains, hills of sand and wildflowers – in particular the wild dwarf rose – and sharp and sinister hollows, covering what appears to be a vast acreage.

To the west is Inishowen Head and the hills of Donegal across the mouth of Lough Foyle; to the north, over the Skerries and across the sea, lies the outline of Islay; and to the east, beyond Rathlin, there is a sight of the peninsula of Kintyre. The Dunluce Course, the championship course, may be the most severe test of all the great British championship courses. The key is driving, which might be said of every golf course in the world, but this is particularly true of Portrush. The fairways are desperately narrow. It is not so much a question of what side of the fairway to be on, it is more a question of

This is the 14th at Royal Portrush, otherwise known as 'Calamity Corner', and one of the most famous short holes in Ireland. It is 213 yards and in place of a fairway has a 50 feet deep canyon between tee and green.

being on the fairway! Almost every fairway turns one way or the other. In championship trim, Dunluce rough is fiercely tenacious. There are no trees on the course, no shelter. It is exposed to all the winds the ocean may blow. And the greens can certainly not be described as large. One peculiar feature in the Dunluce design is the paucity of bunkers, particularly at greenside. However, the greens are either protected by approaches which will run a ball off to the side, or are raised, with steep hollows on one side or the other, and with extremely narrow entrances.

The history of the club has odd similarities with those of its contemporaries, in relation to the acquiring of ground, the laying out of holes, the use of the assets

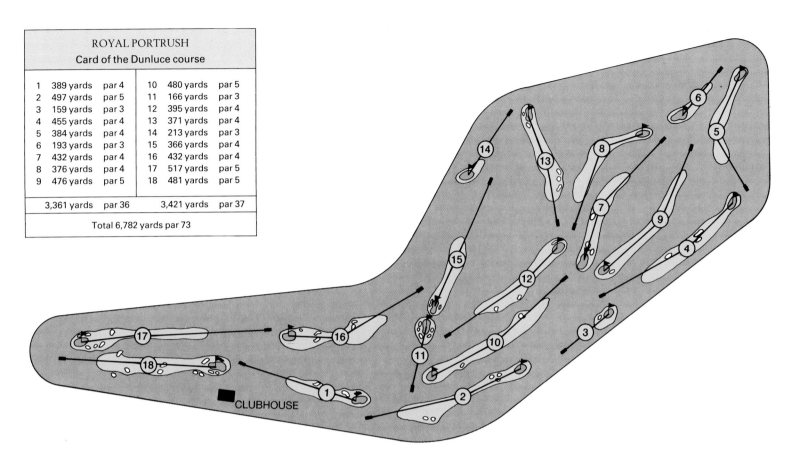

ROYAL PORTRUSH					
Card of the Dunluce course					
1	389 yards	par 4	10	480 yards	par 5
2	497 yards	par 5	11	166 yards	par 3
3	159 yards	par 3	12	395 yards	par 4
4	455 yards	par 4	13	371 yards	par 4
5	384 yards	par 4	14	213 yards	par 3
6	193 yards	par 3	15	366 yards	par 4
7	432 yards	par 4	16	432 yards	par 4
8	376 yards	par 4	17	517 yards	par 5
9	476 yards	par 5	18	481 yards	par 5
	3,361 yards	par 36		3,421 yards	par 37
	Total 6,782 yards par 73				

CLUBHOUSE

and goodwill of the local aristocracy, not to mention Ulster's railway system. Comparisons with Royal County Down are obvious. Royal Portrush was founded in 1888, one year before the Newcastle club. The town of Portrush at that time had a population of 1600 and was already established as a Victorian resort with a fine harbour, a railway terminus – the Northern Counties railway from Belfast – a tramway route out to the Giant's Causeway and even a direct steamer service from Glasgow and the Clyde ports ...and of course, magnificent beaches and sand dunes.

The club started as the County Club, occupying 'The Triangle', 40 acres of ground by the railway station. At one point, members of the County Club could travel first class on a day return ticket to Belfast and have a hot lunch and tea in the Northern Counties Hotel for all of ten shillings (50p). The English master at the Royal Academy in Belfast, George L. Baillie, originally from Musselburgh, resigned as honorary secretary to the Royal Belfast club, where he had helped

introduce golf to Ireland, and became honorary secretary at Portrush. As a founding father, he was very much involved with the landlord, the Earl of Antrim, in extending the course beyond The Triangle and into the natural dune land on the seaward side of the Portrush-Bushmills road. In 1889 Tom Morris, having visited County Down, came on to Portrush, played the existing course and made some suggestions for improving the design. In October that year came the first clubhouse, a hut of wood and zinc which cost £150. And by 1890, there were 18 holes in play, a new professional in Sandy Herd, 250 members and a second 18 almost completed.

The Dunluce course is built on a 'raised beach', a higher shelf of dune left by the receding sea, while the Valley course, the ladies' course, is on lower ground, in some parts below sea level. By 1909, the big course measured 6,608 yards, but not until the 'Twenties did Dunluce take on its present form. In 1923, the remarkable Harry Colt prepared new plans. These were delayed, until 1928 because of

various lease problems and thereafter by cost, but by 1933 the new courses were established, with some superb and taxing holes. The 14th, for example, at 213 yards demands a carry all the way over an evil, 50 foot deep canyon. Dubbed 'Calamity Corner', it is just that, and is one of the most famous short holes in Ireland.

The 5th hole, a dog-leg to the right, needs a careful approach to a green on the very edge of the cliff. In the winter of 1982–3, some 25 feet of cliff behind that green and the neighbouring 6th tee were eroded. The club had to take quick action and launched a fund to help meet the repair cost, estimated at £200,000. Golfers and golf clubs throughout the UK, Ireland and beyond responded, and the work was done.

The club's proudest boast remains the Open Championship of 1951, the only time it has ever been played in Ireland. It was won by the extrovert Max Faulkner, with a surprisingly restrained exhibition of shot-making and putting in highly variable weather.

PORTMARNOCK

Portmarnock is a giant among golf courses, the greatest in the Republic of Ireland. That statement will be challenged immediately by the supporters of Rosses Point, Lahinch, Ballybunion – both courses – Waterville and perhaps even Royal Dublin. And if the claim be extended to all-Ireland, what should we do with Royal County Down and Royal Portrush? But yet again, it must be remembered that we are never quite comparing like with like, and have to fall back on the old disclaimer that rubies are rubies, pearls are pearls and diamonds are diamonds. Like the other selections, Portmarnock must be classified as one of the great golf courses of the world.

The course occupies a peninsula which juts into the Irish sea some eight miles north-east of Dublin, and is arranged in two loops of nine holes through classic links terrain – without the vast sandhills of a County Down or a Ballybunion, but across rolling sandhills of crisp turf on what seems to be an isolated island.

The Wilderness

The origins of Portmarnock are poorly documented, but it appears that in 1894 George Ross and J.W. Pickeman rowed across to the peninsula and, despite the fact that the ground was something of a wilderness, they decided that it had some potential for golf. Before this the Jameson family had their own private course near the shore in the general area of the present 15th hole. John Jameson of Irish Whiskey fame was the local landlord and for many years was first president of the Portmarnock club.

The original nine holes lay more or less as the present opening nine and, within four years, they had a second nine in play and a shack for a clubhouse in place. By 1899 they had a course of 5,810 yards,

Canada Cup 1960. Sam Snead sinks the final putt watched (from left) by Kel Nagle, Arnold Palmer and Peter Thomson. The Americans won the cup by eight shots in Palmer's first ever European tournament.

their first professional tournament, and a notable winner in Harry Vardon, who had scores of 72 and 79. Vardon won the Open at Sandwich later that year. The original clubhouse burned down in 1904, and parts of the present building date from 1905, then the clubhouse was replaced. There have been other changes over the years. Fred G. Hawtree revised the original 18. His son, Fred W., designed a third nine holes in 1964, and new greens have been made at the 6th, 8th, 10th and 18th holes over the years.

In the early days, the club was reached by boat from Sutton, as Ross and Pickeman had done, and the club ferryman was a former naval man and formidable with it. It was said that once on the crossing there was a difference of opinion between himself and a clergyman not of the same faith. The clergyman did not reach Portmarnock. When the Amateur Championship was played at Portmarnock in 1949, the only time it has been played outside the U.K., Henry Longhurst, the

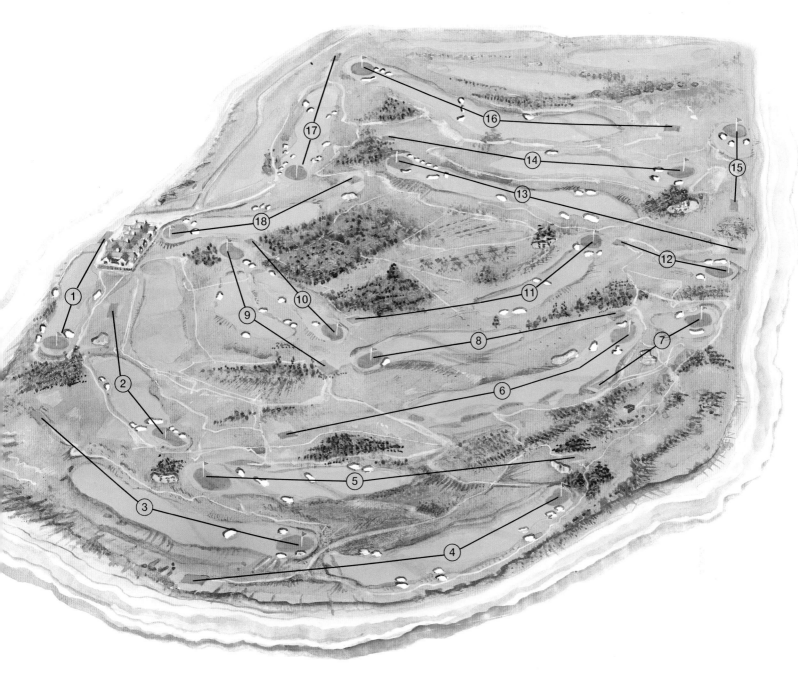

golf journalist, wrote rather pertly about having to show a passport to report the Amateur Championship, which was being played 'in a foreign country'.

An 'Easy' Opening

In championship dress, Portmarnock will play to more than 7,100 yards, with seven of its par-4 holes over 400 yards and two of its three par-5 holes at 565 yards or better. The first three holes run down to and around the very point of the peninsula and if there were easy holes at Portmar-

PORTMARNOCK Card of the course					
1	388 yards	par 4	10	380 yards	par 4
2	368 yards	par 4	11	445 yards	par 4
3	388 yards	par 4	12	144 yards	par 3
4	460 yards	par 4	13	565 yards	par 5
5	407 yards	par 4	14	385 yards	par 4
6	586 yards	par 5	15	192 yards	par 3
7	180 yards	par 3	16	527 yards	par 5
8	370 yards	par 4	17	466 yards	par 4
9	444 yards	par 4	18	408 yards	par 4
3,591 yards		par 36	3,512 yards		par 36
Total 7,103 yards par 72					

nock, it would be these opening three, giving the golfer at least some chance of getting into an early, comfortable stride. On yardage, they are all under 400 yards and therefore theoretically drive and pitch holes, but that ignores the wind, and Portmarnock is seldom without that.

The pin position at the 1st will often be behind the left front bunker. That means the drive should be in the right half of the fairway. But on that side is an area which is out of bounds! The 2nd green is two-tiered, and the 3rd hole doglegs to

the left with a ridge of rough along the left and a lateral water hazard on the right side. The 4th is where the course begins to flex its considerable muscle. The drive is over 150 yards of rough and a little ridge enters a narrow fairway which turns to the left, with pairs of bunkers carefully set up along the right side. Again, accuracy in the tee shot is essential. It must be slightly right to allow sight of the flat green with a narrow approach to it.

Harry Bradshaw, professional at the club for many years, always considered

The 17th hole is lavishly bunkered on both sides of the fairway and the right of the green. Severiano Ballesteros, seen here in the 1986 Irish Open, putts after a perfect second shot to the green.

the 5th the best hole on the course. It is straight, with a blind drive over a ridge demanding a carry of almost 200 yards to the fairway. There is a slight ridge crossing just short of the green and a bunker at the right front of it, just short of a rather small green set across the shot. The

6th is an immense hole of 586 yards, requiring, quite simply, a huge shot smashed off the tee to avoid banks of rough on the left. The second shot should get up to the region of the pond in the left rough – still some 120 yards to the front of the green. The 7th at 180 yards is a pretty and rather straightforward one shot hole, the easiest of the par-3s. The 8th hole offers a selection of Portmarnock characteristics. There is a sandhill on the right, 200 yards out, and a rough-filled hollow as the hole turns left at 250 yards.

death, the course 're-opened', and the Irish Amateur Championship of 1946 was played there. Even if it was not Portmarnock or Ballybunion, there was never any doubt about the quality of Killarney golf. As post-war tourism flourished, it became clear that, as Castlerosse had predicted, a second course would be necessary. The club reclaimed some land between its existing course and the lakeside and the Irish Tourist Board bought enough land for a further nine holes. Fred Hawtree was called in to design a new 18-hole course. Known as the Killeen, it opened in 1971, and the Killarney Golf and Fishing Club was born.

This development was substantially funded by the Irish Tourist Board, but to a large extent directed and inspired by a latter-day Castlerosse, Dr Billy O'Sullivan. 'Doctor Billy', as he is known affec-

Described by Gene Sarazen as 'one of the most memorable holes in golf', Killarney's 18th is certainly the most photographed of all its holes. It is 196 yards, played along the lake shore.

tionately throughout the area, had been a first-rate player in his day. A former Irish champion, Irish international player, club captain and club president, he was still tending to the sick of Killarney in general practice into his late 70s.

One feature of golf at Killarney is the variety of tees, which makes the yardages particularly flexible. The medal tees on the O'Mahony's Point course can play at 6,300 yards, while the championship course stretches to 6,728 yards. A good eight of the 36 holes at Killarney are by the lakeside, opening up marvellous vistas of mountains and of Lough Leane and its

waterfowl. Most of the inland holes are reminders of fine American meadowland golf, and the final three holes of the O'Mahony's Point course make a finish of distinction. The 16th swings downhill towards the lake, turning to the right but with stunning views of the water and the mountains beyond. The hole is 506 yards, without a single bunker, and 80 yards short of the green there is a stream crossing the bottom of a downslope.

The 17th strides along the lakeside, trees on the left, the shore along the right. Again, there is not one bunker on the hole. The 18th is probably the most famous, certainly the most photographed of all Killarney holes: a straight par-3 of 196 yards, with a hit right across the lake shore. It has been described by Gene Sarazen as 'one of the most memorable holes in golf'.

BALLYBUNION

Ballybunion is a small seaside resort in the far south-west of Ireland, at the northern end of the county of Kerry, about 50 miles west of Limerick and 25 miles north of Tralee. It lies on the south bank of the estuary of the river Shannon, and a remote place it is. It is also the place where there is to be found, in the judgement of many serious golfing people, 'the best golf course in the world'. When Herbert Warren Wind, the much-respected American sports writer who has written extensively if not absolutely exclusively on golf, first visited the course, he wrote that Ballybunion 'revealed itself to be nothing less than the finest seaside course I have ever seen'. The much respected British golf writer, Peter Dobereiner wrote '. . . if sheer pleasure is the yardstick, then Ballybunion gets my vote as the best course in the world'. And Tom Watson, the great American champion and lover of links courses, claims that 'it is a course on which many golf architects should live and play before they build golf courses'.

Duneland

Why should there be such a magnificent course in such a remote place? The inexplicable accidents of geography, history, geology and mankind have much to

The 385-yard 17th, on the Old course, shows typical Ballybunion country of high sand dunes, ridged fairways, grassed hollows and the constant presence of the cliffs and the ocean.

do with it. The Atlantic Ocean has pounded the land of the west of Ireland for aeons. The result is stark, standing, crumbling cliffs, georgeous shining beaches and vast stretches of tumbling sand dunes. At Ballybunion, the duneland above the beach is immense, rising in great ridges and peaks, leaving deep valleys and thrusting perhaps 50 feet and more above the beach – a weird and exciting landscape. Unlike dunes in other places, where the sand ridges march in ordered lines parallel with the shore, at Ballybunion they thrust and tumble and heave in all directions, giving valleys for fairways, tops for tees, and the possibility of having greens and tees on the very edge of cliffs, overlooking the strand. Made for golf it was.

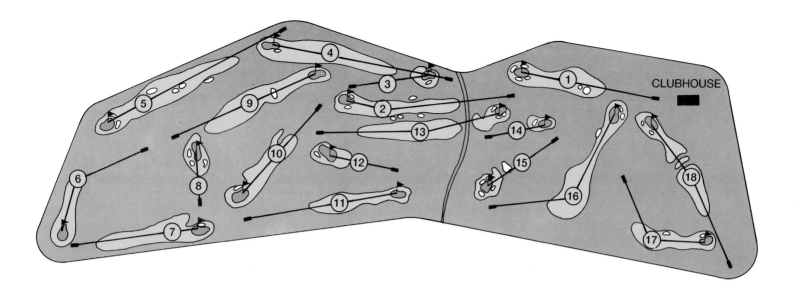

The club started in life on 4 March 1896 – the minute book has been preserved – with George Hewson of Listowel (the nearest town) as president and C. Mark Montserrat, a local estate agent, as honorary secretary. In 1897, Patrick McCarthy, manager of the Listowel and Ballybunion Railway Company, became honorary secretary. Alas, the club had not been organised on a financial footing that could keep it alive and the last entry in the club's minute book came on 13 August 1898.

James Bruen

That might well have been the end of it all but for one Colonel Bartholomew, an Indian Army man who had retired to the area. He formed the present club in 1906, with BJ Johnstone of the Bank of Ireland, Patrick Murphy of the original group, and John Macauley of Listowel, who played Rugby football for Ireland. They retained Lionel Hewson, for many years editor of *Irish Golf*, to make nine holes. The course was extended to 18 holes in 1926, by a Mr Smyth, a designer for Carter and Sons Limited, the London company famous for laying out sports ground; and in 1937 the course was chosen as the venue for the Irish Men's Close Championship. This was the championship memorable for the victory and the emergence of James Bruen, aged 17 and in many ways the greatest of all Irish golfers. He beat

BALLYBUNION					
Card of the Old course					
1	392 yards	par 4	10	359 yards	par 4
2	445 yards	par 4	11	449 yards	par 4
3	220 yards	par 3	12	192 yards	par 3
4	498 yards	par 5	13	484 yards	par 5
5	508 yards	par 5	14	131 yards	par 3
6	364 yards	par 4	15	216 yards	par 3
7	423 yards	par 4	16	490 yards	par 5
8	153 yards	par 3	17	385 yards	par 4
9	454 yards	par 4	18	379 yards	par 4
3,457 yards	par 36		3,085 yards	par 35	
Total 6,542 yards par 71					

another famous Irish player, John Burke of Lahinch, in the final of the tournament.

In preparation for this championship, the club had asked Tom Simpson, the English architect, to review the course. When Simpson saw it, he was astonished and delighted, and did little more than move a couple of greens and plant a bunker in the middle of the fairway at what is now the 1st hole. It was dubbed, quickly and topically, 'Mrs Simpson'.

Friends of the Old Course

Ballybunion has been fortunate that everyone concerned with the existence and wellbeing of the place – from P. Murphy, who was 'employed to look after the ground at 9/- per week', to Jackie Hourigan in the late 1970s, who led a

campaign that saw 'the many friends of Ballybunion' raise £100,000 to check (successfully) erosion on the cliff face – realised the natural merits of the site, and allowed themselves to follow the land. 'The ground determines the play', the old dictum of John Lowe was never more true than at Ballybunion. The course is a mere 6,452 yards, short by modern design standards. But on such an exposed coast, the wind is always thereabouts. When the wind blows as it can, 'Anybody who breaks 70 here', in the words of Christy O'Connor, 'is playing better than he is able to play'!

The course quickly offers the golfer samples in miniature of what is to come. The very first drive, past the graveyard on the right, is downhill to a broad fairway. The hole is 392 yards. There is a huge sand mound off to the left. At 230 yards the first of a pair of bunkers closes out the left side, easing the drive over to the right, to rough and the boundary fence. The 2nd, at 445 yards, has bunkers on either side of the fairway at 210 yards and at 240 yards and the second shot must thread between two huge sand dunes. There is an upslope in front of the green, hollows behind the green, a fall off to the left and another big sand dune to the left – not bad! The 3rd, the first par-3, at 220 yards, has a large dune to the right, hollows in front of the green, bunkers right and left, and a downslope and a public road

running at the back left. At this moment, some players may feel it is time to retire to the clubhouse.

The Vintage Holes

The 4th and 5th are straightforward par-5s, but the 6th swoops out to the cliffs and starts the vintage Ballybunion holes. It is a dogleg to the left of 364 yards. Mounds and hollows mark the inside of the angle, and a mound beyond on the right might stop a really long drive on that line. The green is long, narrow, on the cliff and unprotected save for out-of-bounds on the right. But it does take us to the 7th tee! Here is an outstanding hole, at 423 yards, playing along the cliff tops. There is a mound on the left at around 200 yards. Two big ridges come in from the left further along. There is a grassy hollow just beyond them and the green, hard by the cliff, has a mound in front, hollows at the back and a bunker at the left. The 8th, 9th and 10th play away from the sea in a triangle before returning to the clifftop 11th tee. The 8th, a par-3 of 153 yards, is straight downhill. Tom Watson said of the tee shot; 'One of the most demanding shots I've ever faced'. There are huge bunkers, huge mounds crimping the front of the green, and hollows all around it.

The 11th is one of golf's most dramatic, most difficult, holes, played directly along the cliff top. There is an enormous sand

Above: The 18th at Ballybunion Old, 379 yards, displays all the elements of this famous course: the valley sharply dog-legged; the huge tumbling dunes, and in this case a big cross-bunker.

Right: The 10th, a short par-4, dog-legs left to this green perched high on the edge of the cliffs, with the Irish Sea crashing against them in the background.

dune off the fairway left, at 200 yards. At 245 yards, there are downslopes across the entire fairway. Two huge sandhills straddle the way into the green so that it is almost invisible from off-centre in the fairway, and there are fairway mounds 85 yards short of the green. Playing this hole with a strong wind from the sea hardly bears thinking about!

Holes 14 and 15 are magnificent short holes; 16, 17 and 18 quite startling in the sharpness of their dog-leg turns. The greatest problem the club golfer will have on such a course will be in ignoring his surroundings. They are so dramatic that they may frighten him, may compromise the business of just hitting the ball. The expert players do this so well – concentrating on nothing but the swing and the contact of blade on ball. The ocean, the cliffs, the dunes, the fairways, the air – all of it may be too much. Ballybunion is simply, in the words of a Duke Ellington phrase, 'beyond classification'.

LAHINCH

Old Tom Morris declared Lahinch 'as fine a natural course as it has ever been my good fortune to play over'. And Dr Alister Mackenzie thought that it might come to be regarded as 'the finest and most popular course that I, or I believe anyone else, ever constructed'. Morris and Mackenzie may have been indulging themselves a shade. Both men contributed to its evolution – Old Tom laid out the original course in 1893 and Mackenzie built new and rebuilt old holes in 1927 to put the course into its present shape and sequence.

The pretty village of Lahinch sits on Liscannon Bay on the Atlantic coast of County Clare, some 40 miles from Limerick. Its golf club dates from 1883, formed by officers of the Scottish regiment, the Black Watch, then stationed at Limerick, and of course a few interested locals. The soldier-golfers had been playing on Limerick racecourse, but were searching around for somewhere better. In the

Above: *Barometric billies: Lahinch's goats are the canniest weather prophets in these parts, making for the shelter of the clubhouse if rain threatens.*

Right: *The approach to the green of the par-4 8th is through a bottleneck between dunes some 50 yards short of the green, which is bunkered in front and to the right.*

spring of 1891 one of their officers was able to report that Lahinch, with its beach and sand dunes, was the very place. From then on, the Black Watch made Lahinch their golfing headquarters. Initially they marked out tees and green locations with, of all things, feathers.

When Old Tom Morris arrived in 1893 ('a guinea a day, and expenses, if you please'), he was greatly taken with the quality of the sand dunes and the seaward land, and virtually spurned the inland holes that existed. When he had finished he reckoned Lahinch to be one of the five best courses in the British Isles. No doubt Tom's reference was to the quality of the land as much as to his design, for Lahinch is blessed with vintage golfing ground – huge sand dunes, sheltering dells and valleys and magnificent sea views to the Cliffs of Moher and the Aran Islands.

The course is by any standards a magnificent links. Mackenzie extended the composite course which he created to

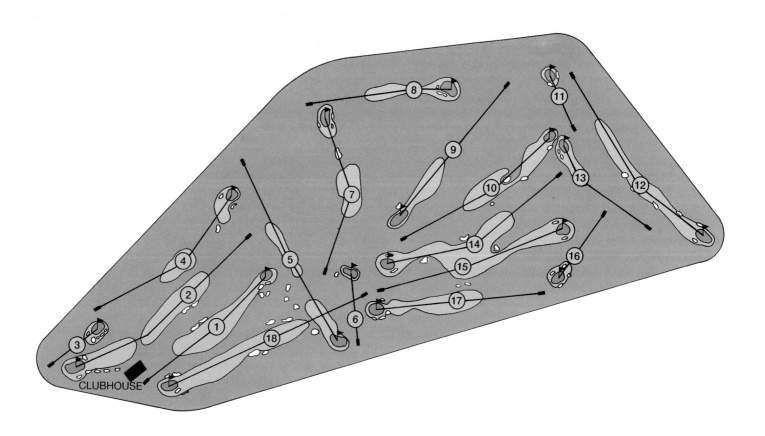

CLUBHOUSE

6,363 yards, and it can now play to just under 6,700 yards. What makes the course and the club so different is the way that it has become wholly integrated with the village. Lahinch is virtually a golf village, with the golf course the justification for its existence.

The course does get a great deal of holiday and tourist traffic, so much so that a second course of 18 holes, the 'Castle' course, designed by John Harris, became necessary and was opened in 1975.

Some holes are magnificent; others infuriating. The 2nd, for example, which plays back up towards and beyond the clubhouse, is a long 512 yards. It demands a drive into a narrow fairway, then an approach to a green which is open, but which has fairway bunkers along both sides, a high mound to the right, downward slopes at the front and to the left, and three fairly inhibiting bunkers. The third is an impish, short hole of about 150 yards with a banked-up front, but falling away at the left and back, and with a string of three bunkers set to the right.

LAHINCH					
Card of the course					
1	385 yards	par 4	10	451 yards	par 4
2	512 yards	par 5	11	138 yards	par 3
3	151 yards	par 3	12	475 yards	par 4
4	428 yards	par 4	13	273 yards	par 4
5	482 yards	par 5	14	488 yards	par 5
6	155 yards	par 3	15	462 yards	par 4
7	399 yards	par 4	16	195 yards	par 3
8	350 yards	par 4	17	437 yards	par 4
9	384 yards	par 4	18	533 yards	par 5
3,246 yards	par 36		3,452 yards	par 36	
Total 6,698 yards par 72					

The best-known holes are of course the 'antiques' – the 5th, or 'Klondyke', and the 6th, the 'Dell'. They remain as Old Tom left them. The 5th is a par-5 of 482 yards, with a drive into a narrow valley with high dunes on either side. The golfer is then faced with a ridge running across the fairway so that the green is completely invisible. This demands a long, blind shot over the ridge towards a fairly flat green. The 6th is a one-shot hole of 155 yards, with the green completely hidden from the tee. A large sand ridge covers the front of the green, another crosses the back, and the green, long and narrow and imprisoned between these ridges, is laid directly across the shot. This is another hit and hope shot – the blind shot still entirely fashionable in golf in the 1890s. When Mackenzie came to re-fashion the course in 1927 he may well have been appalled at what he saw, but he was firmly warned off. The powers in the club announced that these holes were part of the tradition of Lahinch, and they were to remain untouched.

The final Irishism of Lahinch is 'See goats', the sign on the broken barometer in the clubhouse. It seems that when the weather is bad, three ancient goats who have the run of the course will come in from the most distant point to the clubhouse and huddle close to the barometer at the slightest sign of rain. The goats are such reliable forecasters, so why would anyone think of repairing the barometer?

CHANTILLY

France is the doyen of golfing nations in Europe, with more clubs and more players than any other country on the Continent. The game there has an honourable history and there is some evidence, albeit slight, of golf in the Bordeaux area as early as 1767. The first club to be established in France was at Pau in the French Pyrenees, near the Spanish border. It is said that Scottish regiments were stationed there after the Peninsular War and that the Scottish Duke of Hamilton was a prime mover in forming the club in 1856. By 1869 the club had a professional, one Joe Lloyd from the Hoylake area, who may well have been the first British professional to work abroad, and by 1879 Pau had built 18 holes of golf.

Most of the early French courses emerged at coastal resorts – namely, Biarritz in 1888, Cannes in 1891, Valescure, at St Raphael in the south, in 1896 and Dieppe in 1897. Chantilly, the finest course in France, dates from 1908 and within five years it was staging the French Open Championship, which was won by George Duncan, who became Open Champion in 1920. Over the years some impressive names have followed Duncan's: Arnaud Massy, Henry Cotton, Roberto de Vicenzo (twice), Peter Oosterhuis and Nick Faldo have all become French Open champions at Chantilly.

The course is big, some 6,713 yards with a par of 71, and features three big par-5s, four rather stern par-3s (three of them over 200 yards) and no fewer than nine par-4s of more than 400 yards. The 8th and 9th are successive long holes; the 8th straight with forest all along the left side, a barrier of bunkers crossing the fairway at a critical point short of the green, and the green itself set deep in the trees; the 9th, at 460 yards, turns to the right with formidable bunkering in the corner, and, eventually, a not unreasonable opening to the green.

Chantilly is set in one of the great forests of the Ile de France, and there is a sense of splendid separation from the outside world. Moreover, there is a good deal of movement in the ground and, in spite of its lovely woodland, a large part of the course is open. The 1st hole, for example, at 464 yards, plays over a dip and the right, and open, side of its fairway

The 18th green, with the clubhouse and forest beyond, during the 1988 French Open. At 525 yards, the 18th is one of the longest finishing holes in championship golf.

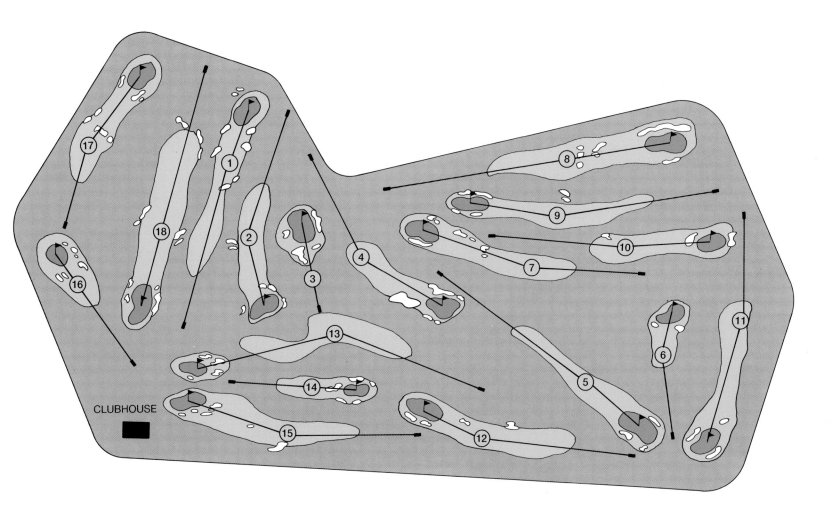

features several bunkers. The 2nd hole reverses direction and, although it turns to the left, it shares these bunkers with the first hole – there being only a narrow strip of rough between the two fairways.

On the other hand, the drive on the 4th is out of a high and narrow chute of trees – almost like the famous 18th at Augusta National. The 5th, in contrast has a completely open drive, then turns right and down a chute of trees to the green.

Chantilly's short holes are difficult, and demand very positive, precise striking. The 6th, for example, is completely screened by the forest. It is 217 yards to a green set diagonally across the shot, with bunkers front right and front left. Hole 14 is 202 yards to a green set in a little valley with two bunkers on either side; the 16th is exactly the same distance with no fewer than six bunkers scattered around it and for the majority of club members these holes demand wood shots off the tees.

Chantilly, 25 miles north of Paris, is in the heart of thoroughbred racecourse

The 14th at Chantilly, set in a tree-ringed oasis. At 202 yards it is the longest of Chantilly's par 3 holes, with a large, distracting central bunker short of the green.

CHANTILLY					
Card of the course					
1	464 yards	par 5	10	437 yards	par 4
2	327 yards	par 4	11	388 yards	par 4
3	153 yards	par 3	12	368 yards	par 4
4	359 yards	par 4	13	424 yards	par 4
5	410 yards	par 4	14	202 yards	par 3
6	217 yards	par 3	15	382 yards	par 4
7	396 yards	par 4	16	196 yards	par 3
8	576 yards	par 5	17	429 yards	par 4
9	460 yards	par 4	18	525 yards	par 5
3,362 yards par 36			3,361 yards par 35		
Total 6,713 yards par 71					

country, like Olgiata (q.v.) in Rome, and it is difficult to resist calling it a thoroughbred among golf courses. Indeed, it does seem to have many of the characteristics of the courses around Ascot in England – the Berkshire, Swinley Forest, Sunningdale and Wentworth. However, despite the similarities, it undoubtedly stands on its own as one of the world's greats.

ROYAL ANTWERP

Golf in Belgium is aristocratic, of course, as it always has been on the Continent – with the exception of the resort golf that has sprung up along the coasts of Spain and Portugal. In fact, it is more than aristocratic, as Belgian golf has had the direct support of a royal family that has included active golfers for several generations. In 1906, for example, King Leopold II donated land and a country house to make possible the founding of the Royal Belgique Club at Ravenstein, near Brussels. Moreover, Leopold III was very keen and played to a high standard, while King Baudouin played his golf at the Royal Antwerp club, under the name of the Comte de Rethy, to a standard good enough to secure selection for the Belgian amateur international team.

Of Belgium's score of golf clubs, almost half of them have the 'Royal' prefix. However, no privilege is involved – when a club celebrates its 50th anniversary it qualifies automatically. Despite having no more than 5,000 golfers, this small country has some outstanding courses and the finest of these is Royal Antwerp, one of Europe's greatest courses. Founded in 1888 by six English businessmen resident in the city – then as now a huge trading post – it is the second oldest club in Europe after Pau in the French Pyrenees. Willie Park, Jr was responsible for the original 18 holes. But in 1924, Tom Simpson and Philip Mackenzie Ross, who were then in partnership, revised the 18 and added nine more.

The Royal Antwerp course is set in gorgeous woodland about 12 miles from the city. The club moved to this location after its original site – on part of an army training ground – had proved less than satisfactory. It is a beautiful piece of heathland reminiscent of Sunningdale; this means sandy subsoil, links-type turf, heather and pine and silver birch. But unlike Sunningdale, Royal Antwerp is virtually flat. However, mounding has been used here and there in the best St Andrews style.

The course plays to 7,026 yards, with a par of 73, and has several interesting

ROYAL ANTWERP Card of the course					
1	331 yards	par 4	10	416 yards	par 4
2	203 yards	par 3	11	483 yards	par 5
3	480 yards	par 5	12	183 yards	par 3
4	380 yards	par 4	13	398 yards	par 4
5	476 yards	par 5	14	477 yards	par 5
6	424 yards	par 4	15	492 yards	par 5
7	185 yards	par 3	16	146 yards	par 3
8	418 yards	par 4	17	377 yards	par 4
9	448 yards	par 4	18	394 yards	par 4
3,345 yards		par 36	3,681 yards		par 37
Total 7,026 yards par 73					

design features. It has five par-5s, all of them on the short side, under 500 yards, and two of them, 14 and 15, coming in succession. Almost all the par-4s are strong holes, demanding a good range of approach iron shots, while the four par-3s become progressively shorter – from the 2nd at 203 yards, with a pair of bunkers on the left close to the line into the green, to the 16th at 146 yards, a short pop to a small green almost entirely ringed with bunkers.

However, generally there is a notice-

Willie Park, Jr, British Open champion in 1887 and 1889, was also a consummate architect of golf courses. He designed the original 18 holes at Antwerp.

able lack of fairway bunkering at Royal Antwerp. Perhaps Simpson and Mackenzie Ross felt them to be scarcely necessary, considering the severity of the dog-legs they built into their fairways. This is a characteristic of Simpson's design work. There is one stretch, through the heart of the course from the 6th to the 14th, where each fairway breaks quite sharply, two to the right, five to the left. In this sequence there are two lovely short holes, the 7th with the ground in front of the green feeding the ball towards a bunker on the right, and the 12th, at 183 yards, protected by three bunkers, thereby putting a premium on accurate striking. Yet Royal Antwerp is not overly restricting and its woodland is neither intrusive nor claustrophobic. Altogether it is a delightful, mature, even sophisticated golf course of great charm.

Tom Simpson, in partnership with Philip Mackenzie Ross, revised the original 18 holes and added nine more. Simpson was a great believer in the dog-leg hole to which the 9th, 10th and 14th bear witness.

FALSTERBO

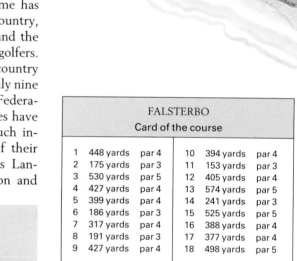

Falsterbo Golf Club is situated 21 miles south of Malmö, on a little finger of land prodding into the sea at Skanör, about as far south as you can go in Sweden. Just a few miles across the waters of the Öresund lies Denmark. There are three golf clubs in the area, the most famous of them being Falsterbo – a course that is almost pure links. Laid out on a flat piece of ground surrounding the old Falsterbo lighthouse, all but a few of the holes are on sandy soil, and a few (4, 5, 11 and 12) are on more marshy ground on the inland side of the course. The entire area is a nature reserve and is particularly blessed with bird life.

The course dates from 1909, when Gunnar Bauer laid out a sequence of holes which is little changed today. However, Falsterbo is not the oldest course in Sweden, a country which was slower than most in Europe – perhaps because of harsh winters and a short season – to take up the game of golf.

In the last two decades, however, golf in Sweden has exploded. The game has grown out of the affluence of the country, the ample spaces it has to spare and the international successes of its golfers. While Sweden is the third largest country in Europe, it has a population of only nine million. Yet the Swedish Golf Federation's coaching and support policies have brought their amateur players much international success, and several of their young professionals, notably Mats Lanner, Ove Sellberg, Magnus Persson and

FALSTERBO Card of the course					
1	448 yards	par 4	10	394 yards	par 4
2	175 yards	par 3	11	153 yards	par 3
3	530 yards	par 5	12	405 yards	par 4
4	427 yards	par 4	13	574 yards	par 5
5	399 yards	par 4	14	241 yards	par 3
6	186 yards	par 3	15	525 yards	par 5
7	317 yards	par 4	16	388 yards	par 4
8	191 yards	par 3	17	377 yards	par 4
9	427 yards	par 4	18	498 yards	par 5
	3,100 yards	par 34		3,555 yards	par 37
		Total 6,655 yards par 71			

Anders Forsbrand, have been successful on the PGA European Tour. Major professional tournaments are now played annually in Sweden and recently the Volvo company has taken on the overall sponsorship of the European Professional Tour.

Falsterbo is almost completely exposed. There are few trees on the course, and those that are there have little influence on the play. The 1st hole requires that the golfer is ready and warmed up, for it is a

Taken from the lighthouse in the centre of the course, this picture shows the clubhouse, the 7th and 18th greens in front of it, and the open and exposed nature of the location.

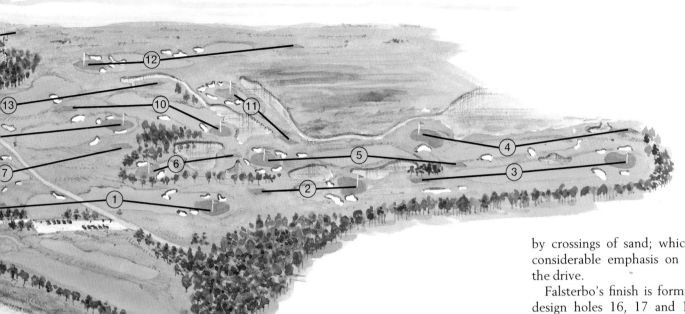

next five holes. The 11th and 12th return briefly to marshland. The 11th, at 153 yards, is a strike over the waters of an inlet all the way from tee to green, with water to the right of the green and five bunkers, no less, covering the rest of it. The 12th, at 405 yards, features two fairway 'islands' in the Pine Valley mode, separated by crossings of sand; which thus places considerable emphasis on the length of the drive.

Falsterbo's finish is formidable, and in design holes 16, 17 and 18 follow the classic oceanside layout – tee hard by the beach, fairway drifting inland then turning back, right in each case, to a green set, like the tee, hard by the beach. Each of the fairways is carefully bunkered at the angle, and each of the greens by the beach is carefully bunkered to protect the hole and distract the golfer.

stiff 448 yards, with a turn to (and an out-of-bounds) on the right, and a fairly tight entrance to the green. The 2nd is a pretty 175 yards to a small green with surrounding bunkers, but the 3rd is a long slog of 530 yards, straight out into the country. The feature here is a very large bunker placed exactly at the centre front of the green, on the premise that the shot arriving will be a high pitch – the golfer's third. For the professional player, reaching the green in two and coping with that bunker will be something of a lottery!

Holes 4 and 5 come back in the opposite direction; the 4th green being set rather close to water, the rough hereabouts being marshy reed grass. On the short 6th we are back in true heather and sand country, and stay with it for the

The 18th green and behind it the dominating feature of the course – the lighthouse. The only true linksland course in Sweden, Falsterbo is one of the finest on the Continent.

CLUB ZUR VAHR

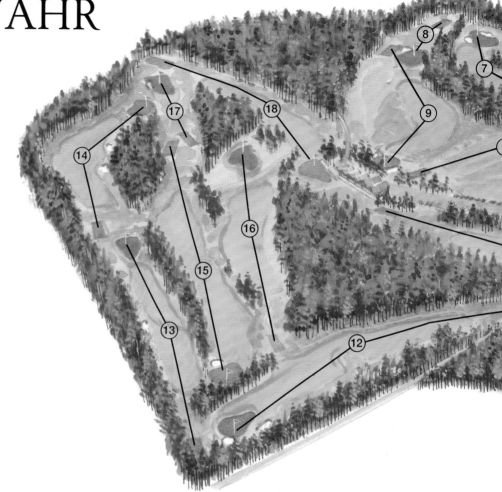

Without being overly romantic, the Garlstedter Heide course of the Club Zur Vahr in Bremen is positively Wagnerian. Indeed, it may just be the best and most powerful course on the Continent of Europe. It stretches 7,265 yards, with a par of 74, is cut through a forest of huge pine and silver birch, and is a magnificent test of driving and longshot golf. At Garlstedt, it is not enough to drive in the fairway – the drive must be long enough to clear the angle of the many dog-legs, and it must be on the correct **side** of the fairway to allow a decent second shot. While there are few fairway bunkers, trees crowd to the very edge of the fairway and are very much an integral part of the course.

The course is part of the Club Zur Vahr, an excellent multi-sports club offering two golf courses, tennis, hockey, skeet-shooting and the like. Its origins are in a few holes played in 1895 on the racecourse at Vahr, a suburb of Bremen, the great international trading port. Foreign businessmen with local merchants teamed up to bring golf to the city, and it became part of the club in 1905. A team from Bremen had played a Berlin team in 1899 in one of the first German inter-city matches, and when Agnes Boecker von

The approach to the green of the long 2nd hole, with the pond and oak tree in the middle of the fairway. Ideally, the tee shot should finish short of the stream immediately in front of the pond.

Kapff won the Danish Ladies' Championship in 1901, she became the first German golfer to hold an international title. In 1921, Dr Bernhard von Limburger won the German Amateur title at the Vahr, which still had only nine holes.

In 1945, the U.S. Army commandeered the course, but the golfers won it back in 1952 and within a few years the membership had grown so much that another course was essential. The local Weyhausen family, notably August Weyhausen who had been German Junior Champion back in 1924, found the land at Garlstedter Heide, 20 km from Bremen on the road to Bremerhaven, and Limburger, an outstanding architect and player, was put to work.

The course was officially opened in 1970, and staged its first German Open in 1971, attracting an impressive field from 23 different countries, and including Peter Thomson, Roberto de Vicenzo, Bernard Gallacher, Peter Oosterhuis, Neil Coles and many others. The cham-

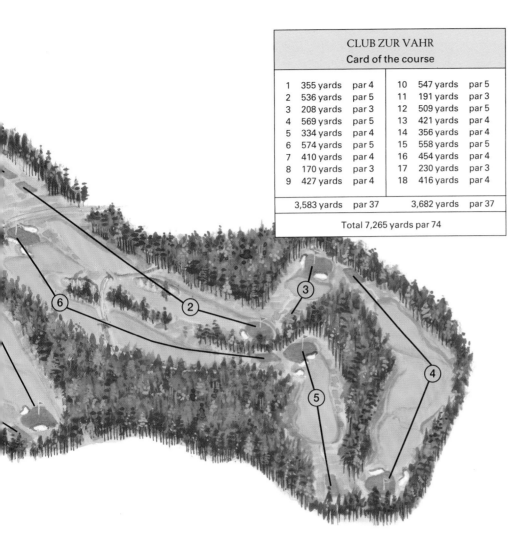

CLUB ZUR VAHR						
Card of the course						
1	355 yards	par 4		10	547 yards	par 5
2	536 yards	par 5		11	191 yards	par 3
3	208 yards	par 3		12	509 yards	par 5
4	569 yards	par 5		13	421 yards	par 4
5	334 yards	par 4		14	356 yards	par 4
6	574 yards	par 5		15	558 yards	par 5
7	410 yards	par 4		16	454 yards	par 4
8	170 yards	par 3		17	230 yards	par 3
9	427 yards	par 4		18	416 yards	par 4
	3,583 yards	par 37			3,682 yards	par 37
	Total 7,265 yards par 74						

fairway and a pond to the left of it. Playing boldly down the left side, to the left of the tree, will see the expert player within reach of the green in two. However, playing to the right will put him out of range. At the 6th, of 574 yards, the stream crosses the fairway again, the hole turning to the right. The player can play down the fairway in two shots, then reach the green to the right with a pitch over two bunkers covering the entrance. The alternative is to cut across the angle with his second shot, leaving a completely open line into the green. But to do that, he would have to carry over a wood!

Over the years, the sophisticated German golfers may have felt that Bremen is less accessible for championships than, say, Munich or Frankfurt. However, their Open was played there in 1975 and again in 1985. During the latter, a rainstorm flooded the course, the championship was reduced to 54 holes, the par to 66, and one kilometre was chopped off the length of the course! But all was well in the end – the winner scoring 183 – 15 under the par of the truncated course – and his name was Bernhard Langer!

West Germany's golfing superstar Bernhard Langer in action at Club Zur Vahr. He won the German Open Championship at Zur Vahr in 1985, when the tournament was reduced to 15 holes because of rain.

pionship was won by Coles with an outstanding score of 279, seventeen strokes under par, and Coles said afterwards: 'I would rate it one of the best championship courses I have played in Europe – altogether an excellent test, forcing you right to the limit all the way'. Over the four days, 6,000 spectators attended – a record at the time for a tournament in Germany.

Almost every hole on the course, save for the 1st, plays into, out of, around, across or over trees, or one single tree. Perhaps Limburger's par-5s – there are six of them – are the most fascinating of the holes; two of them almost avant-garde! The 2nd, at 536 yards, has forest hard down its left side. A stream crosses the fairway just beyond 300 yards and past that there is a tree in the middle of the

OLGIATA

With a population of around 55 million, Italy has less than 20,000 golfers, in comparison to the UK's approximately two million players. Moreover, the question arises as to just how many Italian club members actually play golf, and how many are club members for purely social reasons. In Italian society at all levels, perhaps more so than anywhere else in Europe, style is everything. Thus, and not surprisingly, the old game, with its plebian Scottish ancestry, is elevated to a patrician pastime – and the Olgiata club manifests this as much as any other.

Olgiata is set in pleasantly rolling, heavily-wooded country off the Via Cassia, 12 miles to the north of Rome. The course design and the long, low but spacious clubhouse maintain an aura of Roman elegance. The course is the work of Ken Cotton and Frank Pennink, the English designers, and an interesting pair they make. Cotton was a Cambridge graduate, a scratch golfer and secretary to various golf clubs before founding, in 1946, the golf design firm which became Cotton (CK), Pennink, Lawrie and Partners. He designed the Venice course in 1958, worked in Denmark and Singapore, and made several changes to Royal

The Spanish team of José Rivero and José-Maria Canizares flank the modest World Cup trophy after their victory over a rain-soaked Olgiata in 1984. The tournament was reduced to 54 holes.

OLGIATA
Card of the course

1	377 yards	par 4	10	396 yards	par 4
2	212 yards	par 3	11	431 yards	par 4
3	465 yards	par 4	12	427 yards	par 4
4	399 yards	par 4	13	430 yards	par 4
5	487 yards	par 5	14	170 yards	par 3
6	427 yards	par 4	15	503 yards	par 5
7	195 yards	par 3	16	202 yards	par 3
8	377 yards	par 4	17	520 yards	par 5
9	552 yards	par 5	18	427 yards	par 4
3,491 yards	**par 36**		**3,506 yards**	**par 36**	
Total 6,997 yards par 72					

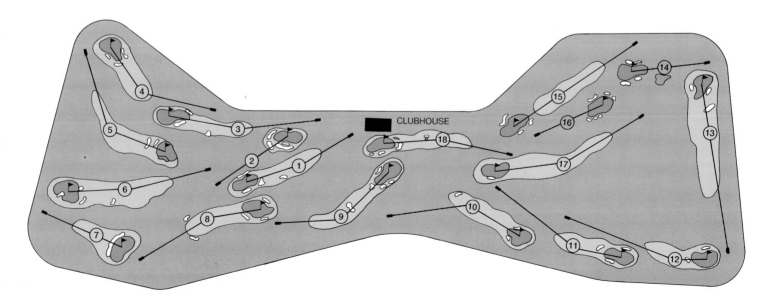

Lytham and Royal Porthcawl.

Pennink was a graduate of Oxford, won the English Amateur Championship twice and was an England international and a Walker Cup player. He had a remarkable career. For many years he concentrated on the 'overseas' commissions of the firm, working mainly outside the UK. He has a surprisingly substantial body of work to his credit and was one of the busiest international designers. One of his finest achievements, with Charles Lawrie, is the Duke's Course at Woburn, in England. He also designed both courses at Vilamoura in the Algarve, in 1969 and 1975, as well as the excellent Palmares, in 1975. And he made changes to three Royals: Liverpool (Hoylake), Lytham and St Annes and St George's.

At Olgiata Pennink and Cotton created a fine, big, mature parkland course of 6,997 yards. And within three years of its opening in 1961, the World Amateur Team championship for the Eisenhower Trophy was played there (won by Great Britain), and in 1967, the Canada Cup – which subsequently became the World Cup – was won by Al Balding and George Knudson for Canada. Balding was winner of the Individual Trophy with an aggregate of 271, 17 under par, on a course with the fire taken out of it by a good deal of rain. In 1984, Olgiata staged the World Cup again, which this time was won by Spain.

Typical of Cotton/Pennink designs are the squeezed landing zones for drives, flanked by bunkers or trees on either side of the fairway. Thus at the 4th, which turns to the right, trees standing tight on the corner push the drive to the left; and the 6th hole, at 427 yards, has a big bunker filling the left half of the fairway at the critical distance. The 8th, at 377 yards, affords the perfect example of bunkers on each side of the fairway, equidistant, squeezing it into a narrow waist. The 11th, 12th and 13th call for tee shots up to raised fairways, and the 12th green is built up and protected by a very narrow entrance. The 15th at 503 yards is one of Olgiata's few straight holes, and 17 and 18 again illustrate the Cotton/Pennink penchant for squeezing the drive with trees and/or bunkers.

Olgiata's outward and inward halves run out and back to the clubhouse, giving the course a long rectangular shape and making the golfer tackle the prevailing wind and weather from changing directions. All told, this is a splendid course that offers a tough and varied challenge in a lovely and elegant environment.

The 16th is a longish one-shotter to a green defended by bunkers on each side. Here José-Maria Olazábal threads his tee shot between the encroaching timber in the 1989 Italian Open.

SOTOGRANDE

Sotogrande, at the western end of the Costa del Sol in Spain, and within sight of Gibraltar, was the first course in Europe to be designed by Robert Trent Jones, the outstanding architect of his time – perhaps of all time. Faced with a property of sand and scrub, wooded with cork and olive trees, which ran gently uphill away from the Mediterranean beach, Jones promptly built an 'American' golf course. That at any rate was the collective critical judgement of the hour when the course came into play in 1965.

Jones had won himself a huge reputation as a golf course architect. Born in England in 1906, he had been taken to America at the age of five, and by 1980, when he was still active, had amassed an enormous body of work – more than 400 courses in 24 countries. His courses featured very long tees, sometimes up to 80 yards, which he said gave the hole 'flexibility'. And he built huge greens, often multi-tiered, with five or six pin positions. Jones planned these pin positions into his designs as targets within the target, and one suspects he always had the great champions in mind when doing it. His

creed, expressed in one sentence, was to: 'Make it difficult for the expert to score a birdie and easy for the club player to score a bogey'. In addition, he was addicted to water hazards: thousands of cubic yards of rock and soil were excavated to make lakes, and he then used the material to make ridges and mounds. He felt that as players attacked the course, it was the architect's duty to defend it. As has been seen at Oakland Hills (q.v.), in 1951, this attitude drew the wrath of Ben Hogan, and probably many others as well.

As his fame grew, Jones' designs became more comprehensive, more expensive, and he became more and more renowned. At Sotogrande, his first problem was to grow and preserve grass in the fierce Andalusian summers. Given an ample water supply and an automatic watering system, and with sunshine and high temperatures guaranteed, Jones ex-

Sotogrande's 10th green, ringed around by five bunkers, illustrates as much as anything how expensive property developments crowd in on these courses along the Spanish coasts.

perimented and eventually decided on a strain of Bermuda grass imported from the U.S. for the fairways, while opting for 'bent' grass on the greens. Jones' success in growing grass in the local climate helped to make possible the development of the game on the Costa del Sol.

The extensive watering necessary meant that the course would 'play American' – that is, the greens would always hold the ball, and thus approach shots had to be hit firmly to the flag. The 3rd hole illustrates this clearly. It is 339 yards, a drive up towards a pair of bunkers, then a half turn left for a simple pitch. But the green is shamrock-shaped, each leaf of it covered by a bunker, thus giving a variety

SOTOGRANDE					
Card of the course					
1	394 yards	par 4	10	453 yards	par 4
2	527 yards	par 5	11	373 yards	par 4
3	339 yards	par 4	12	582 yards	par 5
4	235 yards	par 3	13	214 yards	par 3
5	361 yards	par 4	14	503 yards	par 5
6	517 yards	par 5	15	426 yards	par 4
7	422 yards	par 4	16	388 yards	par 4
8	199 yards	par 3	17	174 yards	par 3
9	363 yards	par 4	18	440 yards	par 4
3,357 yards		par 36	3,553 yards		par 36
Total 6,910 yards par 72					

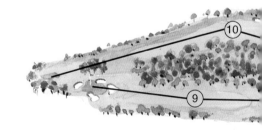

of very tight pin placements.

The first illustration of Jones' severe use of water comes at the 422-yard 7th. The second shot is slightly uphill along a narrow fairway, dog-legged left, and requiring a medium iron. The green is long and narrow, sloping from left to right down to a lake hard by its right side and supported by two right-hand bunkers. There is another bunker at the back left, under the trees, to catch a shot that is overlong. The target here is desperately tight, the margins meagre and the penalties severe.

Water is in play on at least five holes in the inward half. It is as if Jones had had visions of his work at the Augusta National! Whether he did or he didn't we will never know. But what is certain is that at Sotogrande Jones produced a beautiful and significant course.

Another illustration of Trent Jones' harsh use of water is the spectacular 7th at Sotogrande. The green, long and narrow, slopes left to right towards bunkers and lake. The hole is 422 yards, the approach shot a mid-iron.

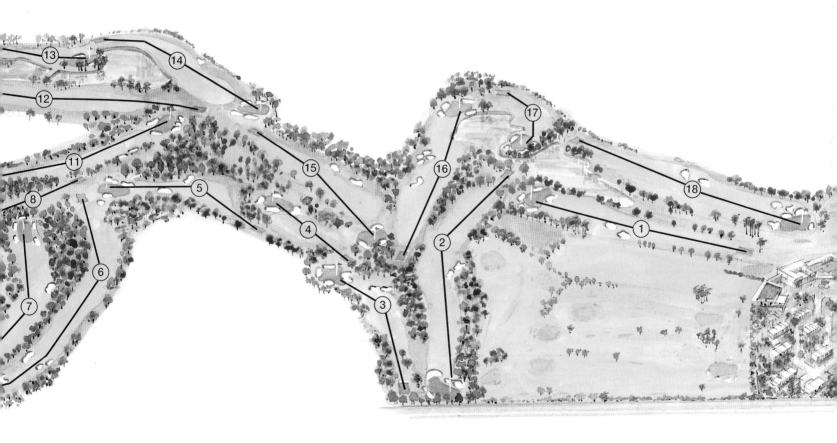

LAS BRISAS

Las Brisas follows on naturally from Sotogrande, opening as it did in 1968. Set in a valley that flows down towards Puerto Banus, a few miles from Marbella, it was a natural progression for Robert Trent Jones in Spain, and contains many of the Sotogrande/Jones features. Yet it is altogether more dramatic, more spectacular and more punishing than Sotogrande – with, for example, typical Jones' greens, which some critics have dismissed as 'unputtable'.

In the wide valley that runs out of the Sierra Blanca, with the peak of La Concha towering over the course, Jones has excavated a water course which dominates the entire golf course. It provides narrow streams, broad streams, lakes, water hazards, lateral water hazards and canals that cross directly in front of putting surfaces to snare the ball that is fractionally short. There are, needless to say, other Jones autographs: notably, large greens with fiercely contoured slopes, huge and evil bunkering and the use of crushed marble in the bunkers, making a silvery contrast with the lush green of fairways and greens.

The clubhouse at the top of the property looks out over a descending and fairly open course; save at its lowest point, where the 12th and 13th fairways run down and the 14th and 15th run back in parallel, to form an arrowhead pointing at the sea. Here, there was deliberate planting of orange trees, olives and eucalyptus, to separate the holes and channel them into narrow fairways.

The famous 12th at Las Brisas, where architect Robert Trent Jones' penchant for the use of water is perfectly demonstrated. No matter how he tackles the hole, the golfer must twice cross a broad stream.

Jones introduces us to the water hazards at the very first hole, allowing a little spur from the main stream on the left to sneak across close to the front of the green. The 2nd hole is 425 yards, with an out-of-bounds along the right and two bunkers and some trees nipping-in the landing zone for the drive. The second shot is uphill to a positively elevated green, with five unfriendly bunkers and a very fierce slope from back to front. A downhill putt of any length is not at all certain to stay on the putting surface – vintage Jones!

The 6th requires a short pitch over a water channel and a front bunker, and there is water close to the left of the green. The 7th is the second of the four par-3 holes; the 4th and the 7th being land-locked, the two others being over water. The 8th and 12th holes are fine examples of Jones' notion of strategic

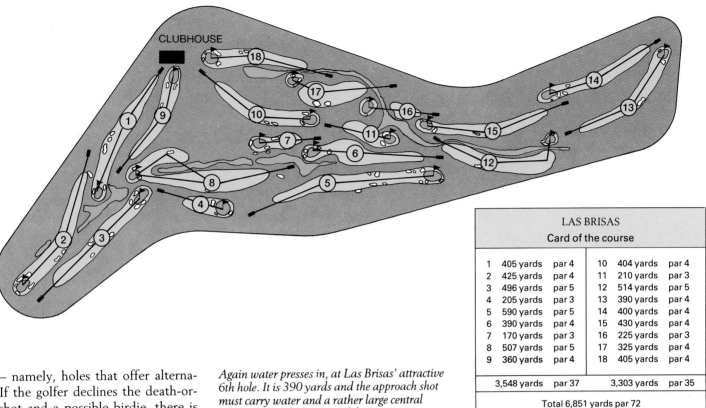

CLUBHOUSE

LAS BRISAS				
	Card of the course			
1	405 yards	par 4	10	404 yards par 4
2	425 yards	par 4	11	210 yards par 3
3	496 yards	par 5	12	514 yards par 5
4	205 yards	par 3	13	390 yards par 4
5	590 yards	par 5	14	400 yards par 4
6	390 yards	par 4	15	430 yards par 4
7	170 yards	par 3	16	225 yards par 3
8	507 yards	par 5	17	325 yards par 4
9	360 yards	par 4	18	405 yards par 4
3,548 yards		**par 37**	**3,303 yards**	**par 35**
Total 6,851 yards par 72				

Again water presses in, at Las Brisas' attractive 6th hole. It is 390 yards and the approach shot must carry water and a rather large central bunker short of the centre of the green.

holes – namely, holes that offer alternatives. If the golfer declines the death-or-glory shot and a possible birdie, there is always a 'roundabout' route which will get him there comfortably, if at the cost of an additional stroke.

Both the 8th and 12th are par-5s. At the 8th, the drive is over a stream, which continues up the right side of a clear and ample fairway. The green is back across the water, as is a spinney of trees some way short of it. The heroic shot would be aimed over the water to the left of these trees, directly at the green. The roundabout route would be over the water to the right of the trees, followed by a pitch to the putting surface. The 12th, at 514 yards, offers much the same challenge. The drive is over a stream, which this time runs along the left side, bulging into the fairway from time to time. The right side of the fairway is open, save for bunkering set to catch the over-long or faded drive. As a three-shot hole, the 12th is simple – another one along the fairway, keeping the water on the left, then a pitch across to an entirely undefended green on the other side of the water. The heroic route directly to the green, however, demands an immense shot, along and over the stream, and across a bunker by the green which Jones has placed directly on the line of flight.

The man has sometimes been considered impish to the point of being evil, and the 16th hole shows why. It is perhaps the ultimate Robert Trent Jones hole. Before it, 13, 14 and 15 are stiff, dog-legged, two-shot holes running through narrow alleyways of trees. The 16th, on the other hand, is par-3 225 yards, with the green positioned above the tee, and sloping wickedly towards the shot. Water lies at the front of the green and huge bunkers are on either side, creating difficult pin positions. This is a fearsome hole – holding the shot on the green is a major achievement – and typical of a magnificent and dramatic course that has been good enough to have held the Spanish Open and the World Cup.

VILAMOURA

When the English architect Frank Pennink was invited to design the first Vilamoura course on the Algarve in Portugal, it was to be part of a huge property and leisure development covering 4,000 acres and which, on completion, would be virtually self-contained with its own farm, airstrip, equestrian centre, marina and so on. The course was opened in 1969, at the end of a decade which had seen the opening of Faro airport and the first explosion of mass tourism on the Algarve. For the Portuguese, it was a time of much optimism. The revolution of 1974, and the years of economic instability which followed, were not foreseen. They did, however, arrive and Vilamoura stood still for a while. Now older, it boasts a second course, an impressive marina, luxury hotels and substantial and on-going property development.

Vilamoura was the third course in the Algarve, after Penina and Vale do Lobo,

both designed by Henry Cotton. Pennink was given a brief to make a championship course of the quality of the better Surrey or Berkshire courses, and given a forest of umbrella pines, a few miles back from the sea, in which to do it. The plot was distinguished by a ridge – a spine – running through its centre, as though it was a transplanted King's from Gleneagles, and Pennink made the most of it, fashioning a lovely and very testing course.

Vilamoura has a par of 73 and is 6,921 yards long. The umbrella pines and cork trees are very much part of it and part of the players' interrogation. They define the margins of every fairway, encroach where necessary and, in some places, one solitary

This shot of the 9th at Vilamoura, a short par-4 of 297 yards, illustrates how the architect Pennink has squeezed the driving zone, his severe bunkering and his use of a distracting single tree on the left.

tree is positioned to affect the line of the shot. Under the trees there is no rough to speak of, nothing but beds of fallen pine needles which absorb the energy from the clubhead when recovery shots are tried. Thus, for the most part chipping out to the fairway is the most intelligent recovery shot.

Yet the trees add greatly to the pleasures of a round at Vilamoura. The umbrella pines are intrinsically lovely. They give each hole a pleasant feeling of isolation, of being divorced from care in the pleasant Portuguese sunshine. And from the top of the course there is the unexpected vista, from time to time, across the tops of this umbrella-like forest to the sea.

Pennink's greens are rather small, and although he is sparing with fairway bunkers, and certainly never uses any simply for cosmetic effect, he does tend to lavish them around the greens. This is particularly important at the par-3 holes. The

VILAMOURA Card of the course			
1	296 yards par 4	10	176 yards par 3
2	494 yards par 5	11	429 yards par 4
3	364 yards par 4	12	536 yards par 5
4	168 yards par 3	13	393 yards par 4
5	455 yards par 4	14	504 yards par 5
6	234 yards par 3	15	168 yards par 3
7	433 yards par 4	16	570 yards par 5
8	469 yards par 4	17	393 yards par 4
9	297 yards par 4	18	542 yards par 5
3,210 yards par 35		**3,711 yards par 38**	
Total 6,921 yards par 73			

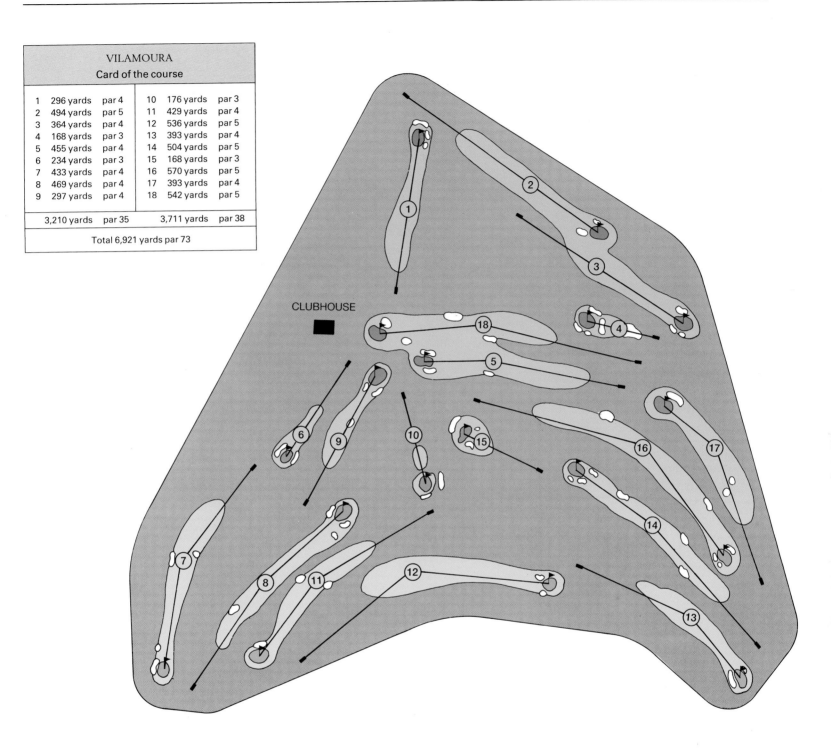

CLUBHOUSE

4th, at 168 yards, is immensely difficult for a hole of that length. The shot is over a lake, a handful of trees insinuate themselves from the right, almost cutting off the line, and the rather turtle-backed green has bunkers left and behind. The 10th at 176 yards seems unprotected, but an unseen depression – a Portuguese Valley of Sin – lies in front of the green. Anything slightly overhit here will be in the trees.

There are two very short par-4s on the outward half. The 1st, at 296 yards, is a downhill dogleg to the left, and the 9th, at 297 yards, is uphill. The temptation to go for the big drive on each of them is hard to resist, but very dangerous. Two trees in the fairway at the 9th, for example, push the drive to the left of the line. Indeed trees are used in this fashion at holes 7, 8, 9, 16 and 17. The inward half, with four par-5 holes, is very testing.

The 16th, at 570 yards, is a great hole which turns to the right from the tee with the landing area constricted by a rather big bunker on the left and trees coming out into the fairway on the right. The green, slightly downhill, is all but smothered by two of Pennink's biggest bunkers. All told, an outstanding golf hole and an outstanding golf course – but if you cannot drive the ball straight you had better stay at home!

REST OF THE WORLD

The old game, which spread from Scotland to England in the second half of the 19th century, was packed in the baggage of regiments and administrators sent abroad in the service of Empire. The Scottish regiment, The Black Watch, was largely responsible for the creation of Lahinch, the stupendous Irish links. Another Highland regiment, the Argyll and Sutherland Highlanders, with the Royal Engineers, started golf in Hong Kong. Sir James Fergusson, the Scottish governor of South Australia, brought golf to Adelaide in 1869.

Thus by the turn of the century, many clubs had been formed in South Africa, India (Royal Calcutta was the first club outside Britain, in 1829), Australia and New Zealand. They followed, by and large, the British pattern of being golf clubs only, no matter how well-appointed, rather than the ornate, all-embracing 'country club', which was favoured and developed in the U.S.

The development of golf in Japan has been phenomenal. It developed first from the long U.S. military occupation of the country following the Second World War and second, from the remarkable triumph of home professionals 'Pete' Nakamura and Kiochi Ono in the Canada (now World) Cup event of 1957. It brought golf in Japan bounding into the 20th century. Now millions of Japanese play or follow the game. Japan is a leader in the manufacture of golf clubs and balls. So precious is land in Japan that architects and constructors literally move mountains to build courses, and the game is enormously expensive.

The 18th green and fairway of one of Japan's foremost clubs, Fujioka. The Japanese attention to detail is very evident in the manicured quality of the course.

KASUMIGASEKI

The first course of the Kasumigaseki Golf Club, some 25 miles from Tokyo, was opened in 1929. It was 'reborn' in 1957, when it was the venue for probably the most significant sports event ever held in the Far East, with greater consequences even than the Tokyo Olympics of 1960, or the Seoul Olympics of 1988 – namely, the Canada Cup tournament, which was won for the first time by Japan. Ever since then, Kasumigaseki has been the most famous club in the country.

Japan's victory in the Canada Cup,

Canada Cup 1957. From right: Torakichi ('Pete') Nakamura and Koichi Ono (winners), Frank Pace, Jr (IGA President) and Dave Thomas and Dai Rees of Wales. The Japanese pair were the only players to master the course.

more recently named the World Cup, made national heroes of its players, Torakichi 'Pete' Nakamura and Koichi Ono, and sparked off a golfing boom that has continued ever since. Now there may be as many as 10 million golfers in a total population of 100 million! The Japan Golf Association has registered 1,500,000 players and 1,300 courses, but many more 'play' only at driving ranges, such is the shortage of courses because of lack of land. Sadly, only the well-to-do can afford to pay, with the average price of a club membership standing at more than

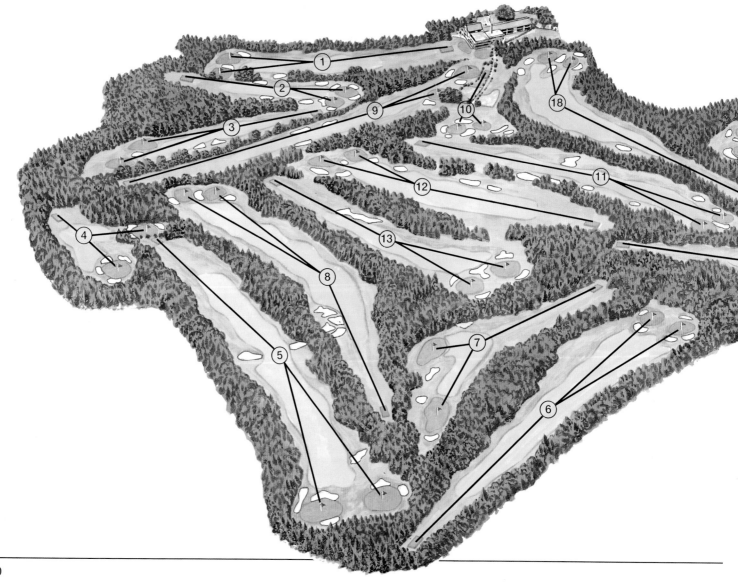

£100,000. This means that most memberships are held by corporations and are regarded as investments. Indeed, there is now a market in these memberships, with 50 traders buying and selling in Tokyo and Osaka. It is all a far cry from the economics of golf in Scotland!

Kinya Fujita's Vision

Nakamura and Ono are responsible for all of this. They conquered the world of golf – the U.S. team was Sam Snead and Jimmy Demaret, and players of the calibre of Gary Player, Roberto de Vicenzo and Dave Thomas were in the field – and they did it through their putting. Nakamura with 274 was 14 under par, Ono with 283 was five under par, and the rest, on the greens, were nowhere. And thereby hangs a tale, a tale of the two-green golf hole and the Japanese talent for lateral thinking.

The Kasumigaseki course was designed

Scotland's Eric Brown tees off at the 1st hole during the 1957 Canada Cup. Kasumigaseki's decorative trees, shrubs and flowers receive the same devoted attention as the greens and fairways.

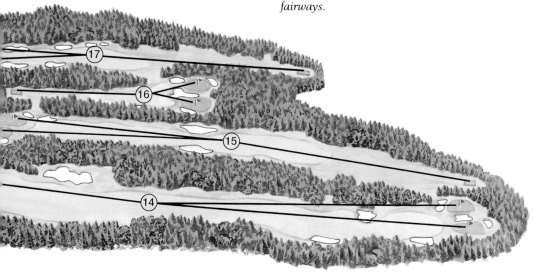

by Kinya Fujita, of a wealthy banking family and a graduate student at the Universities of Chicago and Columbia. He spent some time in America with a silk-importing business, then back in Japan he met Hugh Alison, who was laying out the Tokyo Golf Club course in 1914. Fujita, a talented golfer, became intrigued with course design, and after the war, in 1919, travelled to Britain to study design techniques. Back again in Japan, he organised the Kasumigaseki club and laid out the course. It opened in 1929, but within a couple of years Fujita called Alison in to make a few changes. He introduced some deep bunkering –

KASUMIGASEKI			
Card of the course			
1	388 yards par 4	10	180 yards par 3
2	374 yards par 4	11	433 yards par 4
3	422 yards par 4	12	468 yards par 4
4	158 yards par 3	13	375 yards par 4
5	532 yards par 5	14	593 yards par 5
6	372 yards par 4	15	433 yards par 4
7	220 yards par 3	16	173 yards par 3
8	474 yards par 4	17	349 yards par 4
9	532 yards par 5	18	483 yards par 5
3,472 yards par 36		3,487 yards par 36	
Total 6,959 yards par 72			

which the Japanese had never seen – and to this day, they call a deep bunker an 'Arison'.

The extremes of the Japanese climate created problems on the greens. During the cold season, rye and bent grasses, such as are used in Great Britain and the northern states of America, were fine in Japan, but they could not survive the hot summers – they simply withered away. Korai grass, a stronger version of Bermuda grass, is dormant in winter, but thrives during the hot weather. Its blade is broader, tougher and sharper than its bent grass counterpart, and it is ideal for fairways. The ball sits-up on its spiky points offering a perfect lie. Run your palm over Korai grass and you feel as though it is cutting you. However, on the greens it is the devil to putt. When the pace starts to leave a putt and the line of the ball starts to break, the grain in the Korai grass will make the ball turn to such an extent that on a longer putt the ball will be rolling at right angles to its original line! Korai grain simply goes in all directions. The wily orientals had the world by the tail. Nakamura and Ono knew Korai grass backwards!

Two Greens

To solve this 'problem', the Japanese simply built two greens for each hole – one for winter use, one for summer use. The greens are invariably side by side, although sometimes one behind the other. They share the common drive, then the second shot will be slightly to the right or slightly to the left, depending on which green is in play. This has had an obvious effect on Japanese golf architecture; many holes featuring a bunker or mound to the left of the left hand green, a bunker or mound to the right of the right hand green and a bunker or mounds, or both, separating the greens, but common to both, as it were. All of this, plus the scarcity of good land and the consequent use of hilly or inferior plots, has done little for design and there has been some uninspired course construction. Japanese laws have been very protective of agricultural land, and golf course designers have often had to work with rather banal terrain.

Kasumigaseki, in contrast, was built on

Above: *The 10th has alternative tees, ponds and greens, divided by a line of trees. This is the view from the right-hand tee to a green formidably bunkered at front, back and sides.*

Left: *Kasumigaseki's huge clubhouse, behind the 9th green on the East Course. The picture also illustrates the deep 'Arison' bunker, and the well turned-out caddie, Japanese style.*

View from behind the 10th hole to the tee. This 180-yard par 3 is one of the finest in Asia.

nicely rolling farmland before these restrictions existed. It is also pleasantly wooded. A second course has been built to cope with its 2,000 members, and a ground staff of 200, many of them women, cosset the place as though it were a private garden. Benefitting from the talent the Japanese have for landscaping, the courses are immaculate.

The flowers and the flowering shrubs as well as the ponds, paths and golf courses are all carefully tended. But perhaps the most striking feature of Fujita's East Course is the size and depth and shape of the bunkers, filled with shining silver sand. Charles Hugh Alison was a very talented architect. His notion that a bunker could be deeper than a standing man – commonplace in the west – intrigued the Japanese and was copied throughout the country. Alison's creed was that if a golfer played down the straight and narrow he should not be compromised by trick hazards, and the result is that Kasumigaseki is a fair, honest, open course.

Up and Down in Two

At 6,959 yards, with a par of 72, the course takes a good deal of playing. Nakamura and Ono were not long hitters. Indeed, technically their swings left a lot to be desired. But in putting, and in the short game in general, from 100 yards in to the pin, they were outstanding. Nakamura holed four bunker shots during that 1957 Canada Cup, and *never once* failed to get up and down in two strokes from greenside bunkers. Given the nature of those bunkers, that was a truly remarkable feat. For example, the short 10th hole, at 180 yards, is really two holes in parallel; two tees, two greens, and two lakes to carry, divided by a slender line of trees and the hole in play depending on the season of the year. This is where Alison first surprised his hosts and the foreign teams competing in the Canada Cup with deep bunkering short of the green of the day. Similarly, the 14th features huge bunkers at 250 yards from the tee, huge bunkers 40 yards short of the green, and huge bunkers around both greens. They proved too much for everyone other than Nakamura and Ono, and understandably Kasumigaseki remains to this day the pride of Nippon.

FUJIOKA

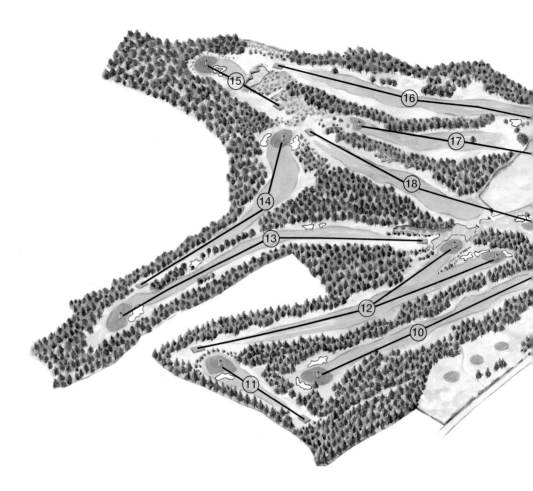

The Fujioka Country Club, near Nagoya, one of Japan's great manufacturing cities, was opened in 1971 and was a look into the future. It introduced lakes and water on a scale never before seen in Japan and it dispensed with the 'two-green' golf holes of Kasumigaseki and other older Japanese clubs. It featured a double green (shared by the 4th and 7th holes) and the fairways were laid with turf in only five months, and as many as 6,000 workers constructed the entire course, which was completed in a year.

The owner of the land, Furukawa, had the notion to build a course that would have the best of modern design, be up to the best international standards, but which would somehow dam the frenzied flood of golf in Japan, of huge clubs with huge clubhouses and huge memberships. His plan was to hold the Fujioka membership to less than 500.

The land was made up in part of pine forests and a tea plantation and there was a large natural lake. A local man, Tameshi Yamada was for some reason appointed the golf course architect. Little is known of him, or of any other work he may have done. However, to advise him, and no doubt to capitalise on the name, Peter Thomson, five times Open champion and winner of 75 professional events around the world, was hired as a consultant. Thomson brought with him, as a 'consultant to the consultant', Mike Wolveridge, an Englishman who had played for a spell on the U.S. professional tour before turning to design work with John Harris. Wolveridge had done excellent work in many countries and by 1980, when he and Thomson were in full partnership, their firm was by far the most active in the Pacific basin.

The Fujioka land had a lot of movement in it, and the design group produced many distinctive holes and distinctive features. More than 40 years on from the work at Kasumigaseki the agronomists had developed a finer strain of Korai grass good for year-round use, so that a normal one-green-per-one-hole system was adopted, save for the 12th hole.

Yamada, with encouragement from the cerebral Thomson-Wolveridge pairing, had done imaginative things with water; Japanese golf architects, unlike their gardeners, have generally been uncomfortable with the use of water. The question mark hanging over the 12th hole was: could they place the green hard by the water, as for example at the 11th hole of the Augusta National course in Georgia?

In the event, there was a compromise. They built two greens, one by the lake and one off to the right at the end of a straight fairway. There is also water at the short 2nd, where it must be carried, and to the left of the fairway at the 3rd.

Moving on, there is a lake to be carried with the drive on 13, a par-5, but at the

At the 395-yard 17th, the drive – one of the four over water at Fujioka – requires a carry of 200 yards to a point on the fairway that opens up the green to the approach shot.

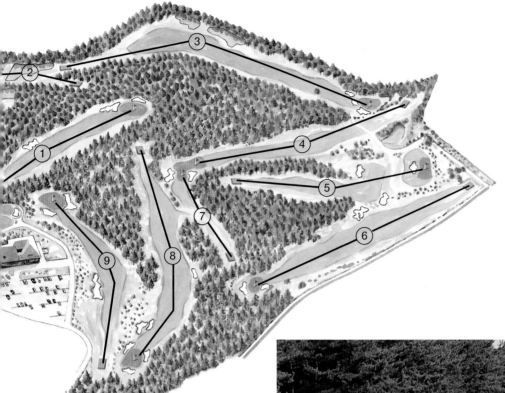

FUJIOKA Card of the course						
1	400 yards	par 4	10	400 yards	par 4
2	190 yards	par 3	11	165 yards	par 3
3	540 yards	par 5	12	440 yards	par 4
4	420 yards	par 4	13	550 yards	par 5
5	350 yards	par 4	14	370 yards	par 4
6	445 yards	par 4	15	190 yards	par 3
7	195 yards	par 3	16	605 yards	par 5
8	500 yards	par 5	17	395 yards	par 4
9	385 yards	par 4	18	430 yards	par 4
	3,425 yards	par 36		3,545 yards	par 36
	Total 6,970 yards par 72				

Fujioka's 18th is a par 4 of 430 yards which runs down a long, narrow undulating fairway, with solitary pines encroaching and a brook crossing some 50 yards short of a raised green.

short 15th the water is merely decorative. However, this hole sports a massive frontal bunker, artistically shaped, with an island of fairway in the centre, its outline copying exactly the outline of the bunker. It is as big as the green itself, and quite beautiful. This is followed by a quite monstrous par-5 16th, at 605 yards, calling for a uphill drive and a long second shot over a rise before the green, guarded by water and sand, comes into view.

Mercifully, one of the delights of Fujioka is the absence of superfluous fairway bunkering. Often a single pine tree, or the movement in the fairway itself, is just as effective. Fujioka's 17th makes the point. It is 395 yards with a carry of 200 yards on the drive across the biggest of Fujioka's lakes. This brings the player to a fairway on two levels, the line of fall being marked by a pine tree, and a split level green ahead to contend with. Positioning of the shots is all. Indeed, it is a rather sophisticated hole on a sophisticated and lovely golf course.

ROYAL CALCUTTA

Royal Calcutta is the oldest golf club in the world, outside of the British Isles. It dates from 1829, when the British Empire was still expanding, and epitomises to some extent that particularly British institution – the gentleman's club. There is some evidence that Scottish troops were involved in the creation of what was originally called the Dum-Dum Golf Club; and since Scots are inclined to the view that a golf course can be built anywhere, and that every golf club has a bar, then this was probably both a club and a golf club!

Royal Calcutta has had a chequered history. It moved from its original home at Dum-Dum, where Calcutta's international airport now functions, and after various moves settled in its present location in the southern suburbs of the teeming city of Calcutta, towards the end of last century. At first the club had 36 holes of golf, but after Indian independence in the late 1940s, the club released 18 holes of land which it could no longer afford to the Bengal government. However, it remains the doyen of India's near-100 clubs, and although Royal Calcutta has no particular authority, the other clubs accept its patriarchal position.

Calcutta's climate is classified as 'monsoon forest', which means simply that it is hot and humid. Royal Calcutta is unlikely to inflict bad bounces on the innocent or have him cry: 'It's not fair, it's not fair!' The greens will be reasonably holding, the fairways will be quite soft, and most of the time there will be not much run on the ball. True, there is a dry season – from December to May – but the course's 7,177 yards on the par 73 championship card can look overwhelming given the lack of run.

One of Calcutta's most prominent features is the huge tees, some 70 yards long or more. The tees and greens are in fact the highest points on a flat course that is basically no more than a few feet above the level of the Hooghly river. Nevertheless, the existence of these raised tees and greens points up the single most striking feature of the Royal Calcutta course – the 'tanks'. The tanks are simply lakes or ponds which are used for the storage of water and are also part of an integrated system of channels and run-off drains which cope with the monsoon rains. The tanks dominate the course, and the soil excavated from them was used to make the raised tees and greens. They number

The splendid clubhouse of Royal Calcutta, home of the oldest golf club outside Britain. The flat course, moderately bunkered, is dominated by its tanks (ponds) and massive trees.

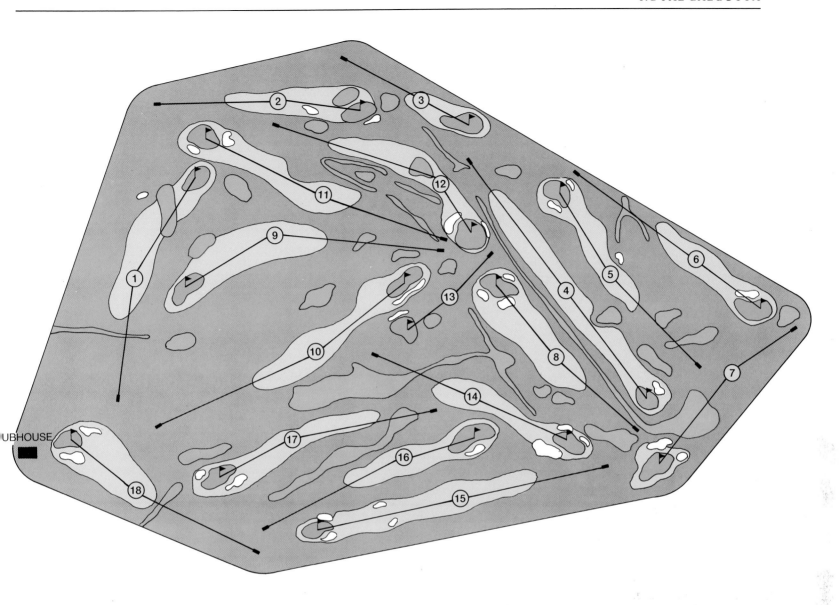

almost 30 and seem to be in play on every hole: one covers the entire fairway in front of the very first green.

Calcutta's tanks have another function in life: they also serve as swimming pools for small boys, who dive for golf balls; and their mothers often use the tanks for washing clothes, children and themselves. Such is India. The tanks take the place of many fairway bunkers, although the greenside bunkers at Royal Calcutta are very large and prettily patterned. At the 2nd hole, for example, five tanks are in the vicinity, none on the fairway, but all visible and all distracting.

However, it is the 7th hole that offers the best example of how water impinges on the strategy of play. The hole is a par-4 of 455 yards. The tee is set in a far corner of the course, behind the 6th green. The

ROYAL CALCUTTA					
Card of the course					
1	366 yards	par 4	10	448 yards	par 4
2	156 yards	par 3	11	508 yards	par 5
3	436 yards	par 4	12	359 yards	par 4
4	525 yards	par 5	13	187 yards	par 3
5	415 yards	par 4	14	431 yards	par 4
6	418 yards	par 4	15	493 yards	par 5
7	455 yards	par 4	16	364 yards	par 4
8	401 yards	par 4	17	374 yards	par 4
9	404 yards	par 4	18	437 yards	par 4
3,576 yards par 36			3,601 yards par 37		
Total 7,177 yards par 73					

hole turns to the left and the drive must carry over a tank in front of the tee, but should stop short of another which crosses the width of the fairway at the 250

yard mark. This tank is some 100 yards across. Finally, the green is protected by a large bunker front right and a smaller one front left. This is a challenging hole, calling for some restraint on the drive followed by a very long second shot. Perhaps the hole has a hint of the Robert Trent Jones about it – though it may be more penal than that as there are few alternative choices; certainly not on that second shot!

But perhaps Royal Calcutta's most significant feature and lasting achievement was its demonstration that grass – in this case dhoob grass, a type of Bermuda – could grow and be maintained in India; indeed in tropical and sub-tropical climates generally. That has encouraged the spread and growth of golf in dozens of countries around the world.

ROYAL HONG KONG

Golf travelled with the British Empire; with its regiments, its administrators and its businessmen. Golf came to Hong Kong in 1889, to Happy Valley on Hong Kong Island where a happy band of enthusiasts tackled an early nine holes. Their 'architect' was Captain R. E. Dumbleton of the Royal Engineers, who was not allowed to build greens or tees, or even dig the holes. The flat and open space, hard to come by on a hilly island, was shared by other sports, including polo, so, therefore, Dumbleton's 'holes' were of necessity portable granite setts – the golfer having to hole out by striking the setts with his ball.

Within a few years the club had 100 members and moved to another site on the south of the island, at Deep Water Bay, where nine holes could be squeezed out of flatland by the shore. Access was gained by sailing around the island! However, the island was soon not big enough to handle the growth in membership, and the search was on for more land to accommodate a 'proper' golf course or two. It was found at Fanling, close to the Chinese border, and what came to be known as the 'Old Course' was built in the early years of the century. Getting there meant adventurous journeys involving walking, rickshaws and

Golf is rarely played in a more beautiful setting than that of Royal Hong Kong, set against the mountains of China. The Championship course is made up of holes from the New Course, built in 1931, and the Eden, completed 40 years later.

launches. However, the railway from Kowloon to the border was opened in 1911 and by 1923, with a club membership of 800, it was time to expand the club again.

The committee proposed building a second 18 holes, which were constructed by one L. S. Greenhill and opened in 1931. It was a more spacious course than the Old, being considered an 'American'-style layout with a meadowland flavour, particularly on the inward half. Not surprisingly the expatriates persuaded themselves that the Old had more of the feel and taste of the Berkshire courses 'back home' in England!

The Japanese occupation from 1941 to 1945 saw the courses neglected and it took several years to return them to

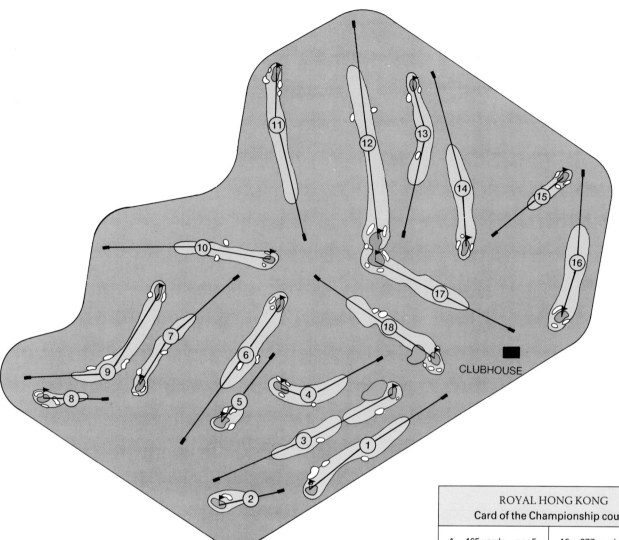

CLUBHOUSE

ROYAL HONG KONG					
Card of the Championship course					
1	465 yards	par 5	10	377 yards	par 4
2	155 yards	par 3	11	469 yards	par 4
3	520 yards	par 5	12	525 yards	par 5
4	295 yards	par 4	13	400 yards	par 4
5	198 yards	par 3	14	426 yards	par 4
6	425 yards	par 4	15	191 yards	par 3
7	385 yards	par 4	16	409 yards	par 4
8	192 yards	par 3	17	412 yards	par 4
9	488 yards	par 5	18	417 yards	par 4
3,123 yards	par 36		3,626 yards	par 36	
Total 6,749 yards par 72					

normal – until 1953, in fact. But by the early 1960s, the 36 holes of the Old and New courses could not handle the demand and the Royal Hong Kong was expanded yet again. Some adjoining land was bought from the Jockey Club next door, and to the design of John Harris and Mike Wolveridge, and under Wolveridge's supervision, a new course was built in 1963.

The new course was named the Eden, after the third course at St Andrews, and features a rather lavish use of water. On 16 of the holes water, in the shape of streams, storm channels and lakes, is on view, if not entirely in play. Fanling sits in a basin with ridges around the sides, and is a network of fairways, little knolls, stretches of rice paddies and screens of

eucalyptus and casuarinas; and all around it Chinese country life goes on.

Within the picturesque setting, the Eden is the shortest of the three courses, but it is modern in design – its greens raised to allow for monsoon run-off – and full of character. The composite course, marrying holes from the Eden and the New, is used exclusively for international championship events. The Hong Kong Open, played annually in late February, attracts an international field. In 1987 the top four places went to visiting 'Brits' Ian Woosnam, Sam Torrance, David Feherty and Ronan Rafferty.

Nowadays the main concern of Royal Hong Kong and its golfers is the concern of the entire colony – namely, 1997 and the attitude of Communist China when it

takes control. What will they make of the decadent, bourgeois, capitalist game of golf? They have allowed Arnold Palmer to build a course in their people's Republic, in the Canton area, with Japanese funding. So, perhaps they are beginning to realise the value of this international game – and hopefully Royal Hong Kong will continue to prosper, as will the colony it serves.

SINGAPORE ISLAND

The Singapore Island Country Club is one of the wonders of golf. It has four big courses and a membership of 7,000, at least 2,000 of whom are active golfers. It is an equatorial Pinehurst or St Andrews. That all this should happen in Singapore, one of the world's smallest nation states (224 square miles!), makes it all the more wonderful. Today's Country Club exists from an amalgamation, in 1963, of the Royal Singapore Golf Club and the Royal Island Golf Club, which in turn have their origins in the founding of the Singapore Sporting Club in 1842.

In 1891 a group of members met to form a golf club, officially started that year with nine holes in the region of the old racecourse and named, simply, the Singapore Golf Club. By 1920, John Sime, a prominent member of the club, had the idea that they should have a proper 18-hole course well away from the restrictions of the growing city. Thus in 1921, a 258 acre site in the jungle by the MacRitchie reservoir was leased to the

club for $1.00 per annum and the original Bukit Timah course was open for play in 1924, having been designed by James Braid – who disliked travelling, so never visited Singapore and designed the course by mail from topographical maps! The jungle clearance was a massive undertaking, but the course was left with a British flavour – English trees were planted.

Members who chose not to go to the Bukit (the word means 'hill') formed the Island Club, which opened in 1932. Both clubs prospered until the Japanese occupation in the 1940s, when much of the ground became farmland and the Japanese forced many members, imprisoned in Changi Gaol, into work gangs to build a road across the courses to a new Shinto shrine they were erecting. After

The well-bunkered 7th green of the Bukit course overlooks the reservoir. Beyond it, dense jungle grows to the water's edge.

the war had ended, the Singapore club, appointed Royal in 1938, reopened in 1947. The Island club took longer to recover, but by 1952 it was functioning again and had also been appointed Royal. Things went so well for the Islanders that they were able to stage the first Singapore Open in 1961.

In 1963, the two clubs merged. The Royal Singapore Golf Club and the Royal Island Golf Club became, simply the Singapore Island Country Club, and in 1968 the Island course and the Bukit course were revised by Frank Pennink. The Bukit was to be the first club in South-East Asia to stage the World Cup, which it did in 1969 – the U.S. team of Orville Moody and Lee Trevino winning the title. And in 1970, the New course, by John Harris and Pennink, was opened.

This splendid club now has four courses: the Bukit at 6,690 yards (the parent course); the Island at 6,365 yards; the New at 6,874 yards, and the Sime at 6,314 yards. The Bukit course, the most

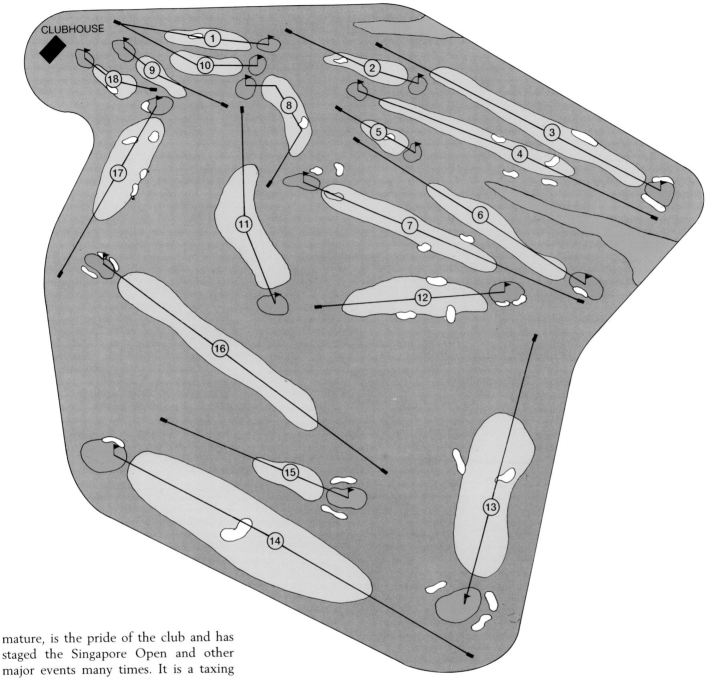

CLUBHOUSE

mature, is the pride of the club and has staged the Singapore Open and other major events many times. It is a taxing course in the Singapore climate, particularly from the back tees. (Singapore, so close to the equator, is hot and humid most of the year.) And Bukit has plenty of rolling, dipping fairways which demand good judgement.

Greenkeeping, too, has its challenges. Hot sun and ample water from the reservoirs mean that there is never any lack of growth – the nearby jungle is testament to that – but controlling it is the game. The greens are on a clay base and seeded, like the fairways, with a strain of Bermuda grass which gives good pos-

SINGAPORE ISLAND Card of the Bukit course			
1	407 yards par 4	10	379 yards par 4
2	205 yards par 3	11	425 yards par 4
3	408 yards par 4	12	223 yards par 3
4	537 yards par 5	13	563 yards par 5
5	175 yards par 3	14	191 yards par 3
6	448 yards par 4	15	501 yards par 5
7	449 yards par 4	16	429 yards par 4
8	366 yards par 4	17	132 yards par 3
9	364 yards par 4	18	488 yards par 5
3,359 yards par 35		3,331 yards par 36	
Total 6,690 yards par 71			

itive lies on the fairways but which, used on the greens as it is, can force the ball to break away from the line. Putting on Bermuda, or any of its varieties, demands a firmer stroke at the ball.

The Singapore Island club has much in common with Royal Hong Kong – large membership, four courses, more than comfortable clubhouses – all legacies of the British. But most of all, they are both marvellous refuges from the stresses and tensions of high-voltage life in these two dynamic island-states.

ROYAL SELANGOR

The Royal Selangor Golf Club in Kuala Lumpur, the capital of Malaysia, can boast of one 'outside agency' that makes Northern Ireland and the West of Scotland seem like drought zones. It is rain – as much as 160 inches of it in a year! It affects all the 10 million inhabitants of the country, of course, but it does create particular problems for golf greenkeepers when you consider the heat and humidity which come with it.

But such trivia never really fazed your honest golf player, and Royal Selangor has been blessed with these ever since 30 keen fellows started the club in 1893 at Petaling Hills, just outside the city. Only once in all that time has the club moved – surprising in the East when one considers the rapid growth of the cities. The move took place in 1918, when the government of the State of Selangor took over the Petaling Hills land for a building project, and in return provided a new course and clubhouse for the club. By 1921 nine holes of golf and the new clubhouse were in place. And in 1931 the 18 holes which later came to be known as the Old course, were ready for the approval of Harry Colt, the famous English architect, who made some minor changes.

The Japanese occupation of 1941–5 was a disaster for the club. There was no

The open nature of Selangor can be seen in this photograph of the 18th fairway (with the 1st fairway to the right).

ROYAL SELANGOR					
Card of the Old course					
1	428 yards	par 4	10	467 yards	par 4
2	405 yards	par 4	11	422 yards	par 4
3	512 yards	par 5	12	391 yards	par 4
4	164 yards	par 3	13	488 yards	par 5
5	346 yards	par 4	14	207 yards	par 3
6	463 yards	par 4	15	579 yards	par 5
7	187 yards	par 3	16	351 yards	par 4
8	388 yards	par 4	17	147 yards	par 3
9	493 yards	par 5	18	435 yards	par 4
3,386 yards	par 36		3,487 yards	par 36	
Total 6,873 yards par 72					

damage to the clubhouse – it was used as a command headquarters by the Japanese Army – but the course was devastated. But Selangor had a remarkable man in Tom Verity, the professional appointed in 1937, who served the club for 27 years. He and the members got down to work, and within a couple of years the club was back in some kind of trim. Nowadays it

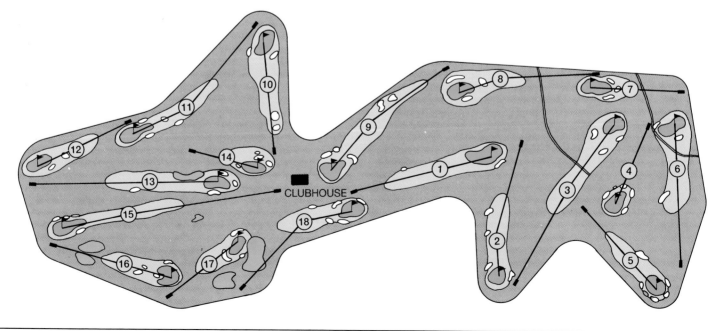

can handle hundreds of people, with its golf, Olympic pool, a dozen lawn tennis and squash courts, and comprehensive restaurant facilities.

The course is quite flat, a definite advantage in the Kuala Lumpur climate, and is also lush and beautiful. Grass here, as in all tropical and sub-tropical climates, has been both a problem and a challenge. Various types of rough grasses and Bermuda strains have been tried and tested to the point where the course now uses a finer grass, albeit a type of Bermuda. All the greens are mounded to throw off rain in the violent storms that are common-place, and concrete-lined water channels cross several fairways. The shapes and contours of these greens call for much more chipping than is normal, since approach shots that are in the least bit

All the greens at Royal Selangor are domed to some extent to allow rainwater run-off in the monsoon. This and the subtle contours of many of the greens enforces accurate chipping.

sloppy will run off the putting surfaces.

The flatness of the course suggests that it will be easier than your average championship test. But it stretches to 6,873 yards, with a par of 72, and the very first hole shows it is no push-over. It is a flat and straight 428 yards to an open green with only one bunker along its right side. But judging distance on the second shot and holding the ball on the green is a good deal more difficult than it may look. Indeed, the start of Selangor is perhaps more challenging than the finish.

The use of water is concentrated on the

inward half, with lakes in play at 13 (where a drainage ditch crosses about 100 yards short of the green), 15, 16, 17 and 18. The 17th is a lovely short hole of 147 yards, played out of a grove of trees and over a lake, water lilies and all. And the 18th is an intriguing finishing hole. At 435 yards, it asks for a drive across a big lake, with trees on the right closing the route across the corner of the dog-leg. From the fairway, a bunker on the left has to be ignored, and a way found into a green with a rather narrow entrance and two bunkers tightening up the right hand side.

With holes such as these it is not surprising that Royal Selangor is a regular and worthy host course to the Malaysian Open Championship; it is clearly one of the finest courses in South-East Asia.

BALI HANDARA

The Bali Handara course rests 4,000 feet up a mountainside in an old volcanic crater on the island of Bali, at the eastern end of Java, the central island of Indonesia. Nine of its holes were laid out on an old dairy farm and nine were hacked out of a tropical rain forest, largely by hand. The course is a one hour drive from Bali's international airport at Denpasar – all of which takes a good deal of explaining. Golf in Indonesia until 1939 consisted of about a dozen courses, almost all of them owned by tea or rubber plantations, most of which were under British management or ownership. Probably the best-known was the Djakarta Golf Club in the capital city. But after the Second World War, the club lost half of its land to a state building project and was left with 18 holes packed into a space only sufficient for nine. However, when Indonesia's President Sukarno was ousted by General Suharto in 1967, the country had an enthusiastic golfer in power.

Not surprisingly, the game started to grow. General Ibru Suharto wanted a prestige golf course and Bali, with a future in tourism, was to be the place. Bali's highest mountain rises to 10,000 feet and Handara, at 4,000 feet, was high enough to escape the coastal heat and thus provide a reasonable environment for growing golf course grasses. The Peter Thomson-Mike Wolveridge partnership was asked to design a course and in September 1973 Guy Wolstenholme, their man, arrived. It was raining!

Wolstenholme was an Englishman who had a distinguished amateur career – English international, Walker Cup team, English Amateur Champion and so on – who turned professional and played quite successfully in the UK and Europe before moving to Australia. He played tournament golf there, but showed a keen interest in design. Thomson-Wolveridge introduced Guy Wolstenholme to the Bali Handara project, and he made a triumphant success of it.

Without machinery, but with a work force of more than 1,000 locals, Wolstenholme fashioned his greens with hand

labour, and had the fairways cleared, cleaned and sown, again all by hand. Bali has two rainy seasons – February-March and September-October – when the rain falls predictably at Handara every afternoon. A very sophisticated drainage system was installed. And Ron Fream, Thomson's American partner, brought from the U.S. a strain of Kentucky Bluegrass seed which was mixed with the local Bermuda to give a quite beautiful fairway texture.

Left: *Guy Wolstenholme (seen here in the 1961 English Close Championship) oversaw the construction of the course at Bali Handara, which he had helped to design.*

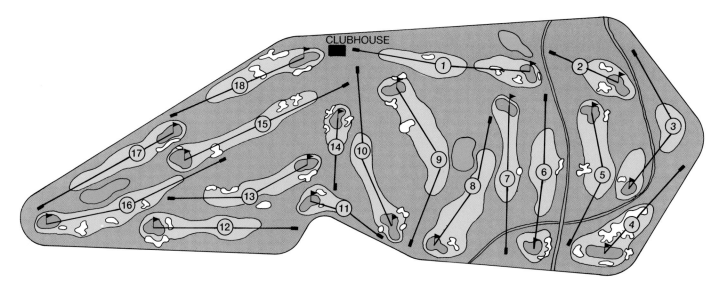

The course is a delight to the eye, as well as a testing pleasure to play – the bunkers cut out in lovely jig-saw patterns set against lush greens; small animals, deer and monkeys cross the fairways; and the whole course is dominated by a heavily wooded mountain. There is also water on the course: a large lake between the 16th and 17th fairways, another between 8 and 9, and a long, meandering stream that crosses the 3rd, 5th, 6th and the 7th. Another attractive feature of the design is the shape of the fairways – waisted here, swelling out there and vanishing in between. At the 1st hole, a par-5 of 500 yards, there is the inevitable bunker on the left to pinch the drive, but somewhere in the middle of the second shot, where a path crosses the fairway, it vanishes and is replaced by a swathe of rough. Further on there is a lovely shamrock bunker short of the green, while the latter is an hour-glass shape set across the incoming shot and severely bunkered. In short, a brilliant hole on a lovely, imaginative golf course.

BALI HANDARA				
Card of the course				
1	500 yards par 5		10	412 yards par 4
2	180 yards par 3		11	180 yards par 3
3	450 yards par 4		12	410 yards par 4
4	180 yards par 3		13	410 yards par 4
5	400 yards par 4		14	180 yards par 3
6	410 yards par 4		15	540 yards par 5
7	400 yards par 4		16	432 yards par 4
8	411 yards par 4		17	442 yards par 4
9	527 yards par 5		18	560 yards par 5
3,458 yards par 36			3,566 yards par 36	
Total 7,024 yards par 72				

The view from behind the 15th green. Although downhill, the hole is a three-shotter for all except those prepared to flirt with the cunningly placed fairway bunker from the tee.

ROYAL MELBOURNE

Alister Mackenzie was born of Scottish parents in Leeds, Yorkshire in 1870. He graduated from Cambridge University with a degree in medicine and served as a surgeon in the South African War. In 1907 Harry Colt, one of the outstanding golf architects of the day, visited Mackenzie's home course, Alwoodley, in Leeds, to carry out some revisions, and stayed overnight with Mackenzie, who showed him various models of tees and greens. Impressed, Colt invited him to assist in the Alwoodley work. From that point, Mackenzie grew more and more interested in golf course design and less and less in medicine. He did return to being an army surgeon in 1914, but after the First World War, became a full-time designer and made his first trip to the United States.

Mackenzie's philosophy was that since good health was of paramount importance to everyone, a pastime such as golf, which provided healthy exercise and clean air, could make an exceptional contribution to human health and happiness. While his motives for embracing the game were admirable, he could scarcely have imagined that by the end of his life, in 1934, he would have been responsible for three masterpieces: Royal Melbourne West, Cypress Point and Augusta National!

The Sand Belt

When Mackenzie arrived in Melbourne in 1926, he found he was working for the club with the longest unbroken history in

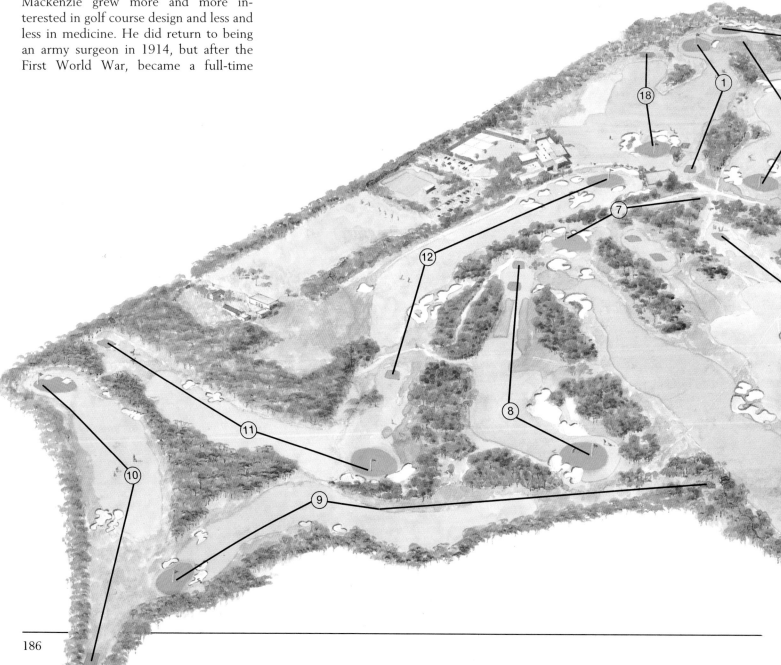

the country. The club dates from 1891 and, after a couple of moves, settled in its present location on Melbourne's 'sand belt' – which is just that, an acreage of sand dunes, heather and bracken, native oak trees and silver-sand subsoil. He could hardly wait to get to work and was lucky to have the help of Alex Russell as an assistant. A local man and a member of the club, Russell as an amateur golfer had won the Australian Open Championship in 1924 – over the existing course.

All the familiar Mackenzie – and for that matter Russell – features are in the

Ben Crenshaw plays from a greenside bunker at the short 7th during the 1988 World Cup. Crenshaw and Mark McCumber won the Cup for the United States, Crenshaw taking the individual prize.

course: great rashes of bunkers in the fairways, around the greens and in the angles of the turns; lightning-fast greens, several of them split-level; only one hole, the 3rd, apart from the par-3s, playing straight; and gently rising and falling ground introducing blind shots and tilted fairways.

But more than any other single factor, the Royal Melbourne greens make the course what it is: an immensely difficult par of 71 over 6,946 yards. The greens are sand-based, cut right down until they are positively sparse, severely contoured and lightning-fast. Mackenzie was already formulating what was to become almost a custodial policy with regard to the speed and contouring of greens, which reached a climax at Augusta National. In this, Mackenzie was much abetted by a greenkeeper, Claude Crockford, whose attitude to greens and putting, and golfers, was exactly that of Mackenzie and Russell.

Mackenzie's Melbourne

The 1st hole plays into a fairly wide patch of fairway, turns slightly to the left and goes up to a reasonably flat green with one bunker front right. The 2nd hole is a

ROYAL MELBOURNE					
Card of the Championship course					
1	424 yards	par 4	10	460 yards	par 4
2	480 yards	par 5	11	455 yards	par 4
3	333 yards	par 4	12	433 yards	par 4
4	440 yards	par 4	13	354 yards	par 4
5	176 yards	par 3	14	470 yards	par 4
6	428 yards	par 4	15	383 yards	par 4
7	148 yards	par 3	16	210 yards	par 3
8	305 yards	par 4	17	575 yards	par 5
9	440 yards	par 4	18	432 yards	par 4
3,174 yards		par 35	3,772 yards		par 36
Total 6,946 yards par 71					

The fearsome 6th hole at Royal Melbourne West. The right-angled dog-leg has clusters of bunkers and scrub in the angle, and the raised, subtly-controlled green is another trade mark of the architect, Alister Mackenzie.

quality par-5. It turns to the right and a huge, jigsaw-patterned fairway bunker sits on the driving line. It must be carried if the green is to be reached in regulation and up ahead there are similar sized bunkers on either side of the green.

The 3rd is a Russell hole of 333 yards. A drive downhill over a crest, then on to a green split into two levels – high on the right, falling down to a very deep bunker just off the left side. For one so short, this can be a complicated hole with a very difficult shot to the flagstick. The 5th hole has one of the most common Mackenzie characteristics at a short hole: a sharp downslope at the front of the green, so that the short ball will roll back off the putting surface and into whatever dis-comforts have been left there for it. This one, 176 yards, plays over a hollow, is firmly bunkered on either side and slopes rather sharply from the back down.

The 6th is a superb golf hole of 428 yards, turning to the right. In the angle is a mass of bunkering and natural scrubland tempting the player to carry the corner. The second part of the hole goes up a hill with a slightly adverse camber, to a green tucked under trees and protected by heavy side bunkering.

The 8th hole is a perfect illustration of what can be done with a short par-4. This is 305 yards. From a high tee, it crosses a valley to a plateau fairway, and turns to the left. Lining the entire inside of the turn, on a direct line to the green, is an enormous lateral bunker. You are invited to carry it, reach the green and putt for, at least, a birdie! On the direct line there are, of course, no other bunkers. On the indirect line, however, played wide of that lateral bunker, there are bunkers at the right front of the green for any incoming pitch.

Trevino Scores a Nine

The 9th, 10th, 11th and 12th holes, all in the mid-400 yard range, form the heart of the round. The 9th turns left and has a wicked green on two levels – higher at the back. The 10th demands a drive over huge fairway bunkers – the driving zone pinched between a large bunker on the right and a sandy valley on the left. The 11th goes out to a rise at around 250 yards, then turns left across a dip of 200 yards to a green completely closed off on the right. The main feature of the 13th is that the green falls off at the back – a gambit Mackenzie has used elsewhere. The 14th is one of Melbourne's most provocative holes – at 470 yards only just a par-4. The drive is played blind, over a rise which has a long ridge of bunkers on the skyline. The hole then turns quickly to the right, the fairway running downhill and tilted right to left. The second shot must carry rough in the corner, then a file of bunkers guarding the right front of the green and another big one, on the same line, on the left side.

Royal Melbourne's finish is very tough. The 16th is 210 yards, slightly uphill to a palette-shaped green. It is heavily but not closely bunkered across the front left and is played over scrubby ground. The green is quite long and the pin position might well call for two clubs more in selection. At 575 yards the 17th is a long slog – the longest on the course – with bunkers crossing the fairway at approximately 400 yards. And the 18th is a fine finishing hole of 432 yards; a dogleg left to a green that is ringed with bunkers, save at the back on the left, where it falls away. This hole has undulations typical of Royal Melbourne – a course that demands the utmost concentration, positive thinking and definitive shot-making.

The closing par-3 on Royal Melbourne's East Course, at 168 yards, is as pretty as any short hole could be. It is a simple, but not easy hole. A rather small green is surrounded by large bunkers, and is primly contoured.

ROYAL ADELAIDE

Royal Adelaide is big. It runs to just under 7,000 yards, and has a look of Muirfield about it – Muirfield with trees, that is. A sandy subsoil, marram grass in the rough, even some modest sand dunes, give it the look and feel of a links. It is a superb course, with just an occasional echo of Pine Valley as well. Such a pedigree could hardly be better, especially since the good Dr Alister Mackenzie also ran his stethoscope over it.

It has been suggested that golf came to Adelaide as early as 1869, in the person of Sir James Fergusson, new Governor of South Australia, a Scot from Edinburgh. After five years he left, and golf in Adelaide seemed to lapse, but the club was revived in 1896 and 18 holes were constructed at Glenelg, their creation helped along by one Francis Maxwell,

another expatriate Scot, who was the brother of the amateur champion, Robert Maxwell of the Honourable Company of Edinburgh Golfers.

In 1904 the club moved to its present site at Seaton – 204 acres around a railway station and a single track line which linked it to the city, half an hour away. The club also, and sensibly, appointed as its first professional a Carnoustie man named Jack Scott, who stayed with them for 20 years as an excellent teacher and clubmaker. When Alister Mackenzie looked over the course

A diagonal of no fewer than six bunkers marches across the front of Royal Adelaide's 7th green. Others at back right and back left crowd the target green, only 29 yards long on the 156-yard hole.

in 1926 he rearranged the routeing so that none of the holes played over the railway line, and of course put in some typical, and large, Mackenzie bunkering. The course has been modified here and there since, notably after visits by the Thomson-Wolveridge partnership, and there are some very fine holes.

The 1st, at 382 yards, is perhaps a shade short for an opener, but it is a modest classic of its kind. The drive is into a narrow fairway which turns to the left. On the inside of the turn are sand dunes thick with marram grass. On the outside are two bunkers on the edge of the rough and the green is slightly angled, with a very big and deep bunker covering the left side, the 'inside' line from the fairway – simple, but effective.

Adelaide has three par-3s, but five

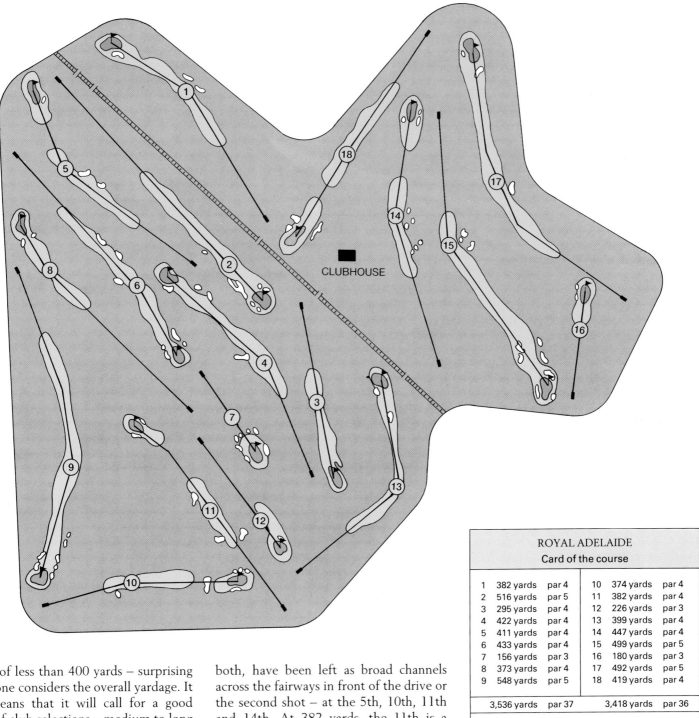

ROYAL ADELAIDE				
Card of the course				
1	382 yards	par 4	10	374 yards	par 4
2	516 yards	par 5	11	382 yards	par 4
3	295 yards	par 4	12	226 yards	par 3
4	422 yards	par 4	13	399 yards	par 4
5	411 yards	par 4	14	447 yards	par 4
6	433 yards	par 4	15	499 yards	par 5
7	156 yards	par 3	16	180 yards	par 3
8	373 yards	par 4	17	492 yards	par 5
9	548 yards	par 5	18	419 yards	par 4
3,536 yards par 37			3,418 yards par 36		
Total 6,954 yards par 73					

par-4s of less than 400 yards – surprising when one considers the overall yardage. It also means that it will call for a good range of club selections – medium to long irons – on the par-4 holes. Of the shorter holes, the 3rd at 295 yards is a real challenge. The drive is blind, covering a path that leads from the tee, travelling between trees and cresting a rise. The green is undefended save for some rippling fairway short of the putting surface. For the long hitters, the drive is at the mercy of the bounce of the ball.

At several holes, swatches of Adelaide's silver sand, or rough, or a combination of both, have been left as broad channels across the fairways in front of the drive or the second shot – at the 5th, 10th, 11th and 14th. At 382 yards, the 11th is a particularly good example. The drive must skirt two large mounded bunkers on the left of the fairway while the second shot must carry a broad band of sand and rough to a green with flanking bunkers near the highest point on the course.

The 15th and 17th are outstanding par-5 holes, in the sense that trees, dunes or bunkers will push the tee shots to the outside of dogleg turns; then the classic fairway bunker short of the green will close out the long second shots seeking to get home in two, forcing them short or wide and thus necessitating a little pitch for the third shot. And finally the 18th, at 419 yards, almost straight, with no fairway bunker but ridges and humps and hollows in front of the green, makes a perfect finish to this lovely 'inland links'.

ROYAL SYDNEY

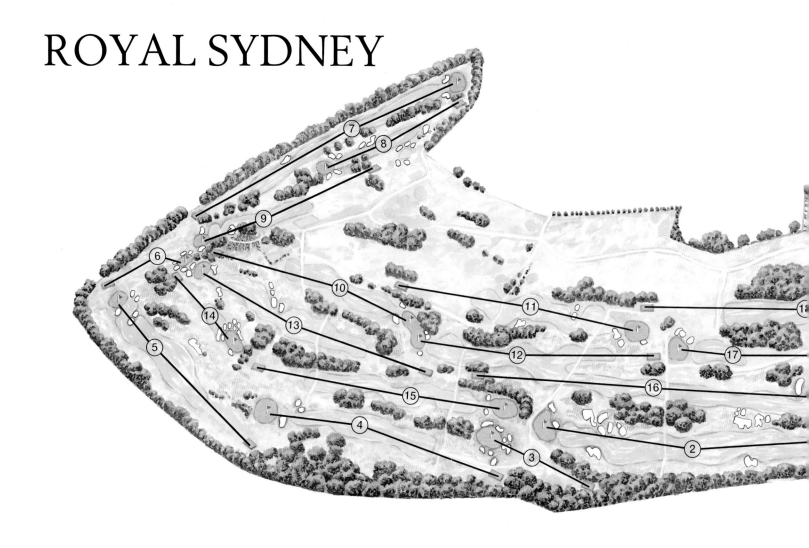

When a golf club has 5,000 members, you may be sure that it is something out of the ordinary. Royal Sydney started in 1893 as a men-only club. Now it is a golf, tennis and social club which is an intrinsic part of the fabric of the biggest Australian city, and is only a ten minute drive from the city centre. The plan of the course is not unlike that of the Old Course at St Andrews: turn right at the first green, then straight out, a loop at the end, then come straight back. However, the Old Course is only two fairways wide, where Royal Sydney is four. The original nine holes played round the outside of the present layout, but in 1896, after James Scott joined the club as its professional, the course was extended to 18 holes. A year later it acquired the Royal prefix.

Just as a links course will set its tees by the beach, so Sydney set its tees on that

ROYAL SYDNEY					
Card of the course					
1	280 yards	par 4	10	420 yards	par 4
2	547 yards	par 5	11	440 yards	par 4
3	173 yards	par 3	12	387 yards	par 4
4	426 yards	par 4	13	509 yards	par 5
5	435 yards	par 4	14	194 yards	par 3
6	154 yards	par 3	15	443 yards	par 4
7	554 yards	par 5	16	563 yards	par 5
8	302 yards	par 4	17	211 yards	par 3
9	359 yards	par 4	18	410 yards	par 4
3,230 yards	par 36		3,577 yards	par 36	
Total 6,807 yards par 72					

original nine holes on the very edge of the property, the holes playing inwards and occasionally turning back so that the green was set on the perimeter and the approach shot would be slightly uphill. The second nine of the course were built

inside these holes and on sandy soil. With a sea breeze blowing most of the time, it had much of the flavour of a links.

The original design is credited to one S.J. Robbie, but in the 1920s, when Dr Alister Mackenzie spent some time in Australia, he was asked to revise the bunkering. This he did with a vengeance, digging deep, wide pits in Sydney's white sand. In combination with fierce rough, narrow fairways, small greens and strategically placed trees, and a yardage of 6,566 yards for normal play with a par of 72, Royal Sydney is no ordinary course!

The straightest hole on the course is the very first. At 280 yards it is within reach of the stronger player, although there is a tiger tee set further back beside the clubhouse. No fewer than six bunkers line the right side of the fairway, with three more around the green. The course then turns right and 2, 3, 4 and 5 run along the

Right: *Mark Calcavecchia of the U.S. hoists the hulking Australian Open trophy in 1988, having won over the Royal Sydney course with the remarkable score of 19 under par – 269.*

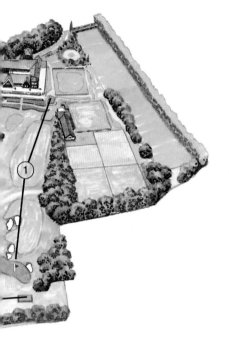

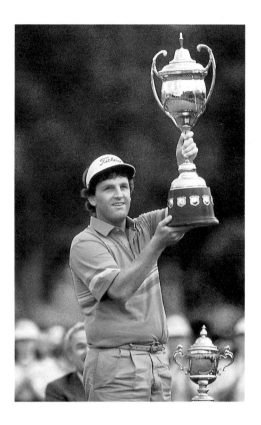

rim of the property – the players driving down into valleys, then hitting up to the greens. There are bunkers galore on this stretch of very fine holes. The 6th hole, a one-shotter of 154 yards, turns towards the loop, which includes the long 7th of 554 yards, with little in the way of hazard but very narrow.

The inward half is longer by 500 yards and two strokes on the card, with two 'back-to-back' long holes at 15 (443 yards), and 16 (563 yards). The closing hole of 410 yards and a sharp dogleg to the left, makes for exciting championship finishes. The second shot is played up to a large, raised green, with bunkers short of it on both sides. Just as intriguing in its fashion is the 17th, at 211 yards. The defences are against the faded shot, three big traps being sited to the right of a fairly small green.

Royal Sydney is a fine old course that has kept abreast of the times. But, like any other course in the world, it cannot repel the onslaught of the modern professionals when conditions are right. Thus in the Australian Open of 1988, Mark Calcavecchia (Open Champion in 1989) won with 269 – 19 under par!

Below: *Greg Norman plays a short iron to the 18th in the 1988 Australian Open. He has drawn his tee shot round and beyond the dog-leg, which lies some 170 yards from the green.*

PARAPARAUMU

Peter Thomson, who ought to know, described Paraparaumu as 'the only true championship links in New Zealand or Australia'; and Bob Charles, who also ought to know, claimed that its 5th hole was 'the equal to any short hole in the world'. Yet Paraparaumu is something of a freak. Why it should be the only links course in New Zealand or Australia is a mystery, since both countries have miles and miles of beachland and dunes.

The course is situated in North Wellington, about an hour's drive from the city centre, on the west coast beneath the big Tararua range in which Mount Hector goes up to 5,000 feet, and in the shelter of Kapiti Island, which lies close offshore.

A course of sorts existed in the area for many years, but seems not to have been very successful, until one day in 1946 Douglas Whyte and Alex Russell looked down on the property from a nearby sandhill and were inspired to do something about restoring it. Whyte was a member of the Royal and Ancient of St Andrews and had played to scratch, so he had some insight into the make-up of a good golf course. Alex Russell had nothing to prove about the craft of building

golf courses. He had worked very closely with the famous Dr Alister Mackenzie on the magnificent West Course of Royal Melbourne in 1926, and at Yarra Yarra in 1929. And he had designed the East Course of Royal Melbourne in 1932.

A Classic Links

By 1949 Russell's endeavours at Paraparaumu Beach were finished and the course was in play. It was quickly seen as a thing of beauty, both artful and artistic and a classic links as typical as anything in Scotland, but one to which modern design thinking had been applied. The

fairways ran in general along shallow valleys, with dunes rather than huge sandhills – Birkdale-style – screening the sides. In general, there were no ferocious carrys from the tees and there was a striking absence of bunkers, both in the fairways and at greenside. Five of the par-4 holes were less than 400 yards. The par-3s were of sensible length and the whole thing ran to no more than 6,500 yards. Wherein then did Paraparaumu's greatness lie?

First and foremost it lay in the wind. During one period of ten days embracing a New Zealand Open and a match play

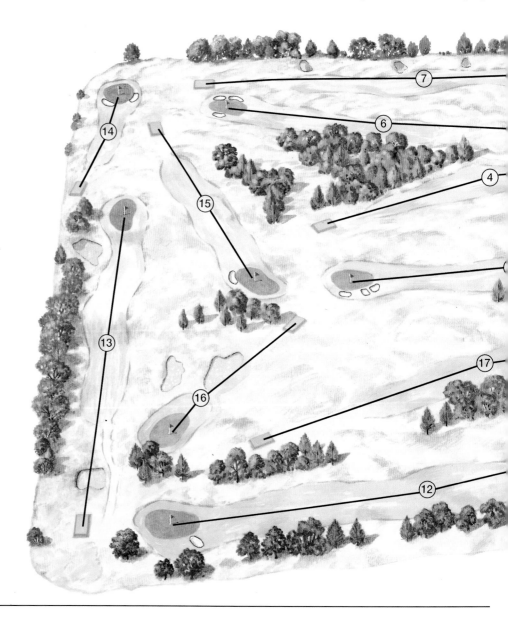

Paraparaumu's 400-yard par-4 13th hole is typical of the course. Its fairway undulates severely and it requires two precisely placed shots to obtain par.

event, the wind blew variously around 270 degrees, from north to west to south to east. And while Para does have some trees, it is as exposed as, say, Carnoustie. Secondly, it lay in the fact that Russell had used the heaving, undulating terrain to artful effect. His dogleg angles, save perhaps on the drive and pitch holes like 8 and 9, were never abrupt. Russell placed his tees so that, where he needed it, the drive would be checked by an up-slope. In other places, at the 449-yard 13th, for example, he demands that a long drive reach a plateau in the fairway from which an equally long second is needed to get to an undefended green. And Russell's greens on the whole are small. Indeed, the more closely one looks at the structure of this course, the more fascinating these holes become.

The Outward Nine

The drive at the first hole passes through a gap in low dunes to a wide expanse of fairway, moving slightly downhill and giving a clear view of the green. There is no bunker on this hole. The test here is in the putting, there being plenty of movement in the green. The 2nd hole has similarities to the 5th, at least in construction. In each case the green has been formed by chopping off and levelling the top of a dune. At 200 yards, to a long but rather narrow green which has two pot bunkers at the front left, this can be a demanding tee shot, depending on the conditions. The famous 5th hole, which Bob Charles so admires (the man has won the New Zealand Open and other events here), has a small, sitting-up green, no bunker, but slopes falling away all round,

particularly at the front. There is something of the flavour of the 5th at Gleneagles King's, or the 16th at Carnoustie, or the 17th at Troon here, although the latter two are much more critical holes.

The 6th hole, at only 309 yards long,

PARAPARAUMU Card of the course					
1	419 yards	par 4	10	312 yards	par 4
2	200 yards	par 3	11	427 yards	par 4
3	420 yards	par 4	12	517 yards	par 5
4	446 yards	par 4	13	449 yards	par 4
5	167 yards	par 3	14	151 yards	par 3
6	309 yards	par 4	15	379 yards	par 4
7	496 yards	par 5	16	140 yards	par 3
8	369 yards	par 4	17	440 yards	par 4
9	379 yards	par 4	18	470 yards	par 5
3,205 yards	par 35		3,285 yards	par 36	
Total 6,490 yards par 71					

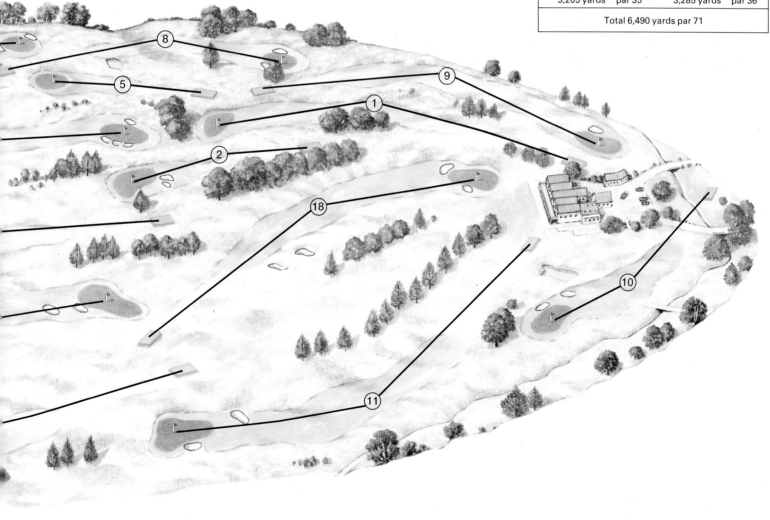

depends entirely on the bounce which the fairway gives to the tee shot. It has many humps and hollows, and again there is no fairway bunker. Indeed, it is quite astonishing that, discounting the bunker placed 25 yards or so short of the green, there are no fairway bunkers anywhere on this course! There are two bunkers in the angle of the 18th hole, some 150 to 200 yards out from the tee – but they are in the rough.

The 7th is probably the least glamorous hole on the course. The drive needs a carry over some dunes but the hole, a par-5 of 496 yards, requires little more than hard hitting. But 8 and 9 are exciting holes, short par-4s at 369 and 379 yards respectively; both turning fairly sharply to the right. On the 8th, the drive should get out a good 200 yards to climb up to a raised fairway to see a raised, small green with flanking bunkers and heavy rough around it. To 'see round the corner' at the 9th, the tee shot will have to go further, better than 200 yards, and fairly solid mounding closes the angle on the right of the fairway. The 10th is a straightaway

Above: The famous 5th hole, so admired by Bob Charles, rivals the Postage Stamp at Troon or the 11th at St Andrews. It has a small raised green, no bunkers, but slopes all the way round.

Right: Home grown talent and the greatest left-hander in the game, Bob Charles has won the New Zealand Open and many other tournaments at Paraparaumu, and holds the course record, a phenomenal 62.

drive and flick, but there is a stream and an out-of-bounds line hard along the left side. The out-of-bounds persists along the 11th and 12th as they run out along the boundary of the course.

Magical Finish

Paraparaumu's finish is superb. The 13th is a straight, strong par-4 of 449 yards. A really long – 250-yard – drive from the very back tee will catch a downslope. Short of that, the drive will stop on a level plateau giving a good look at the green, still a long shot away. The green is undefended, but small, with a dip immediately in front of it. And in the rough

on the left, in hooking territory just short of the green, is an unseen pond!

The 14th and 16th make a marvellous pair of one-shot holes of 151 and 140 yards respectively. They are short pops when there is no wind – the 14th over rough ground to a rectangular green, its entire front defended by sand; the 16th over a pond to a tilted rectangular green, its entire back defended by sand. At 15, 379 yards long, the driving line is tightened between dunes at 180 yards, forcing the ball to the outside of the turn. The approach is to a slender green, only 24 yards long, with a bunker front right, and a downslope off to the left – a very fine hole indeed.

The final holes, 17 at 440 yards and 18 at 470 yards, both turning right, demand precise driving into uneven fairways and long seconds which will be hard pressed to hit their targets. At 17, the green is 32 yards long, but is so set across the line that it becomes a target only 21 feet deep! All in all, Paraparaumu Beach is a marvellous golf course and well worth emigration to Wellington.

DURBAN COUNTRY CLUB

The existence of the Durban Country Club arises in part from the misfortunes of its predecessor, Royal Durban. Golf in South Africa started in 1882 when a Scottish regiment laid out six modest holes near Cape Town, and within a few years the Cape Golf Club, the first in South Africa, had been formed. Others quickly followed: in 1885 the Pietermaritzburg G.C.; in 1888, Bloem-fontein; in 1889, Aliwal North; and in 1892 what was then the Durban G.C. was formed. A nine-hole course was laid on the flat, inside the racecourse, and golf in Natal was under way. However, it was soon evident that the city of Durban was in need of more golf than one club could provide; a fact that was underlined when, during the national championships of 1919, the Royal Durban club became totally water-logged in a rainstorm; drainage at the low-lying course had always been a concern.

Thus, Laurie B. Waters, the 'father of South African golf', was asked to design a course on a piece of duneland close to the shore. A native of St Andrews, where he had been apprenticed to Old Tom Morris, Laurie had emigrated to South Africa in 1901. He introduced grass greens, won the South African Open more than once and designed Royal Johannesburg West in 1910. Helped by George Waterman, he had the Durban Country Club course in play in 1922. Two years later, it staged the first of many South African Open Championships.

The Durban course had two distinct sectors: the area near the clubhouse, which featured considerable movement in some of the fairways, making the

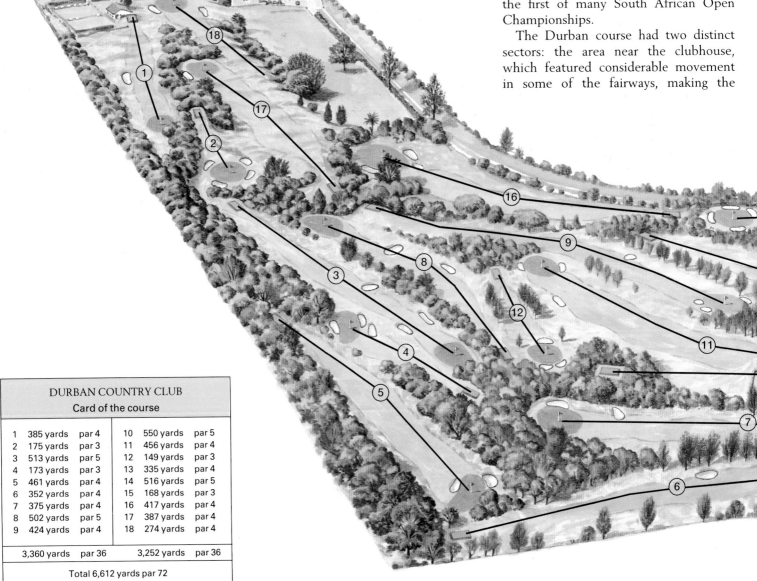

DURBAN COUNTRY CLUB					
Card of the course					
1	385 yards	par 4	10	550 yards	par 5
2	175 yards	par 3	11	456 yards	par 4
3	513 yards	par 5	12	149 yards	par 3
4	173 yards	par 3	13	335 yards	par 4
5	461 yards	par 4	14	516 yards	par 5
6	352 yards	par 4	15	168 yards	par 3
7	375 yards	par 4	16	417 yards	par 4
8	502 yards	par 5	17	387 yards	par 4
9	424 yards	par 4	18	274 yards	par 4
3,360 yards par 36			3,252 yards par 36		
Total 6,612 yards par 72					

humps and hollows of the Old Course at St Andrews look positively tame; and the other area, distant from the clubhouse, and known as the flatlands.

Stafford Vere Hotchkin

Waters' course has been reviewed a couple of times, first by the splendid Stafford Vere Hotchkin in 1928. Hotchkin was born (and died) at Woodhall Spa, near Lincoln in England, and served in the 17th Lancers in the First World War, reaching the rank of Colonel before he retired from service. In 1922–3 he was a Conservative Member of Parliament and for many years served on the Lincolnshire County Council. He purchased and re-modeled his famous home course at Woodhall Spa in 1920 – one of the finest inland courses in England.

Hotchkin formed a company which embraced all aspects of the golf course business, including design, construction, maintenance, equipment, seed and other materials. In the mid-Twenties he made an extended tour of South Africa, designing Maccauvlei in 1926, Humewood in Port Elizabeth in 1929, and Port Eliz-

abeth G.C. He also remodeled East London, Mowbray and Royal Port Alfred. Many South Africans thought him the best architect who had worked in the country. Bob Grimsdell, who designed the Royal Johannesburg's East Course, Swartkop in Pretoria, and other courses, revised the Durban course in 1959; but his and Hotchkin's changes left Laurie Waters' layout essentially unchanged.

The course has seen much derring-do over the years. Gary Player won the first of his many South African Open titles at Durban in 1956, and Bobby Locke and

Bob Charles have been among its South African Open Champions. The unusually short 18th hole, at 274 yards, has made for many a spectacular finish. The hole may be short, but it is not simple. The right side of the fairway falls off down a steep bank into bushes and towards the practice area. The drive must be held up on the left side of the fairway, and when conditions are right the green can be driven. The most dramatic finish to any South African Open came at this hole in 1928. Jock Brews drove the green and holed a 15 foot putt for an eagle two. He

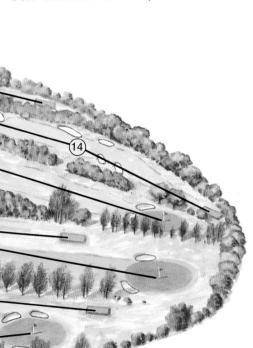

Golf in an urban setting. Durban Country Club amid the heaving escarpment of its 17th and 18th fairways within sight of downtown Durban, and squeezed between highways.

won the championship by one stroke – from his brother, the more famous Sid.

Lunar Landscape

The course plunges straight into its lunar landscape – this moon is green – at the 1st hole. There is an out-of-bounds along the right side and a big deep bunker also on the right which should be passed, narrowly. If the drive is too far left, the second shot, indeed any sight of the green, may be blocked by a large dune. The short 2nd hole is from a tee on a ridge in a copse, across a hollow to a green on a ridge in a copse! The 3rd hole is from the highest point on the course, a commanding tee that looks across a valley, then moves along a series of undulations in the fairway for the rest of its 513 yards. There is a mounded fairway bunker on the left at driving range and others on either side just short of the green. These first three holes have run straight out through the dunes, but the short 4th turns back and plays out into the flatlands. From a high tee looking down to a bunkered green it looks shorter than its 173 yards.

The Wind Factor

The 5th, 6th and 7th, forming a triangle around a wood at the end of the course, are fair and honest holes – the first a drive and mid-iron; the next two a drive and a pitch, that is, in still conditions. It must be said that Durban Country Club, close by the sea, seldom has still conditions! Most of the time there is some kind of wind. The 8th hole makes a sortie back into the 'high country', a par-5 that turns left, with a fairway bunker on the outside of the angle, and further on featuring a very big centre-fairway bunker to be carried with the second shot. At 502 yards, with a fairway rising to an oval green, this is a big-hitting hole. The 9th hole turns back and makes a sortie out of the 'high country' back to the flatlands, turning right and easing downhill to the green, 424 yards from the tee.

The 10th at 550 yards and the 11th at 456 yards are similarly orthodox; solid hitting holes without fairway hazards and with reasonably receptive greens. But the 12th is a rather difficult one-shotter of 149 yards. The green is on a flat-topped

Above: *Gary Player, seen here on home territory in a match against Arnold Palmer, won his first South African Open championship at Durban in 1956.*

Right: *Durban's first five holes run more or less parallel to the ocean. The 5th, seen here from behind the green, requires two straight shots with a driver and medium iron.*

dune with fall-off in all directions, a big bunker to be carried at the front, smaller ones back left and right and a very large tree ominously close behind. The 13th and 14th – flatland holes – take us round to the seaward side of the course and after a short pop of 168 yards at the 15th, we are in the duneland again, and into Durban's unusual finish.

The classic finish on a championship course is to have a long par-4, a long par-3, and a long par-5 in one combination or another over the final three holes. At Durban, they are all under 400 yards. The 17th, nevertheless, is something of a terror. A valley falls off to the right just as it does on 18. The fairway on the left drops into hollows and undulations which might well hide the green, so the drive must be placed precisely – so high but no higher – on the right side of the fairway. All told it is a fascinating finish to a great course of infinite variety.

ROYAL JOHANNESBURG

Golf came late to Johannesburg. From its simple start in the Cape in 1882, golf spread in the 1880s to Bloemfontein, Pietermaritzburg and other places, but Johannesburg, in time to become South Africa's greatest city and financial and industrial heartland, had other things, or more accurately, one other thing, on its mind – gold!

In 1890, when the first course was laid, Johannesburg was no more than a mining camp; but a mining camp with a vengeance and one that was to experience over the next few decades a boom scarcely paralleled in history.

To say that the first course was 'laid out' in 1890 is something of an exaggeration. It was virtually no more than a few cans in the ground, and with the city expanding in all directions, it was not until 1906 that the club, with the help of

the industrialist Sir Abe Bailey, found a proper and reasonably secure piece of land. Laurie Waters built the original course and in 1933, when the club decided on a second course, Bob Grimsdell was commissioned to produce what has become the East, the championship course. More recently, revisions were made by the Rob Kirby-Gary Player partnership, and the course is now a modern parkland layout as spacious as anyone could imagine.

One of the first and major efforts expended on the course was the removal of the native Kikuyu grasses in favour of

Royal Johannesburg's 13th hole is one of two par-4s under 400 yards but it is lined with vast bunkers, deep enough to make the loss of a stroke inevitable.

strains less rough, and then maintaining these through Johannesburg's hot summers. Even now, with great advances in agronomy, the grasses are a good deal less fine than the fescues of Western Europe, and putting on the greens of the Transvaal is an art in itself. The grain in the grass is strong, substantially affecting the run of the ball and requiring a great deal of study. Perhaps that is why golfers from the Rand – Gary Player and above all Bobby Locke – have been such successful putters when they went abroad. They are, of necessity, experienced in the business of 'reading' the lines of putts very closely.

Royal Johannesburg's East course extends to 7,465 yards, a fearful prospect for most visitors; but the fact is that in this thin air, at 6,000 feet, the ball will fly much further (10–20 per cent further) than it does at sea level. The course moves

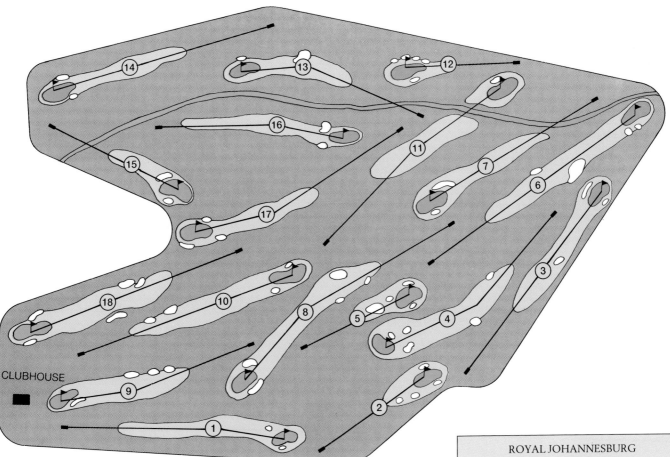

Gary Player is one of a long list of superb South African golfers who have had success worldwide. Player is a master with the sand iron and has to be at Royal Johannesburg with its massive bunkers.

along over rather gentle undulations, with little in the way of abrupt slopes, and it is nicely tree-lined, the trees often used to influence the line of the shot. On the 517-yard straight 1st hole for example, some trees edge in from the right about 100 yards short of the green. They have no serious effect on the line to the green, but the golfer is well aware of their existence.

Only two of the par-4 holes are less than 400 yards long, which is not too surprising at this altitude, and interesting holes they are too. The 13th, at 393 yards, turns to the left and calls for a drive to the left of a big right-side fairway bunker. From there, the green is but a pitch away, but a spinney edges in from the right and there is a pond at the front left. The 17th turns the other way, with the drive carrying up a rise in the fairway. The hole is 387 yards long and the pitch is critical –

the green being protected left front, left rear and right middle, with trees crowding in at the back.

All told, Royal Johannesburg East is a big and not ungenerous course that demands, above all, careful driving. And as a prime Transvaal location for the South African Open Championship, it lists the cream of South African golf among the winners: Bobby Locke, Gary Player, Bobby Cole and Harold Henning.

ROYAL JOHANNESBURG					
Card of the East course					
1	517 yards	par 5	10	513 yards	par 4
2	249 yards	par 3	11	511 yards	par 4
3	457 yards	par 4	12	203 yards	par 3
4	486 yards	par 4	13	393 yards	par 4
5	159 yards	par 3	14	435 yards	par 4
6	580 yards	par 5	15	218 yards	par 3
7	420 yards	par 4	16	490 yards	par 4
8	535 yards	par 5	17	387 yards	par 4
9	400 yards	par 4	18	512 yards	par 5
	3,803 yards	par 37		3,662 yards	par 35
Total 7,465 yards par 72					

ROYAL RABAT

The game of golf has been played in Morocco after a fashion for most of this century. But its expansion into eight 18-hole courses and three nine-holers, with several other projects in hand, has been consolidated with the coming of the jet aircraft, the overcrowding of Spain and Portugal, the desire of tourists to travel further and experience different cultures, but, above all, because of the enthusiasm for the game of King Hassan II. The king, anxious to promote his tourist industry, ran the rule over the standards of all golfing facilities in Morocco, which are excellent, and which at the same time have been kept relatively inexpensive for the foreign visitor. What's more, caddies are plentiful and the courses are kept in immaculate condition.

The pride of Moroccan golf is the Red course at Royal Rabat, 10 miles from the city of that name and the nation's capital. It has a grounds staff of 500 to ensure immaculate fairways and greens; 300 days of sunshine; and, in abundance, mimosa, fuchsia, bougainvillea, orange and apricot trees, monkeys and flamingos.

Robert Trent Jones had perhaps the dream briefing for a golf course architect: a 1,000-acre forest of cork trees in which to build two and a half courses. Jones had never been one to allow a budget to come between him and his ambitions and his work here has been characterised – with his client's blessing, of course – by the movement of vast quantities of earth, either in the excavation of lakes or the building of huge mounds, or in raising the

fairways and greens; all of this as a consequence requiring even more sophisticated drainage, watering and maintenance systems.

His Red course opened at Rabat in 1971, and appropriately was king-sized at 7,329 yards in length with a par of 73. Its three short holes were each 200 yards or more. Its par-5 holes, with one exception, were massively over 500 yards each. Only two of the par-4s were less than 400 yards, and then only slightly. It seemed that Robert Trent Jones was making some kind of point.

The Moroccan Open, a PGA European Tour event, was played on the course in 1987. It was won by Howard Clark with a score of 284 against a par of 292. Only nine players were under par, and only

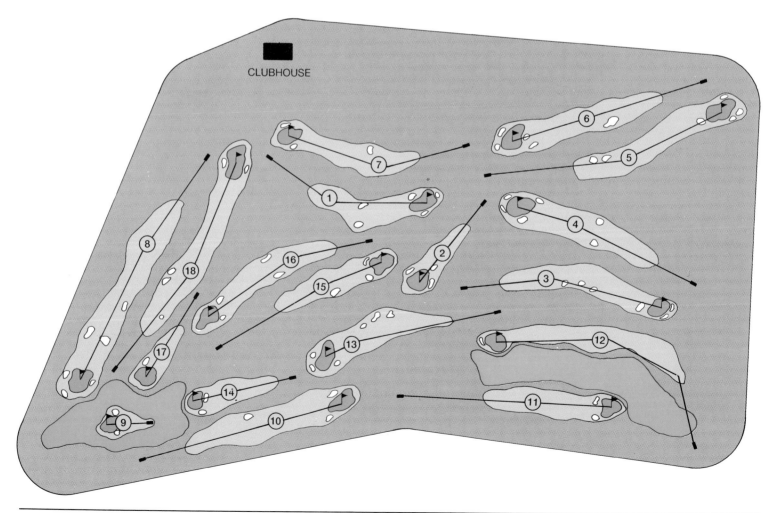

four players scored better than 290 – Clark, Mark James, Peter Baker and Sam Torrance. Clark scored 73, 73, 66 and 72 and, on this course, that 66 bordered on the miraculous.

Apart from sculpting the fairways and greens, Jones retained the forest to give him avenues of cork trees, laid down flamboyant bunkering, and on the far side of the course created another Jones speciality – lakes. One of them has given him the opportunity to build what many people consider a positively bizarre hole, but one which has been much copied since. His much-photographed 9th hole is an island in a lake, connected to the tee by slender wooden bridges. The hole is listed as 199 yards, but can be played from shorter tees, spotted at different positions around the lake.

Apart from the par-3 holes, almost

ROYAL RABAT					
Card of the Red course					
1	400 yards	par 4	10	481 yards	par 5
2	232 yards	par 3	11	467 yards	par 4
3	443 yards	par 4	12	526 yards	par 5
4	404 yards	par 4	13	384 yards	par 4
5	565 yards	par 5	14	206 yards	par 3
6	440 yards	par 4	15	390 yards	par 4
7	420 yards	par 4	16	424 yards	par 4
8	582 yards	par 5	17	225 yards	par 3
9	188 yards	par 3	18	552 yards	par 5
3,674 yards	par 36		3,655 yards	par 37	
Total 7,329 yards par 73					

every hole turns or is dog-legged to a greater rather than a lesser degree. The 1st hole puts the course completely into character. It is 400 yards lined with cork trees and turns to the left. At the corner a

The climax to Royal Rabat's longest hole, the pitch to the 582 yards par-5 8th, with the tee of the 9th, the famous 'water hole', in the foreground.

huge bunker on the left forces the tee shot wide to the right. The green has a huge bunker covering the left front and side, there is a little flash trap at the back and a big bunker wide to the right.

One of the really typical Trent Jones holes is the 12th which is 526 yards long; it turns left, a lake all along the left side, and for anyone bold enough to shoot for the green with a second shot, James has allowed a spur of the lake to cover the left half of the green. And there are bunkers at the back, of course! Royal Rabat certainly is a course regal in its power, and very forbidding.

ACKNOWLEDGEMENTS

The Publishers wish to thank the following photographers and organisations for their kind permission to reproduce their photographs:

Allsport/D Cannon 1, 8-9, 33, 49, 61, 82, 83, 96, 122-3, 125, 187, 188, 189, 190, 193t, 197, 198, 199, 200, 201/Simon Bruty 120/Vandystat 152; Chris Ayley 194; Bali Handara Country Club 184-5; Paul Barton 70-1; Charles Briscoe-Knight 6, 40, 87, 106-7, 128; Club de Golf Mexico 69; Club Zur Vahr 158, 159; Colorsport 72, 73, 78-9, 85 top, 100, 104, 118, 126, 127; Jerry Cooke 77; Peter Dazeley 2, 46, 48, 54-5, 86, 91, 107, 126 bottom, 145, 146, 148 top left, 148-9; Mikael Kristersson 156, 157; Fujioka Country Club 168-9; Golf World Magazine/Robert Green 153; Matthew Harris 54 top, 62-3, 173, 174, 175; Hobbs Golf Collection 24, 132-3, 150, 151, 154, 155; Hulton Deutsch/UPI/Bettman 81, 94, 112 bottom, 121; Illustrated London News 102; The Jockey Club, Argentina 76; Marcel Joubert 199; Lagunita Country Club/Gustavo Machado 74, 75; Bruce Longhurst/Pocket Pro 64, 65; Popperfoto 88, 101, 122, 200; Royal Calcutta Golf Club 176; Royal Dornoch Golf Club 115, 117; Royal Hong Kong Golf Club 178; Royal Montreal Golf Club 66; Phil Sheldon 4, 11, 12-3, 16, 17, 18, 21, 22, 24, 24-5, 26, 27, 28-9, 32, 33, 34, 35, 41, 43, 47, 51, 56, 90-1, 95, 98, 99, 104-5, 110-111, 112, 113, 132, 138, 160, 161, 162, 163, 164, 165, 166, 205; Singapore Island Country Club 180; Isaac Smith 136-7; South African Golf Journal/Seef Le Roux 202, 203, Bob Thomas 46 top, 92, 129, 130; Topham Picture Library 85 bottom, 109, 114, 140, 184; Tony Roberts Photography 15, 37, 38, 39; United States Golf Association 10, 14, 20, 52, 58; Stuart Windsor 182, 183; Yours In Sport, Lawrence Levy 57, 135, 137, 193.

ILLUSTRATORS

The Publishers would like to thank the following illustrators: Linda Rogers Associates/Terry McKivragan: 22-3, 26-7, 52-3, 58-9, 80-81, 84-5, 88-9, 96-7, 98-9, 100-101, 102-3, 108-9, 114-5, 124-5, 186-7; /Frank Nichols: 130-31, 140-41, 154-5, 156-7, 158-9, 162-3; /Tony Morris: 20-21, 36-7, 66-7, 74-5; Nicholas Skelton 10-11, 30-31, 44-5, 170-71, 174-5, 192-3, 194-5, 198-9.

All diagrams completed by Oxford Illustrators.

USA
1 Shinnecock Hills
2 The National
3 Oak Hill
4 Baltusrol
5 The Country Club
6 Oakmont
7 Merion
8 Pine Valley
9 Pinehurst
10 Oakland Hills
11 Muirfield Village
12 Augusta
13 Olympic
14 Cypress Point
15 Pebble Beach

CANADA
16 Banff
17 Royal Montreal

MEXICO
18 Club de Golf Mexico

DOMINICAN REPUBLIC
19 Cajuiles

BERMUDA
20 Mid Ocean

VENEZUELA
21 Lagunita

ARGENTINA
22 The Jockey Club

ENGLAND
23 Royal St George's
24 Royal Lytham and St Annes
25 Royal Birkdale
26 Formby
27 Ganton
28 Sunningdale
29 Walton Heath
30 Wentworth

SCOTLAND
31 St Andrews
32 Muirfield
33 Royal Dornoch
34 Carnoustie
35 Royal Troon
36 Turnberry
37 Gleneagles (King's)

WALES
38 Royal Porthcawl

NORTHERN IRELAND
39 Royal County Down
40 Royal Portrush

EIRE
41 Portmarnock
42 Killarney
43 Ballybunion (Old)
44 Lahinch

FRANCE
45 Chantilly

BELGIUM
46 Royal Antwerp

SWEDEN
47 Falsterbo

WEST GERMANY
48 Club Zur Vahr

ITALY
49 Olgiata

SPAIN
50 Sotogrande
51 Las Brisas

PORTUGAL
52 Vilamoura